LLEWELLYN'S
HERBAL
ALMANAC
COOKBOOK

LLEWELLYN'S
HERBAL
ALMANAC
COOKBOOK

A Collection of the
Best Culinary Articles and Recipes

Llewellyn Worldwide
Woodbury, Minnesota

First Edition
First Printing, 2015

Book design by Bob Gaul
Cover illustration and interior art by Rena Ekmanis
Editing by Ed Day

Llewellyn Publications is a registered trademark of Llewellyn Worldwide Ltd.

Library of Congress Cataloging-in-Publication Data
Llewellyn's herbal almanac cookbook: a collection of the best culinary articles and recipes.—First edition.
   pages cm
   ISBN 978-0-7387-4563-3
1. Cooking (Herbs) I. Llewellyn's herbal almanac. II. Title: Herbal almanac cookbook.
   TX819.H4L57 2015
   641.6'57—dc23
                                         2015007857

Llewellyn Worldwide Ltd. does not participate in, endorse, or have any authority or responsibility concerning private business transactions between our authors and the public.

   Any Internet references contained in this work are current at publication time, but the publisher cannot guarantee that a specific location will continue to be maintained. Please refer to the publisher's website for links to authors' websites and other sources.

Llewellyn Publications
A Division of Llewellyn Worldwide Ltd.
2143 Wooddale Drive
Woodbury, MN 55125-2989
www.llewellyn.com

Printed in the United States of America

Contents

Disclaimer   ix

Introduction   1

Back to the Basics

Edible Weeds in Our Garden *by Delores Duchen*   4

A Kitchen Herbal Primer *by Caroline Moss*   12

Get Cooking with Herbs *by Deborah C. Harding*   33

World Spice Blends *by K.D. Spitzer*   46

The Herbs and Spices of India *by Carolyn Moss*   52

Garnishes and Gremolata *by K.D. Spitzer*   62

Cooking with Magical Intent *by ShadowCat*   68

The Herbal Flavors of Greece *by James Kambos*   72

Great Herbal Snacks *by Dallas Jennifer Cobb*   84

Beverages

Have a Homebrew *by David L. Murray*   102

Herbal Syrups for Beverages *by Carly Wall*   113

Herbal Tea Parties *by Cindy Parker*   119

Bhang: The Sacred Drink of Shiva *by Magenta Griffith*   129

Yarrow Beer *by Chandra Moira Beal*   133

Herbal Wines and Liqueurs *by Chandra Moira Beal*   140

Making Magical Herbal Teas *by Jonathan Keyes*   149

Dandelion and Chicory Coffee *by Tammy Sullivan*   160

Main Dishes

A Gala Herbal Breakfast *by Caroline Moss*   168

An Herbal Thanksgiving Celebration *by Lynn Smythe*   173

Herbal Comfort Foods *by Dallas Jennifer Cobb*   187

Soy and Tofu Tucker *by Zaeda Yin*   198

Stew on This: A History of Ingredients *by Nancy Bennett*   210

Breakfast and Brunch Delights *by Lynn Smythe*   215

Condiments

Herbal Vinegars: Aromatic Delights from Your Garden
by Susun Weed   226

Making Herbal Butters *by Carly Wall*   237

Herbal Salad Dressings *by Caroline Moss*   241

Herbal Honeys and Honey-Candied Herbs *by Sara Greer*   247

Jams, Jellies, and Condiments *by Tammy Sullivan*   257

Flowers and Herbs

Recipes with Violets *by Delores Duchen*   270

The Lucky Carnation *by Carly Wall*   272

Cooking with Lovage *by Carly Wall*   276

Lovely Lavender *by Chandra Moira Beal*   284

The Story of the Edible Herbal Flower *by Lynn Smythe*   287

Sage: The Wise Herb *by Magenta Griffith*   303

Cooking with Southwestern Herbs *by Chandra Moira Beal*   312

Herbal Treats Beat the Summer Heat *by Elizabeth Barrette*   325

Afro-Caribbean Greens *by Stephanie Rose Bird*   336

Sweet, Sweet Stevia *by Dallas Jennifer Cobb*   341

Feasting on Rosemary *by Anne Sala*   351

Disclaimer

The publisher and the authors assume no liability for any injuries caused to the reader that may result from the reader's use of content contained in this publication and recommend common sense when contemplating the practices described in the work.

The old-fashioned remedies in this book are historical references used for teaching purposes only. The recipes are not for commercial use or profit. The contents are not meant to diagnose, treat, prescribe, or substitute consultation with a licensed healthcare professional. New herbal recipes should be taken in small amounts to allow the body to adjust.

Introduction

Why an *Herbal Cookbook?*

Everybody eats. It's as simple as that.

Our first almanac about herbs, *The Organic Gardening Almanac*, was published more than two decades ago. While being a good steward to Mother Earth is still important, many things have changed, including the increased popularity—and need—for organically raised produce. A few years later, the *Herbal Almanac* emerged, reflecting the fact that using herbs as medicine, in beauty products, and in craft projects were gaining acceptance (or re-acceptance, as the case may be), as many people had become more aware of the impact their activities had on the environment.

The one use that never went out of style is eating.

Herbs can enhance ordinary dishes and make good recipes absolutely delectable. Also, in the *Herbal Almanac Cookbook,* you might find unexpected ways to use herbs—in liqueurs, as a sweetener, and even as a unifying ingredient over several courses of a meal. With contributions from Elizabeth Barrette, Stephanie Rose Bird, James Kambos, Anne Sala, and Tammy Sullivan, this book includes recipes for beverages, main dishes, and condiments, as well as the multiple uses for several herbs, flowers, and spices.

In addition, many of the recipes in this compilation go beyond cooking instructions and explain the importance of the herbs used. Where did it originate? Why was it revered? What was the folklore behind it? Who introduced it to mainstream culture? Some authors sometimes expound on their personal reason an herb is especially important to their traditions. Others offer a way to make a meal magical.

So whether you enjoy foraging for edible weeds, making yarrow beer, or judiciously adding herbs to a brunch menu, remember that there is a often a story that goes along with it. If there isn't, it's a chance to create a story of your own.

BACK TO
THE BASICS

EDIBLE WEEDS IN OUR GARDENS
by Deborah Duchen

In some ways, weeds are plants with which gardeners have a very close relationship. We hold them and pull them and hack them and uproot them. In fact, we possibly have more physical contact with our weeds than with our ornamental plants. But how much do we actually know about them?

Too many gardeners don't think of weeds as "plants." They are simply "weeds"—unwelcome trespassers in our domain. But have you ever wondered why some wild plants make weeds of themselves? They almost seem to prefer human company to life in the untouched wild. Well, in many cases, that is because these plants were naturalized many centuries ago for use as food, medicine, or other purposes. In a sense, they are semi-domesticated. Although we abandoned their use as our lifestyle changed, they faithfully continue to follow us.

In this article, we will look at a few of the most common weeds found in gardens throughout North America. In each case, we will examine the history of the plant itself, its historical uses, and suggestions for present-day usage.

Dandelion *(Taraxacum officinale)*

Dandelions, although they seem to grow everywhere, are not native to North America. Like most Americans, the dandelion is an immigrant. It was brought here by the earliest English settlers (maybe even on the *Mayflower*!), because it was considered absolutely essential to survival. It provided food, medicine, and wine for the whole family. No self-respecting English housewife would be caught without dandelion in her kitchen garden. But the history of dandelion goes back to before Plymouth Rock.

Probably originating in Asia Minor, the dandelion spread throughout the known world before written history began. In China, it was called "earth nail" for its long taproot. In Japan, it is still considered highly ornamental, as more than 200 varieties in colors ranging from white to copper are cultivated by florists. The Greeks learned to grow the tender greens and dandelion even took a place in Greek mythology. The Romans, typically, mimicked the Greeks. But they also noted its usage in the places they conquered. When Caesar (an amateur botanist himself) invaded the British Isles, he found the dandelion in use among the Celts, who made wine from the flowers, a favorite country wine in England to this day. The Gauls, today's French, appreciated the greens.

The very name—"dandelion"—is a reminder of the Norman Conquest. Remember that many French names, which were considered refined and upper-class, replaced traditional Anglo-Saxon names, which were (and still are) seen as crude. Such was the case with "dandelion," an Anglicized version of the French "dent-de-lion," or tooth of the lion, referring to the jagged edge of the leaf. The Anglo-Saxon name, "piss-a-bed," referred to the plant's effectiveness as a diuretic.

Medicinally, dandelion has been used for such diverse ailments as rheumatism, dropsy, chronic skin disorders, liver and gall bladder disorders, poor digestion, and kidney stones. Its scientific name refers to its traditional use as medicine.

Once settlers brought dandelion to the Colonies, it spread rapidly, its winged seeds riding in the wind. In fact, it moved west faster than the pioneers. And as dandelion moved west, the Indians found new ways to use it. When the settlers finally caught up, they found such tribes as the fierce Apache organizing scouting parties to go in search of this popular new herb.

Dandelion has many uses. In fact, every part of the plant, except for the flower stalk, is usable. The young leaves in early spring make a delicious green vegetable to be eaten raw or cooked. Harvest the leaves before the flower appears, or they will taste very bitter. If you find the raw leaves too bitter for your taste, blanch them before eating. The roots may be dug at any time. Boil them like parsnips. Or you may use them as a caffeine-free coffee substitute, or coffee-stretcher. Here's how. Cut the cleaned roots into small pieces and roast in the oven at 400 degrees F until dark brown. Cool, then grind them in a coffee grinder or blender on "coarse." The flower buds, sautéed in butter, make an interesting side dish. Shred the flowers into salads for color and flavor.

With our modern-day appreciation of nutrition, dandelions are making a comeback. A ⅓ cup serving of the cooked greens contains 45 calories, 2.7 grams protein, 1.6 grams fiber, 187 mg calcium, 3.10 mg iron (about the same as spinach), 36 mg magnesium, 88 mg phosphorus, 397 mg potassium, 35 mg vitamin C, and 14,000 IU vitamin A. Their diuretic property makes dandelion greens a boon to dieters and those with a tendency to retain water.

Plantain *(Plantago major)*

The familiar lawn weed plantain is another plant of Eurasian origin, brought to the New World by early settlers. Plantain seeds are a favorite among birds, so the plant spread quickly from settlers' herb gardens into the surrounding fields and beyond.

In fact, it seemed to the Indians that it sprang up wherever the white man stepped. They named it "white man's footprint." English settlers in Australia and New Zealand also took plantain with them. The Aborigines there made the same observation, naming the plant "Englishman's toe."

The young leaves were valued as a cooked green. To prepare them as a green, simply boil the most tender young leaves in water for a few minutes. Try mixing them with other edible greens, such as dandelions and/or spinach, for a tasty side dish. Some people prefer to eat the young leaves raw, adding them to salad.

Plantain is also a good herb for outdoor first aid. The leaves can be used to take the sting out of bee stings and the itch out of insect bites. The classic way to use it is to macerate, or chew, the leaf, then spread it on the sore spot. It really works!

If you want to attract birds and other wildlife to your yard, let the plantain in your lawn go to seed. It prefers full sun and rich soil.

Humans can eat the seeds too. In fact, if you use a fiber laxative, you are simply ingesting the seeds of another species of plantain that grows in another part of the world, *Plantago ovata*. You can save money and get the same effect by gathering the seeds of plantain and adding them to your diet for bulk. They're also nutritious.

Purslane *(Portulaca oleracea)*

Also known as "pusley," this common garden weed is rich in flavor and nutrients. A popular vegetable in many parts of the world, including Holland and France, it has never caught on in the United States—which is unfortunate. In fact, part of its scientific name, *oleracea*, actually means "like a garden vegetable." No less a personage than Henry David Thoreau praised purslane in the classic *Walden* when he wrote, "I have made a satisfactory dinner off a dish of purslane, which I gathered and boiled. Yet, men have come to such a pass that they frequently starve, not for lack of necessaries but for want of luxuries."

Purslane prefers sunny spots in sandy, rich soil. It carpets the ground, rarely growing more than 5 inches high. The succulent, purplish-green leaves range from ½ to 2 inches long. The tender red stems bear tiny five-petaled yellow flowers at their tips. The whole plant is edible. Some purslane lovers have found that they can use one plant from June until frost just by snipping off the tips of stems. A fast grower, the plant soon replaces them.

The most common way of eating purslane is as Thoreau did it, by boiling the stems and leaves (no need to remove flowers or seeds). Some people like to mix the cooked greens with bacon and vinegar. It has a tangy flavor and a mucilaginous quality like okra. Because of this, it can be used as a thickener like in gumbo, soups, or stews. If you don't like the "slimy" texture, you can counteract it by breading and frying, a delicious variation.

Raw purslane has a pleasant crunch and is a good salad green. An interesting "purslane cole slaw" can be made by chopping up the raw leaves and stems, mixing with chopped carrots or other raw vegetables, and blending with a commercial cole slaw dressing.

Purslane's great taste, high level of nutrition, and low caloric content (the plant is 92 percent water, similar to cabbage) make it a favorite. The famous Euell Gibbons was particularly fond of purslane and liked to experiment with it, as reported in his famous book, *Stalking the Wild Asparagus*. Among other things, he discovered that it pickled well. He packed two-pint jars with purslane stems and leaves, then covered them with a mixture of 1 cup white vinegar, 2 cups cold water, ¼ cup salt, and ½ teaspoon alum. Then he added 2 dill flowers, a clove of garlic, and 1 small red pepper. After sealing the jars, he let them sit in a dark place for at least one month. "No cooking, no processing, no fuss, no bother," he states. Other people have found that any good dill or bread-and-butter pickle recipe works well.

The seeds are edible, too, as a grain. They can be gathered, ground, and cooked into mush or mixed 50/50 with regular flour to use in breads, etc. Although tiny, they are numerous. One plant can produce as many as 52,000 seeds. An easy way to collect them is to harvest several plants. Then, just lay them down on a piece of plastic. Over a period of a few days, the seeds will ripen and the seedpods will burst open on their own. Shake them out over the plastic and strain to remove the seeds from the chaff. This was said to be a popular food among the Indians of the Southwest at one time.

A one-cup serving of cooked purslane yields 1.7 grams protein, 78 mg calcium, 39 grams phosphorous, 67 mg magnesium, 488 mg potassium, 3.5 mg iron, 2,500 IU vitamin A, and 25 grams vitamin C—and only about 20 calories. Additionally, purslane is a good source of heart-protective omega-3 fatty acids.

So, when the purslane appears in your garden this year, don't fight it. Consider yourself blessed with one of the finest vegetables to be found anywhere.

Pokeweed *(Phytolacca americana)*

Pokeweed is one of the best-known edible weeds around. It is also one of the most complex and misunderstood. A tall perennial—it can grow to seven feet in one season—it is poisonous if eaten raw. A traditional Native American medicinal plant, it is finding a place in the modern pharmacopeia.

The traditional way of eating pokeweed is to pick the very young leaves in the spring. Add them to a pot of boiling water and cook for a very short time—3 to 5 minutes. Then pour off the water and rinse the greens. Add them to another pot of boiling water and cook for a few more minutes, although some people add meat or fatback and cook longer. Strain the greens and lay out on a platter. Sprinkle with chopped, hard-boiled egg and vinegar or hot sauce. This is a Southern delicacy.

You may also cook the greens as above and mix with a cream sauce or canned mushroom soup. They have a rich, tangy flavor all their own. Most people find well-prepared pokeweed to be very pleasant.

You might have heard of pokeweed being called "poke salad." Well, that is an incorrect name, the result of changes in our language. You see, the Old English name for this traditional favorite was poke "salat," sometimes spelled "sallet," which was a word meaning "cooked vegetable." As mentioned earlier, do not eat the raw plant. Also, do not eat the berries, the seeds of which are very poisonous.

Poke is a Native American plant and was a favorite of the Indians. Indian healers discovered that the juice of the plant was useful in treating skin cancer. In the 1970s, a group of researchers tested it in the lab and found that the juice of pokeweed indeed could shrink tumors—all kinds of tumors, not just skin cancer. It is now one of the medicines used in the chemotherapy arsenal. More recent research has revealed that a protein found in pokeweed can kill viruses, including the HIV virus that causes AIDS.

Although further testing must be done, it appears that this old Indian remedy still can serve us in the twenty-first century.

Nutritionally, poke, even cooked twice, is valuable. A ⅓ cup serving yields 20 calories, 2.3 grams protein, 53 mg calcium, 1.2 mg iron, 33 grams phosphorous, 82 mg vitamin C, and 8,700 IU vitamin A.

Lamb's-Quarters or Pigweed (*Chenopodium spp.*)

Closely related to spinach, lamb's-quarters are just as good to eat and a lot easier to grow. Lovers of disturbed soil, they are among the first weeds to appear in the garden every spring, their pale green leaves, shaped like a goose's footprint, sprinkled with a grainy, white powder. Try them raw. They're milder than spinach, containing less of the oxalic acid that gives its more famous cousin its "bite."

Although they can be eaten raw as a nibble or salad, most people prefer them slightly cooked, like spinach, in just a little water. Eat them as is or mix them with a simple cream sauce. The leaves are also good added to chicken broth. Try adding lamb's-quarters leaves in your favorite quiche recipe. This is one of the most versatile volunteer vegetables around.

There are several species of lamb's quarters. Some are Native American, others were brought here by early settlers. Depending on what part of the nation you live in, you may be blessed with one or several species in your own garden. It is not necessary to differentiate, however, as all the species are edible. The only possible exception is a species known as Jerusalem tea, epazote, or wormseed, *Chenopodium ambrosoides*. This particular species has fleshy leaves and a strong, rather unpleasant scent. It looks different than the other lamb's-quarters and is rarely identified as one and the same with its kin. Although it is edible in small quantities, it is not recommended that it be eaten in the same amounts as the other lamb's-quarters.

Nutritionally, lamb's quarters is a winner. A ⅓ cup portion of the cooked greens yields 32 calories, 3.2 grams protein, 1.8 grams fiber, 258 mg calcium, 45 mg phosphorous, 37 mg vitamin C, and 9,700 IU vitamin A. It contains all of the essential amino acids.

There are only a few of the many "wonderful weeds" that are tasty and nutritious. Remember, many weeds are actually forgotten foods. They come up in the spring ready to provide us with vitamins, minerals, and even medicine. Since they are easy to grow, requiring no special treatment, we can benefit from their presence. Rather than treating them like trespassers, we should welcome them into our midst and use them like our ancestors did.

....

A KITCHEN HERBAL PRIMER
by Caroline Moss

When planning herb gardens for others, as it is my pleasure to do, I always ask what uses are expected for the herbs. Occasionally I get the answer "for medicines" or "for potpourri." Even more rarely comes the reply "for dyeing" or "to make natural cosmetics." However, by far the most frequent response is "for cooking." Even those who claim not to like "fancy" food or not want an herb garden will enjoy a little parsley or thyme, but we can do better than that! Now I will help you give yourself a real treat.

In the depths of a cold winter, make a cup of your favorite tea, put a few cookies on your prettiest plate, and take a blank piece of paper, some colored pencils, an herb reference book, and some specialist herb nursery catalogs. Sit at a table and start planning your dream herb garden.

This little exercise is a many-layered pleasure. You have the delight of a very special few hours in the planning. You will have the great sense of fun and achievement later in the year of getting the garden up and running. You will also have the continued joy, for many years to come, of tending, altering, adding to, and of course, harvesting from your very own herb patch.

In designing your garden, much will, of course, depend on the space available. You can have a lovely selection of herbs to use throughout the year with nothing more than a few pots or a window box. You could set aside a very small, semi-formal herb patch by using a template in which to plant. This could be an old ladder with a plant in each gap, a cart wheel, or paving slabs laid out leaving chessboard spaces of earth. One could plant in a more casual way, while always being aware that the blowsy, cottage garden look still involves careful planning of height and regular tending to ensure that some element of control is maintained. Then again, if you are sure you have a considerable amount of time to spend on maintenance, then you could even try a knot garden, where intricate patterns are achieved by working with carefully trimmed herb hedges, often box *(Buxus sempervirens)*. Make full use of varying leaf coloring and even colored gravel carefully placed to bring out the pattern. Begin with the following:

- An idea of space available, but beware! Once you get the bug, your herbs will take over your entire garden.

- Information on what plants are possible in your locality. It's no good trying to plant a tree-sized lemon verbena to over-winter outdoors in Vermont.

- A list of the plants you definitely want to include. It would be a shame to plant up a wonderful herb patch only to have to purchase rosemary at the market.

- Details of basic growing patterns, such as the expected heights of plants and any particular requirements. For example, you might want to plant mint in a container or in a separate area.

We now want to get on to the herbs you could include in your garden. As I work in England, I deal with growing in a middling sort of climate. If you have very long, harsh winters or are in the desert states, you will need to check local growing guides to ascertain what plants you can deal with, or any extra care they may need.

We will look at how to grow and use several lovely plants that will help you in the kitchen. There are, of course, many dozens more herbs, but these are a good basic selection with which to start, with one or two that are perhaps slightly more unfamiliar. I have only included culinary uses, but many of these herbs do, of course, have valuable medicinal or scented qualities.

Basil *(Ocimum basilicum)*

Traits: Half-hardy annual, six to 12 inches tall.

Natural Habitat: India.

History and Folklore: Basil is connected with scorpions in astrology and the ancient herbals. The scorpions were said to enjoy lying under, and even breeding under, the basil.

Varieties: There are numerous varieties, including lemon, spice/cinnamon, holy, Greek/bush, opal, purple ruffles, green ruffles, and lettuce leaf basil.

Growing: It is easily grown from seed. Do not overwater, but do think to avoid transplanting. Grow indoors as a pot plant in all but the warmest of conditions.

Harvesting: Pick leaves from the top to avoid flowering and thus prolong life.

Preserving: Please don't dry basil—dried basil is horrible. Some basils freeze after painting leaves on both sides with olive oil, although I prefer to treat it as a summer herb and just use it fresh. Infuse the leaves in olive oil or white wine vinegar to add to cooking and salad dressings.

Uses: Tear leaves coarsely over tomato salads. Use basil pesto as a pasta sauce or on pizza.

Basil Pesto

2 oz. fresh basil	Salt
4 oz. extra virgin olive oil	2 oz. butter, softened
2 oz. pine nuts	4 oz. freshly grated Parmesan
2 cloves garlic	

Blend the basil, oil, pine nuts, garlic, and salt in a food processor. Blend in the butter and Parmesan. This makes enough for 1½ pounds of pasta. Add a little hot water if mixing with pasta. It can also be used on chicken or on vegetables such as peppers, tomatoes, or eggplant.

Bay (*Laurus nobilis*)

Traits: Evergreen perennial, over 20 feet tall.

Natural Habitat: Mediterranean.

History and Folklore: Bay was sacred to Apollo, the Greek god of prophecy, poetry, and healing. Indeed, Apollo's temple at Delphi had a roof constructed of bay as a guard against disease, witchcraft, and lightning. A wreath of bay became a mark of honor for scholars and athletes, and the word *laureate* means to crown with laurel.

Growing: Bay really needs to be in containers when small and must be brought under cover if frosty. It is hardy when mature but the leaves will die in a hard winter. Grow from cuttings (in April) or layering (April or August). Plant in full sun, protected from winds in a moist soil. Be patient. It is slow-growing.

Varieties: Look for a golden bay *(Laurus nobilis "Aurea")*.

Preserving: The leaves dry most successfully.

Uses: The leaves are used extensively in cooking. The savory uses of bay are well known, but try adding a leaf to custards or rice pudding. A leaf placed between each piece of meat or vegetable in kebabs is good. Bay is essential in a bouquet garni (along with thyme and parsley). A leaf placed in the flour bin effectively repels weevils and other bugs.

Bouquet Garni

A jar of these muslin bags makes a good present.

12, 4-inch squares of muslin	12 tbsp. dried parsley
12 bay leaves	12 peppercorns
12 tsp. celery seeds	6 tsp. thyme
24 cloves	

Divide the ingredients equally between the squares of muslin. Tie with heavy twine, leaving a long string attached with which to fish the bundle out of the stew pot.

Chives *(Allium schoenoprasum)*

Traits: Hardy perennial, 6 inches tall.

Natural Habitat: Northern Europe and northeastern North America.

History and Folklore: Chives were used in China as long as 5,000 years ago and introduced into Britain by the Romans.

Growing: Chives will take in virtually any conditions, although they need to be watered well in very dry weather. Feed the soil occasionally and divide clumps every couple of years. This plant will keep in a pot all year round.

Preserving: Use only fresh chives.

Uses: Finely chop the stems into salad dressing, particularly for potato, tomato, or egg salad. Add to anything where a mild onion flavor is required. Also delicious chopped into cream cheese.

Coriander/Cilantro
(Coriandrum sativum)

Traits: Annual, from 18 inches to 36 inches tall.

Habitat: Native to southern Europe.

History and Folklore: The name comes from the Greek *koros*, meaning an insect, due to the smell of bed bugs in the leaf. The leaves are certainly pungent, but I cannot actually vouch for what a bed bug smells like. As with so many herbs, coriander was introduced into Britain by the Romans, who used it as a meat preservative. In the Middle Ages it was added to love potions, and the Chinese believed that the seeds conferred immortality. The Greeks, notably Pliny, said the best coriander came from Egypt.

Growing: Plant seeds in full sun in well-drained, fertile soil. The leaves can be used when desired. The seed is ready for use in late August. Treat it as a salad crop with several plantings as soon as it goes to seed.

Uses: The leaves are widely used in Eastern foods, and the seeds are essential in spice and curry mixes and crushed in boiled basmati rice. Use the leaves in moderation in salad dressings. Some find the flavor of the leaves something of an acquired taste, others love it. Coriander flavors certain German sausages and is wonderful in a carrot soup. To keep leaves fresh in the fridge, Madhur Jaffrey recommends pulling up a whole plant, roots and all, and placing it into a jar of water and covering the lot with a plastic bag. Discard yellowing leaves daily and the bulk should keep for weeks.

Spicy Cheese Dip (Not for the faint-hearted)

1 lb. grated cheddar cheese	1 red onion, finely chopped
1 carton sour cream	1 tomato, chopped
3 cloves crushed garlic	1 bunch fresh coriander
1 chile, seeds removed and finely chopped	Avocado slices

Mix the cheese, sour cream, garlic, chile, and half the chopped onion. Bake in a greased dish in a hot oven until melted, stirring occasionally. When melted, add the tomato and broil until bubbling. Sprinkle with the remaining onion and coriander. Garnish with avocado slices. Use as dip for tortilla (corn) chips or crackers.

Dill *(Anethum graveolens)*

Traits: Hardy annual, up to 5 feet tall.

Natural Habitat: Southern Russia and surrounding countries.

History and Folklore: Dill was used in the Middle Ages on St. John's Eve as a protection against witchcraft. It was known as "meetin' seed" by early American settlers as it was given to young children to chew in long religious meetings. The name kill is derived from a Norse word, *dilla*, meaning "to lull."

Growing: Plant in full sun, protected from the wind, in a rich and well-drained soil. Grows well from seed planted in spring up to June. Do not plant near the closely related fennel, as it will cross pollinate. Thin seedlings to 1 foot apart.

Preserving: The leaves should really only be used fresh, but the seed may be dried or preserved in vinegar.

Uses: Add seeds to soup, fish dishes, pickles (such as the famous German-American dill pickles), cabbage, sauerkraut, seed cake, or apple pie. The seeds can be chewed to aid digestion after a meal. The chopped leaf can be added to potato salad, cream cheese, salmon, eggs, or grilled meat.

Dill Pickles

Fill sterilized jars with baby cucumbers or gherkins. Quarter the cucumbers lengthwise if they are too thick. Place a clove of garlic and a flowering head of dill in each jar. Boil the following solution, fill jars, leaving a half-inch of head space, and seal in a boiling water bath for 20 minutes.

3 oz. salt   8 oz. white wine vinegar
24 oz. water

Label and date. Keep in cool place for six weeks before using.

Fennel *(Foeniculum vulgare)*

Traits: Hardy perennial, up to 4 feet tall.

Habitat: Mediterranean.

History and Folklore: Hippocrates suggested that fennel be used by wet nurses to increase their milk supply. In medieval times, bunches were hung on Midsummer's Eve to ward off evil spirits, and keyholes were filled with the seeds to keep out ghosts.

Growing: It will take some shade but likes a rich, well-fed soil. It self-seeds throughout the garden and may be grown from seeds or propagated from root division.

Varieties: Bronze fennel (*F. vulgare "Purpurascens"*) has a lovely purple-brown tint and is most attractive in the garden. Florence fennel (*F. vulgare var. dulce*) has a larger bulb that can be eaten raw in salads or cooked as a vegetable.

Preserving: Dry the seeds, but otherwise use fennel fresh.

Uses: Fennel seeds aid digestion and can be an ingredient in baby's gripe water. The leaves may be finely chopped into mashed potato, salad dressings, or sauces for fish. Use sprigs of the leaf in salads with other greens for a marked aniseed note.

Goosefoot Family/Good King Henry (*Chenopodium*)

Natural Habitat: Europe, North America, and Mexico.

Varieties: *C. bonus-henricus* (Good King Henry, English mercury, goosefoot, smearwort, allgood), *C. album* (fat hen, lamb's quarters, dirty dick, baconweed, pigweed), *C. rubrum* (red goosefoot, sowbane), *C. ambrosioides* (wormseed, American wormseed, epazote, Mexican tea, herba Santa Maria), *C. quinoa* (quinoa).

History and Folklore: Good King Henry may take its name from Germany, where a poisonous but similar plant is known as "Bad Henry." The Brothers Grimm (as in fairy tales) said the "Henry" came from the elves of Heinz and Heinrich, who had magical powers of a malicious nature, whereas others say it was named for Henry IV of France who promised a chicken in every peasant's pot. This herb was used to fatten the fowl. Fat hen has been found in the stomach of a preserved Iron Age man. Various varieties were commonly used in feeding-up livestock, hence such names as fat hen, pigweed, and bacon weed.

Growing: Grow Good King Henry in sun or very light shade in a well-drained, well-dug, rich soil. Plant seeds in spring or take root divisions in the fall. Plant or thin to 1 foot apart and fertilize. This is an outdoor plant only.

Flower: Tiny, green, seed-like flowers in spikes.

Uses: Steam Good King Henry flowers lightly and toss in butter like broccoli for an excellent source or iron and vitamins. The very young leaves may be used in salad and older leaves cooked like spinach. It may be added to quiches, soups, and stuffings, and the stems boiled and peeled like asparagus.

Lemon Verbena *(Lippa citriodora)*

Traits: Tender perennial. Can reach 6 feet tall in a pot to 10 feet outside in subtropical conditions.

Natural Habitat: South and Central America, where it is known as *herba luisa*.

Growing: Grow lemon verbena in a large pot with rich soil. It must be fed from late winter to summer. It will sit outside during the summer in virtually all zones, but needs protection from frost in winter when it must be kept in a light, cool, moist situation. Take cuttings when well established. Lemon verbena may be grown as a house plant. When all the leaves drop off in winter it is not dead! Keep it moist and it will sprout again in February.

Uses: This herb has the strongest lemon scent of all the many lemony herbs. The leaves will drop in winter. Save them for tea or potpourri. Try adding just one or two leaves to a pot of ordinary tea. Use in fruit punches or add to any sweet or savory dish where a hint of lemon is required.

Lemon-Glazed Cake

2 tbsp. warm water	Zest of one lemon, grated
3 drops vanilla essence	Water or lemon juice if necessary
A few lemon verbena leaves	Crystallized lemon for garnish, if desired
8 oz. icing sugar	

Combine water, vanilla, and lemon verbena and soak overnight. Strain out leaves and stir in sugar and zest. Add water or lemon juice if required to reach a pouring consistency. Pour over a plain sponge cake (a firm pound cake, butter sponge, or Madeira cake is best). Garnish with lemon verbena leaves and crystallized lemon.

Lovage (Levisticum officinale)

Traits: Hardy perennial, up to 7 feet tall.

Natural Habitat: Mediterranean, Greece, south of France.

Growing: Lovage will take some shade and likes a rich, well-drained soil. It self-seeds easily and can be grown from seeds planted in late summer. Plant them soon after they have been collected as they go bad if kept to plant the following spring.

Preserving: Freeze leaves. Dry seeds and roots.

Uses: Lovage seeds can be used in baked foods and on mashed potatoes. However, I really grow the plant for its leaves, which are most useful in salads, on chicken, in soup, on their own, or added to other herbs. The leaves are also good chopped over a tomato salad. Try anywhere where a celery flavor would be appropriate.

Note: Lovage is not to be taken during pregnancy or by anyone with kidney problems.

Lovage Dip

½ lb. cream cheese	1 tbsp. chopped chives
½ c. chopped lovage leaves	Salt and pepper

Blend together. Serve with raw vegetables, chips, and bread sticks.

Lovage Cordial

Steep lovage seeds in brandy and add sugar to taste. This makes an excellent medicine to warm and comfort the stomach. It is also good for a cold. Lovage cordial can be bought commercially. You can also mix it in with brandy for a warming drink.

Marjoram (Origanum majorana)

Traits: Hardy perennial, up to 2 feet tall.

Natural Habitat: Mediterranean and western Asia.

History and Folklore: The name "oregano" comes from the Greek *oros* (mountain) and *ganos* (joy). The Greeks planted it on graves to bring joy to the departed, and the Romans felt it symbolized happiness and wove it into head circlets for young couples.

Growing: Marjoram likes the sun and can take a poor soil, as long as it's well drained. It self-seeds easily and can be grown from seed or cuttings.

Varieties: Marjoram varieties are notoriously confusing, but anything labeled "oregano" or "Greek marjoram" should have a good strong flavor. Wild marjoram (*O. vulgare*) does not have such a good flavor. Golden marjoram (*O. onites "Auereum"*) is a very attractive garden plant with the same culinary uses. Dwarf marjoram (*O. onites "Compactum"*) is low-growing with an attractive full and bushy habit and is useful for window boxes or small gardens.

Preserving: The leaves dry well.

Uses: A wonderful plant for attracting bees, marjoram can be used in many savory dishes. It is used extensively by Germans, Italians, and Greeks to flavor sausages, salami, pizza, spaghetti sauces, and stuffings.

Mint *(Mentha)*

Traits: Hardy perennial.

Natural Habitat: Pretty much worldwide.

History and Folklore: Mint is named for the nymph Menthe, who was turned into the mint plant by the jealous Proserpina when she learned of Pluto's passion for her.

Growing: This robust plant will take some shade and prefers a rich, damp soil. It spreads violently and sprigs pulled from established plants will root easily. Try sinking large plastic bags or pots in the soil to contain the roots, and don't plant different varieties too close or they may cross-pollinate and lose their character.

Varieties: There are too many to mention, but here is a selection: Spearmint (*Mentha spicata*) and peppermint

(*M. x piperita*) are the two standard forms. Corsican mint (*M. requienii*) has minute leaves and forms a fresh-smelling carpet. Pennyroyal (*M. pulegium*) is a pretty plant for between paving stones, but do not make into tea as it was formally used, with considerable effect, to induce abortion. Eau de Cologne mint (*M. x piperita citrate*) has a lovely fragrance.

Preserving: Freeze leaves. They are not good dried, but available fresh for most of the year.

Uses: Mint adds a freshness to grilled chicken and is popular in Middle Eastern dishes. A strong, sweet mint tea is also widely drunk in the Middle East, and one of the sharpest, freshest scented mints is often marketed as "Moroccan mint." It is the traditional English sauce with roast lamb, finely chopped and mixed with vinegar and a little sugar. The oil or flavoring is, of course, widely used in sweet dishes.

Parsley *(Petrsolinum cirspum)*

Traits: Hardy biennial, up to 1 foot tall.

Natural Habitat: Southern Europe.

History and Folklore: Said to take so long to germinate as it must go to the devil and back again seven times and only then, if the woman is master in the home, will it grow. The Greeks thought the plant sprang from the blood of Archemeus, the forerunner of death, and thus used it to decorate tombs rather than to eat.

Growing: Parsley does not like full midday sun. Plant in a rich, well-drained soil. It is notoriously slow to germinate, so soak seeds in hot water for a few minutes prior to planting and ensure seeds do not dry out at all prior to shooting. It grows very vigorously in "grow bags."

Preserving: Parsley freezes well in entire sprigs in plastic bags and can be crumbled, still frozen, into cooking. Despite being available in shops, the dried form doesn't really taste good.

Uses: Use parsley chopped in salad dressings, sauces, soups, and especially in fish dishes. Use it in a mixed herb bunch for bouquet garni, and try deep-frying sprigs quickly in hot oil for an unusual, crisp, and delicious garnish. Drain well on absorbent kitchen paper before use. Not recommended for consumption by people with inflammatory kidney disease.

Rosemary (*Rosmarinus officinalis*)

Traits: Usually a evergreen perennial, 3 to 6 feet tall.

Natural Habitat: Southern Europe.

History and Folklore: Rosemary is the symbol of love and friendship. It is also the herb for Christmas and weddings, as it symbolizes remembrance. The normal plants have blue flowers. It is said that originally they were all white-flowered, but the Virgin Mary dried her blue cloak on a rosemary bush and since then almost all have been blue and grow for only 33 years (the life of Jesus) or to around 6 feet (the height of Jesus).

Growing: Plant in a sunny, very well-drained site, protected from wind. Bring indoors in bad winters or when small. Rosemary likes a lime soil but can take poor conditions. Grow from cuttings, layering, or from seed.

Varieties: Look out for the new tall tree type, a prostrate type (try this in hanging baskets), and white or pink flowered varieties. There are also variegated forms with green and gold leaves.

Uses: Indispensable with roast meats (chicken, lamb, or pork), rosemary is also delicious in roasted or sautéed potatoes. Some add it to fruit purée, although I don't, but do try herb butters and oil or vinegar infusions. Save branches from which you have removed the leaves to scatter on a barbecue, and use the very sturdy stems as barbeque skewers. Include rosemary with vegetables.

Sage *(Salvia officinalis)*

Traits: Hardy evergreen perennial, 1 to 2½ feet tall.

History and Folklore: Sage has often been associated with longevity, hence the proverb: "How can a man grow old who has sage in his garden?"

Growing: Grow sage in full sun on a dry, well-drained soil. It grows well from cuttings. Cut it back in late summer and replace woody plants every five years or so (like lavender).

Varieties: There are many, including: *S. lavadulifolia* (narrow leaf sage), *S. officianalis* "Tricolor" (variegated—green/ white/red), *S. officinalis* "Purpurea" (purple/red sage), *S. elegans/rutilans* (pineapple sage), *S. officinalis* "broad leaf" (broad leafed sage), and *S. officinalis* prostrates (prostate sage). There are many varieties of the *Salvia* family.

Uses: This is an indispensable culinary herb. Use it in stuffings with cheese dishes, or with sautéed liver. The leaves may be coated in light batter and deep fried for an unusual Italian nibble with drinks. Try in oil, vinegar, and herb butters, but do beware that sage needs to be used with moderation as it can overpower other flavors. The woody branches add a savory aroma to a barbeque.

Salad Burnet
(Sanguisorba minor, S. officinalis)

Traits: Hardy perennial, up to 2 feet tall.

Habitat: The mountain areas of Europe as far north as Norway.

History and Folklore: Salad burnet was carried to the New World by Pilgrim Fathers. The herbalist Gerard said it would "make the hart merry and glad, as also being put in wine, to which it yeeldeth a certain grace in the drinking." The botanical name comes from *sanguis*, blood, and *sorbeo*, to staunch, indicating its early use as a wound herb. Culpeper rated it only one step below betony as a valuable herb.

Growing: Plant seeds in sun or light shade in a well-drained lime *(alkaline)* soil. Thin to 9 inches apart. It will self-seed prolifically if allowed to flower.

Preserving: Never used dried salad burnet. Salad burnet should be available virtually all year round unless the weather is particularly harsh.

Uses: Salad burnet is decorative in the garden with pretty, delicate leaves, as long as kept under control. It is high in vitamin C and gives a mild cucumber flavor to salads. Add it to herb butters, cream cheese, cream soups, and cream sauce for fish. Infuse it in vinegar (white) to use for salad dressings.

Summer Savory (*Satureja hortensis*) and Winter Savory (*Satureja montana*)

Traits: Summer savory is an annual up to 18 inches tall, and winter savory is a hardy perennial up to 9 inches tall.

History and Folklore: Savory was regarded as the herb of the satyrs, hence the botanical name *Satureja*.

Growing: Savory needs full sun and a well-drained soil. Sow seeds outside in late spring or take cuttings, which root easily. Take winter savory cuttings from close to the roots. Savory, like so many herbs, responds well to being picked for use and will give several harvests in a season. Grow summer savory as a pot plant.

Uses: Winter savory is a good edging plant and is virtually evergreen. Both varieties are largely culinary herbs. The leaves have a slightly peppery flavor and can be used in any bean dish (green or haricot type), rice, soup, stuffings, sauces, bouquet garni, salads, and dressings. Winter savory is traditional, not to mention delicious, with trout. Try making a bread and onion dressing with savory instead of sage, and roll it into small balls to bake or fry.

Smallage (*Apium graveolens*)

Traits: Hardy biennial, up to 3 feet tall.

Natural Habitat: Southern Europe—found wild on marshland, primarily near the sea.

History and Folklore: Smallage was used to crown victors of the Nemean games held in honor of the Greek god Zeus, but when the son of the Nemean king was killed by a snake concealed in smallage it was used as a funeral wreath. Smallage was popular throughout history and particularly with the American Shakers, who were expert herbalists, for their medicines.

Growing: Grow in sun or partial shade in a rich, moist, well-drained soil. Plant seeds in spring. The germination will be slow and may benefit from heat. Transplant to over 1 foot apart. Smallage will not do well indoors.

Uses: The seed may be ground with salt as celery salt, or added to soups and pickles. The Romans puréed the stems with lovage, oregano, onions, and wine, and used the leaves with dates and pine nuts to stuff suckling pig. The chopped leaves may be put to good use in green salads, cream cheese, or chicken salads, and may be added to milk when poaching white fish.

Note: Avoid consuming high levels during pregnancy, and use with caution if suffering from renal disorders.

Tarragon *(Artemisia dracunculus)*

Traits: More of less hardy perennial, 2 to 3 feet tall.

Natural Habitat: Parts of Russia, Mongolia, and China.

Growing: Tarragon likes a sunny, rich, and dry site. French tarragon (the preferred variety) grows from cuttings only, so avoid tarragon seeds, which are the coarse Russian tarragon and has no culinary value. Protect your plants in winter with straw mulch and bring them indoors in very harsh weather.

Preserving: Tarragon leaves may be frozen, dried, or infused in oil or vinegar.

Uses: Tarragon is an essential ingredient of the French seasoning mix *fines herbes*, with parsley and chervil. Chop it into Béarnaise, tartar, and hollandaise sauces, or mix it into herb butter for steaks and fish. Chop fresh tarragon into omelettes and salad dressings, and try adding it to your favorite chicken dishes. A good starter or light supper is to put a pat of tarragon butter into mushroom caps and bake them uncovered.

Note: Tarragon is a member of the *Artemisia* family, which includes the mugworts, wormwoods, southernwoods, and other decorative forms.

Thyme *(Thymus)*

Traits: Hardy perennial, up to 8 inches tall.

Natural Habitat: Mediterranean, Greece, south of France.

Growing: Plant in full sun on a well-drained soil, like many Mediterranean herbs, such as sage and marjoram. Thyme will grow from seed, or propagate easily from cuttings.

Varieties: There are dozens of varieties, and indeed a whole garden could be devoted to thymes with great effect. Look for: Common thyme (*Thymus vulgaris*), with green leaves and mauve flowers; broad leaf thyme (*T. pulegioides*), with dark oval leaves and dark pink flowers; miniature thyme (*T. minimum*), with tiny leaves, a ground creeping form; and lemon thyme (*T. x citriodorus*), with a lovely lemon scent. Look also for forms with yellow or variegated leaves and bright flowers, often found in the Alpine section of nurseries rather than with the herbs.

Preserving: The leaves dry successfully.

Uses: Can be added to many cooked, savory dishes such as soups, stews, and sauces. Use it in dressings for roast chicken or turkey. Include a sprig in bags of mixed herbs or bouquet garni for authentic French casseroles.

· · · · · · · · · · · · · · · · · · · ·

GET COOKING WITH HERBS
by Deborah C. Harding

Herbs can enhance the flavor of any meal. A plain salad or pot roast can be invigorated by the addition of fresh or dried herbs. Vegetables and fruits can become taste temptations through the use of herbs. Herbs can be baked into breads, cookies, and cakes to create something special and unusual. Herbs are truly a versatile culinary tool that no kitchen should be without.

Herbs can be purchased or grown and preserved for use several different ways.

Fresh: Fresh herbs can be purchased at most grocery stores. Herbs are also easy to grow in a garden or in pots on a patio or on a windowsill.

Dried: Dried herbs can be purchased at grocery stores or homegrown herbs can be dried.

Frozen: Pick herbs from the garden or take leftover fresh herbs purchased at the grocery store and freeze. Clean, whole sprigs or leaves can be thrown into a freezer bag and into the freezer for future use. Leaves can also be chopped and placed into ice cube trays filled with water. Use these cubes in soups or stews.

In oil: Some herbs can be blended with cooking oils, such as olive oil, to be used in cooking. Some of these herbal cooking oils can be purchased in specialty stores.

In vinegar: Herbal vinegars are very popular and can be found in any specialty store. They are very easy to make as well. Fill a jar ¾ full of herb leaves and top off with vinegar. Place plastic wrap over the opening of the jar before placing the cap on. Vinegar coming in contact with the metal lid will cause an undesired chemical reaction, so care must be taken to ensure they do not touch. Place the jar in a sunny windowsill for several weeks. Be sure to shake the jar at least once a day. Strain the vinegar through a coffee filter until it comes out clear and place in a bottle or jar with a fresh sprig of the herb. Experiment with different vinegars and herbs. These work well in marinades and salad dressings.

There are also a few very important factors to keep in mind when cooking with herbs:

Use twice the amount of fresh herbs as dry herbs in any recipe. The drying process concentrates herbal oils, making flavor stronger in dried herbs. Most recipes list measurements for dry herbs unless otherwise specified.

When using dry herbs, crush or crumble the leaves while adding them to your recipe. This will release the oils and their flavors.

In most cases, herbs should be added near the end of cooking time. Flavors tend to fade in herbs when heated.

Store dried herbs in a dark area away from heat. Do not store them above or near the stove. Bright light and heat dissipate the herbal oils, rendering them weak and tasteless. When home drying herbs, try to use dark jars for storage.

The Culinary Possibilities of Herbs

Here are some basic culinary possibilities for a few common herbs.

Basil

Basil is an aromatic herb most associated with Italian and Mediterranean cooking. It is native to India, Africa, and Asia. The name basil comes from the Greek word *basileus*, meaning "king." In India it is a sacred herb to Vishnu and Krishna. In Italy it was considered a sign of love. A pot placed on the balcony was a signal that a woman wished to see her lover. Basil is considered a protection herb and is said to attract prosperity.

There are many different varieties of basil and most are useful in cooking. The best variety is common basil *(Ocimim basiicum)*, but lemon, anise, and cinnamon-flavored varieties are also useful. Basil has a spicy, almost peppery flavor. Leaves can invigorate veal, lamb, fish, and poultry. This herb works well with salads, pasta, rice, tomatoes, cheese, and eggs. Try it with zucchini, squash, eggplant, potatoes, cabbage, carrots, cauliflower, and spinach. Basil is a great addition to soup, stews, and sauces (especially tomato sauces). Its strong flavor does intensify during the cooking process. Start out by adding just a bit in recipes and keep tasting as you cook, adding more accordingly.

To preserve fresh basil, pull off all the leaves from a sprig and place them on a paper towel, making sure they do not touch each other. Place another paper towel on top. Microwave on high for 1 minute, then reduce power to 50 percent and microwave at 30-second intervals until the leaves feel dry. Remove from microwave and let cool for about 5 minutes. Store in an airtight container. Leaves can be air dried by hanging in bunches in an airy dry place out of direct sunlight. The leaves will turn black and it will take about 1 to 2 weeks for them to dry. Basil leaves can be frozen for use in soups and stews. Basil vinegar makes a lovely marinade for meat and it can be combined with oil for use in flavoring meats, vegetables, and sauces.

OLD WORLD PASTA WITH BASIL

Original Italian dishes didn't use a sauce. Instead pasta was tossed with fresh produce. This recipe is one in the old style.

4 large tomatoes, seeds removed, sliced	Vinegar
4 cloves garlic, sliced	Pepper to taste
1 green pepper, halved, seeded, cut into strips	1 lb. rotini, cooked per package directions
20 fresh basil leaves, shredded	Mozzerella
½ c. salad oil	Grated Parmesan

In a large bowl combine tomatoes, garlic, green pepper, basil, oil, vinegar, and pepper. Cover and let stand at room temperature. Drain cooked pasta and put back into the pan without rinsing. Sprinkle mozzarella over top and toss until the cheese melts slightly. Add to tomato mixture and toss well. Serve at room temperature topped with Parmesan cheese.

Chives

Chives are a very old herb dating back more than 5,000 years. The first recorded account of chives comes from the Orient. The ancient Greeks also enjoyed the mild flavor of chives. Chives were thought to drive away illness and it was not unusual to see bunches of the herb hanging over doorways to ward off evil.

Chives can be dried or frozen, but they are best used fresh. Chives add flavor to poultry, fish, and shellfish. They combine well with potatoes, artichokes, asparagus, cauliflower, tomatoes, corn, peas, carrots, and spinach. The also add variety to cream sauces, cheese, and eggs. Add chives to soups and stews or any hot dish right before serving. Their flavor weakens if cooked for long periods of time. Chive butter is lovely on hot bread, and chive vinegar is a great addition to any salad dressing. The flowers of this plant are also edible. Add them to salads.

Chive Broccoli Potatoes

2 lbs. potatoes, peeled, sliced, and cooked	½ c. sour cream
6 tbsp. butter or margarine	½ c. cream cheese
¼ c. milk	1 tbsp. fresh basil, chopped
10 oz. fresh broccoli, chopped	Salt and pepper to taste
1 egg, beaten	1 c. shredded cheese of choice
4 tbsp. fresh chives, chopped	

Cook potatoes and mash with butter and milk. Place back into the pot. In another pot cover with broccoli with boiling water, let sit for 5 minutes, and drain. Add to potatoes along with the egg, chives, sour cream, cream cheese, basil, salt, and pepper. Put half of this potato mixture into a greased two-quart casserole. Add half the shredded cheese, then the rest of the potato mixture, and top with remaining cheese. Bake at 350 degrees F for 40 minutes. Let sit 10 minutes before serving.

Mint

Mint can be grown by anyone just about anywhere, as it grows like a weed. Mint is a common flavoring in mouthwashes, breath fresheners, and toothpastes because of its clean and fresh taste, and it was treasured long ago by Romans and others. The Pharisees paid tithes with sprigs, and Greeks used mint in their temples and as a remedy for clearing the throat and curing hiccups. Because of its fresh scent, sprigs of mint were strewn on the floor in kitchens. Mint water was sprayed about the medieval home to give it a pleasant scent.

Mine was used in the nineteenth century for many remedies, including colic and stomach discomforts. It was also applied to wounds to prevent infections. Tea was used for headaches, heartburn, and insomnia. Placing a mint leaf in a wallet or purse is said to guarantee prosperity. Wearing a sprig of mint at the wrist will keep illness at bay, and kept indoors it will protect the home from any malady.

There are many different varieties of mint. The best varieties for culinary purposes are peppermint, spearmint, applemint, pineapple mint, and any of the citrus mints. Make mint water or mint lemonade by adding a sprig to a glass or pitcher. Peppermint is the best for this because of its strong, cooling taste. Spearmint is a bit milder than peppermint. It can be used with meats, eggplant, beans, lentils, fruit salads, cucumbers, creamy vegetable soups, peas, in jellies, and with chocolate. Flavored mints are a good addition in drinks, fruit, and cottage cheese. Add apple or lemon mint to melon balls with a little sparkling apple cider drizzled over top for a wonderful summer salad.

Mint is better used fresh. When dried, the flavor weakens. Mint can be grown in a flower garden or in a pot. It is better to place in a container as it has a tendency to spread all over the garden. Mint can be frozen or dried. Dry by hanging bunches upside down until dry and crispy, then store in an airtight container. Dab a bit on the face on a hot day for a fresh pick up.

Vegetable Mint Salad

1 medium red or
yellow pepper, diced

1 medium green bell pepper, diced

4 large tomatoes, seeded and diced

¼ c. fresh parsley, chopped

1 can garbanzo beans (chickpeas),
drained and rinsed

1 medium red onion,
peeled and sliced thin

½ c. fresh mint, chopped

¼ c. olive oil

3 tbsp. fresh lemon juice

In a bowl combine peppers, tomatoes, parsley, garbanzo beans, onion, and mint. Drizzle olive oil and lemon juice over top. Toss to coat and serve.

Oregano

Oregano is associated with Italian cooking, and is now very common, but remarkably this herb wasn't popular in the United States until after World War II when soldiers came home bragging of the food they enjoyed in Italy. Oregano has a hot, peppery flavor. It is used in dishes in Italy, Greece, Mexico, Spain, Cuba, and South American countries. Oregano combines well with eggs in omelets, frittatas, and quiches. It can give new taste to yeast breads, vegetables, mushrooms, beef, pork, poultry, and shellfish. Try it with black beans, zucchini, eggplant, and tomatoes. Oregano is commonly confused with its milder tasting relative, marjoram. These herbs look very similar and they can be interchangeable in cooking, though marjoram is milder. If marjoram is to be used as a substitute for oregano, twice as much must be used.

Oregano's early uses were primarily medicinal. Greeks used leaves to relieve sore muscles. Romans used oregano for scorpion bites. The tea was used for coughs and asthma, while oil was used for toothaches. Oregano is easy to grow and lends itself well to container growing. Snip off the leaves as needed. Oregano can be dried by hanging in bunches. Once dried, run fingers down the stem to remove the tiny leaves and store them in airtight containers. Oregano can also be frozen. Oregano oil can add flavor to meats and be used when making omelets. Oregano vinegar is useful in meat and vegetable marinades.

LEMON OREGANO CHICKEN

4 chicken breast halves with bone, skinned	3 tbsp. fresh oregano or 1 tsp. dried oregano
1 clove garlic, peeled	Salt and pepper to taste
⅓ c. fresh lemon juice	¼ c. melted butter
⅓ c. olive oil	

In the morning remove the skin from the chicken breasts and rub each with the peeled garlic clove. Place in a china or earthenware bowl. Do not use plastic or metal or the flavor will be altered.

In another nonmetal bowl, combine the lemon juice, olive oil, oregano, salt, and pepper. Add the garlic clove used to rub the chicken breasts. Pour this over the chicken, cover, and refrigerate. Turn the chicken breasts a few times during the day.

Preheat a broiler to high or prepare a grill. Arrange chicken on a broiler pan or on the grill and baste with the melted butter. Broil or grill on both sides, basting often, alternating with the marinade and the butter until done. Serve hot.

Parsley

Parsley is best known for its garnishing abilities, but it is also a very tasty herb. But there is a good reason parsley is used for a garnish. The herb is a natural breath freshener. Just chew a bit of it after the meal is over for fresh breath. Romans placed it on each plate because they thought it would guard against contamination. Early Greeks prized parsley. They would make garlands for use in funeral ceremonies because parsley was associated with death. It seems parsley sprouted from the ground where Greek hero Archemorus was killed by serpents. Triumphant athletes were crowned with parsley wreathes since it was thought to be one of Hercules' favorite herbs. In the Middle Ages, parsley became popular as a medication being used to relieve kidney and liver complaints and to aid digestion. Parsley is a protection herb and is said to stop misfortune if used in purification rites.

These are two different types of parsley commonly used in cooking. One is curly leaf parsley, used primarily for garnish, and flat leaf parsley, which has more flavor. Both are grown easily in gardens or containers; both grow well from seed though they are often slow to sprout. (An old saying tells that parsley goes to the devil seven times before it sprouts; it can take up to six weeks for germination.) Snip fresh sprigs as needed and bring your harvest in to dry before the first frost. The best way to dry your parsley is in a gas oven with a pilot light. Tear the parsley leaves from the sprig and place them on an oven sheet. Stir the leaves around occasionally until dry. It should take a few days.

Parsley can be combined with butter and used when cooking eggs or vegetables. Parsley can also be frozen for soups and stews. Parsley has a delightful, mild flavor that blends well with anything except sweets. It is used in Middle East, French, Swiss, Japanese, and Mexican cuisines. Instead of placing parsley on the plate as a garnish, put parsley in your recipes. Parsley combines especially well with all meats, poultry, and fish as well as with any vegetable, rice, or pasta.

PARSLEY PARMESAN POTATOES

4 tbsp. butter

½ c. fresh Parmesan cheese

3 tbsp. dried parsley, chopped,
   or 6 tbsp. fresh parsley, chopped

¼ c. flour

1 tsp. pepper

½ tsp. salt

1 can peeled whole potatoes or 3 baking
   potatoes, peeled and sliced thin

Parsley potatoes are a mainstay of banquet dining. This recipe adds a little cheese for a different flavor. Preheat oven to 350 degrees F. Melt butter in a 2-quart casserole. In a resealable 2-quart freezer bag combine Parmesan cheese, parsley, flour, salt, and pepper. Place potatoes or potato slices, a little bit at a time, in the bag and shake to coat. Place potatoes in the casserole, sprinkle with the remaining coating mixture, and bake 20 minutes. Remove from oven and turn potatoes. Return to oven for another 15 to 20 minutes or until potatoes are tender.

Sage

Sage is very popular around the American Thanksgiving because of its ability to combine with traditional turkey and dressing. Many ancient cultures associated sage with immortality, longevity, and wisdom. It is one of the Native American sacred herbs used to purify and cleanse the spirit. It was also used by the Native Americans as a medication. Sage has many medicinal uses, including fighting epilepsy, insomnia, and seasickness. A legend says that a full garden bed of sage brings bad luck, so it is best for it to share the bed with another plant. To see if a wish will come true, write it on a sage leaf and place it under your pillow, sleeping on it for three nights. If you dream about the wish it will come true. If not, the leaf should be buried in the ground so it can do no harm.

Sage has a pleasant bitter taste somewhat reminiscent of camphor. There are several varieties, but most are not suitable to cooking. Common, or garden, sage *(Salvia officianalis)* is the best, but pineapple sage adds a bit of zip to some recipes as well. Almost every culture, from the Mediterranean—where sage finds its origin—to Europe, Asia, and North and South America utilizes this herb. The leaves blend well in salads, with eggs, soups, yeast breads, and in marinades. Try adding sage to sausage, poultry, and pork. Of course, it is traditional in poultry stuffings, but you may also try it in pork stuffings. Sage works well with any meat, with tomatoes, asparagus, carrots, squash, corn, potatoes, beans, cabbage, citrus fruits, and cheese.

Sage is a bit difficult to grow since it takes about two years for the plant grown by seed to become harvestable. Sage is a shrub and tends to get old and woody after about three years and must be replaced. Sage leaves can be hung to dry and stored in airtight containers. Dried sage is as good as fresh in any recipe. Frozen leaves can be used as well. Sage vinegar makes a great marinade for chicken or pork and also makes a delicious addition to green beans or beets.

SAGE POT ROAST OR THE WISE ROAST

5 lb. boneless beef chuck roast	1, 12 oz. can beef broth
1 clove garlic, crushed	5 potatoes, peeled and quartered
2 tbsp. olive oil	4 carrots, cut in 2 pieces
1½ tsp. dried sage	2 onions, peeled and quartered
½ tsp. salt	5 tsp. cornstarch
¼ tsp. pepper	¼ c. water

Sage is known to be more compatible with chicken or pork, but this recipe highlights its use with beef. In an ovenproof Dutch oven or other deep ovenproof pan, brown the roast in the oil and garlic. Season with sage, salt, and pepper. Add the broth. Cover and bake in a preheated 325-degree F oven for 2½ hours. Add potatoes, carrot, and onion. Cover and bake 1 hour longer. Remove roast and vegetables to a service platter and keep warm.

In a cup combine the cornstarch and water. Stir into the pan juices and cook, stirring constantly, until thick and smooth. Serve over the roast.

Thyme

Thyme is probably the most versatile of all herbs. It goes with practically everything, grows easily, and it has a dependable medicinal reputation. *Thymus* means "courage" in Greek. Thyme represented elegance to ancient Greece and was placed in banquet halls before feasts. The knights of the Middle Ages considered thyme a symbol of chivalry. Placing thyme under the pillow is said to ensure a restful sleep. It is also said women who wear a sprig in their hair are irresistible. A legend states that wearing thyme will enable one to see fairies. Thyme was used in the fight against every plague that came along and swept Europe. It was also used as an antiseptic all the way up until World War I.

There are many different varieties of thyme with different flavors and scents (camphor, caraway, nutmeg, lemon) and with different looks for landscaping (silver, creeping, and woolly). The best type to be used in cooking is common thyme (*Thymus vulgaris*). Thyme lends itself well to container gardening, but it is better to purchase a plant rather than plant from seed because the seeds are very picky about their conditions. Snip fresh thyme whenever needed, and harvest before a frost. Tie the sprigs in bundles and hang to dry. Remove the tiny leaves from the stems and store in airtight containers. This is another herb where using fresh is just as good as using dried in cooking. Frozen is also acceptable in most dishes. Thyme vinegar makes wonderful marinades and salad dressing. Thyme butter gives a delicate taste to breads, and using it in egg dishes is pure pleasure. Thyme oil is good for browning meats.

Thyme tastes earthy, clean, and faintly clovelike. French cuisine is fond of this herb, and it is prevalent in Creole and Cajun dishes. But practically every cuisine makes use of this herb. Thyme combines well with veal, lamb, beef, poultry, and fish. It is a welcome addition to stuffings and patés. Include it in sausage, stews, and soups. It will bring out the flavor in cucumbers, tomatoes, onions, carrots, eggplant, parsnips, mushrooms, green beans, broccoli, potatoes, corn, peas, cheese, egg, and rice.

EASY THYME CHICKEN POUQUI

4 boneless, skinless chicken breast halves
Salt and pepper to taste

Sauce

2½ tbsp. butter, divided	½ tbsp. dried thyme, crumbled
1 clove garlic, crushed	3 tbsp. dry white wine
1 tbsp. olive oil	⅓ c. cream of chicken soup
½ c. onion, chopped	⅓ c. half and half

In a heavy skillet, melt 1½ tablespoons butter over medium heat. Add garlic and sauté until slightly brown. Pat chicken dry with a paper towel and season with salt and pepper to taste. Place in the skillet and cook on both sides until done (about 7 to 10 minutes). Transfer to a serving plate.

In a heavy medium saucepan melt the remaining butter with the oil. Add the onion and thyme and sauté until the onions become translucent. Add the wine and cook until the liquid is reduced by half. Add the soup and half and half and stir until heated through. Spoon over cooked chicken and garnish with a little dried thyme.

These are just a few of the wonderful world of culinary herbs used to enhance the flavor of food. They will bring your old recipes back to life with new tastes and vitality in a healthy way. So, what are you waiting for? Get cooking with herbs!

·····················

WORLD SPICE BLENDS
by K. D. Spitzer

We tend to think of herbs as indigenous plant tops of leaves that are grown for human consumption. We see this happening commonly in backyard gardens, along wild roadsides, or in open woodland groves.

But more intriguingly, we can also think of herbs as exotic spices made from roots, barks, and berries grown in far away and mysterious lands. In fact, the trade of exotic spices comprises a long, romantic, and often bloody chapter in human history. Originally brought by caravan from the Far East through roads in the Middle East to peoples of the Mediterranean, herbal spices played a key role in the spread and growth of civilization. It is difficult to imagine—now that such herbs are now nearly omnipresent in even the most remote corners of the planet—that there was a time when they were not entirely known everywhere.

Herbs in World Cuisine

Some historians have thought that the medicinal efficacy of herbs came before their use as flavorings, but just the opposite is probably true. People were eating greens long before they moved into settlements; they actually probably dried them in order to carry these flavorful plants more easily on their nomadic wanderings. The Romans carried seeds all the way to Britain, and the Brits brought them to the New World. It was a fair exchange because the Americans returned allspice, chilies, cayenne and paprika, sweet and hot peppers, and chocolate and vanilla to the Old World. Today these flavors are found in cuisines around the world.

Before refrigeration, herbs and spices were used not only to mask the odors of rotting meats, but also to preserve meat, dairy products, and even bread in hot climates. We think of cinnamon as a sweet spice, but it was first used for its antibacterial qualities in the preparation of meats in India and the Middle East. Drop a stick into your beef stew, and people will question the surprising magic you have wrought.

A key ingredient in Mediterranean cooking, thyme was rubbed on or used in the process of making meat in order to keep all kinds of vermin from entering the larder. And in fact, its name in Greek means "to fumigate." Today, thyme's reputation as an antibacterial is long-standing as the distilled tops produce a strong disinfectant more potent than carbolic acid.

Caraway, meanwhile, was and is commonly used to season cabbage and pork dishes. It is also useful for its help with the indigestible side effects of a fatty dish. Its marriage with these ingredients is ambrosial, and its reduction of flatulence after dinner makes it a gift of the Goddess.

Specific herbs and spices have an affinity for one another. These classic combinations even stretch back several thousand years. Many of these mixtures are used in cooking food, such as meats, that require cooking over a long slow fire. Other mixtures are used in pickling, another useful and traditional food-preservation method.

In any herb combination, be sure to use freshly dried spices and herbs. If purchasing such mixtures from a natural food store or herb shop where the prices are assuredly cheaper, be certain the herbs have not been on the shelf for a long time. Buy a good quality product instead, and make it organic if you can find it. Do not store containers on your stovetop or in the sunlight. Keep the lid tightly secured, and rotate your stock of herbs regularly to help maintain freshness.

Buying whole spices or peppercorns and grinding them yourself can produce a greater flavor sensation than purchasing preground ones. For this, a marble or granite mortar and pestle grinds seeds and roots more readily than a wooden one. An electric grinder is even better if you grind in short bursts. Be aware: if the blade gets hot it will heat up and affect the oils of the herb of spice, thus ruining its flavor and properties. You can also place your herbs in a plastic bag and crush with a rolling pin or edge of an iron skillet. Some herbs, especially seeds, are toasted in a dry skillet to bring out their full flavor before grinding.

Recipes

The distinction among world cuisine relies not upon differing ingredients but in the subtle use of them. Chicken, rice, onions, garlic, and tomatoes can make your supper in Rome or New York, Calcutta, or Mexico City, but the use of herbs in differing proportions will blend these ingredients into entirely unique ways—and bring a completely different taste to your mouth! And long-distance differences are not the only ones you will find. In France, an experienced palate can tell the region by the flavor of the dinner. This is true in many countries, where regional differences have much to do with the local variance in traditional herbs and spices.

Below are some recipes you can sample to begin your exploration of the great diversity of flavor in herbal spices. You can use these as a starting point to examine the use of herbs in the endless and exotic cuisines around the world. Happy hunting!

Garam Masala

Aromatic garam masala is a spice blend from northern India. Your homemade version of garam masala will be far superior to anything you have bought in a store. Also, because of the variety of herbs and complicated flavor in the mixture—and the possible variations of flavor ranging from subtle to fierce—it is worth experimenting to produce a combination of spices in this mixture that is suitable to your own palate.

In Indian dishes, you can also add one part garam masala to three parts curry for a depth of flavor unobtainable by just using curry. The following is fairly mild, but still suitable for a meat curry. Indian spice blends are always best when used fresh. (Makes about ⅓ cup)

20 green cardamom pods	2 tsp. whole cloves
3 cinnamon sticks	2 tbsp. black peppercorns
4 bay leaves	2 tsp. freshly grated nutmeg
4 tsp. cumin seeds	

Remove the small dark seeds from the cardamom pods. Discard the papery outer husk. Crush the seeds. Break the cinnamon stick into smaller pieces. Crumble the bay leaves.

Add all the spices except the ground nutmeg to a dry skillet and shake over medium heat for 2 to 3 minutes. Shaking or stirring with a wooden implement will prevent burning. If you can take the mouthwatering scent, you can also toast the spices in a 200 degree F oven for 35 to 40 minutes, stirring occasionally. Place the mixture in a bowl and let cool completely. Add the nutmeg and then grind to a fine powder in small batches in a mortar and pestle or electric grinder. Store the spice mixture in a sterilized jar, seal, and label. Refrigerate if you are not going to use it right away.

Note: The freshly grated nutmeg is well worth the slight extra effort. You will immediately realize the superiority of scent and flavor of this fresh spice.

Hot Curry Powder

(Makes about 1½ cups)

½ c. ground turmeric	½ c. coriander seeds
5 tbsp. black peppercorns	1 tbsp. whole cloves
2 tbsp. cumin seeds	2 tbsp. decorticated cardamom seeds
1 tbsp. mace	1 tbsp. cinnamon
1 tbsp. ground fenugreek seeds	1½ tsp. ground ginger
1 tsp. ground cayenne pepper	

Shake all ingredients in a heavy skillet for 5 minutes, or toast in a 350 degree F oven for 20 minutes. Let cool and then grind coarsely. Store in a sterilized jar, seal, and label. Refrigerate. You don't need to cook it before using.

Herbes de Provence

The French have added several herb blends to world cuisine. Probably the most famous and expensive is the imported herbes de Provence. Made up of herbs commonly grown in the soil of Provence, this herbal bouquet is marked in particular for its inclusion of highly fragrant lavender. In fact, the province is well known for this flowery herb.

You can use herbes de Provence by tying it up in tiny cheesecloth bags, or by measuring a teaspoon or so into a tea ball and tossing it into a stew along with some red wine. It is also suitable for use as a rub on a roast. (Makes about 1 cup—use freshly dried herbs if available)

3 tbsp. summer savory	3 tbsp. thyme
3 tbsp. marjoram	1 tbsp. rosemary
1 tbsp. basil	1 tsp. sage
1 tsp. fennel seed	½ tsp. lavender

Mix all of the herbs well. Store the mixture in a sterilized jar, seal, and label.

Italian Seasoning

The Italians have their own wonderful herb blend that is perfect for throwing into a minestrone, rubbing on a lamb roast, tossing into a cannellini bean soup, or using to season a pizza. You can add fresh minced garlic to the mixture as you use it to bring out the flavors of the green herbs. (Makes about 1 cup)

8 to 12 bay leaves	3 tbsp. sage
3 tbsp. Italian (flat leaf) parsley	3 tbsp. thyme
2 tbsp. hot Hungarian paprika (optional —you can use less if you choose)	3 tbsp. freshly ground black pepper
3 tbsp. Greek oregano	

Crush the bay leaves to a fine powder. Mix all the ingredients together and pack in a sterilized jar, seal, and label.

Note: Dry fresh flat Italian parsley in the microwave in 30-second bursts until dry. This has better flavor than the dried curly parsley sold in glass jars. Lemon thyme plants can be grown in small containers and have wonderful flavor. Dry this herb in the microwave.

Multipurpose Sweet Spice Blend

Spice up your pies and cookies with your own spice blend. Sweet spice mixtures have been popular for centuries. Try this one as it's written, and then next time change the proportions to suit your own tastes. Add in place of the cinnamon and other spices when making a pie, or instead of the spices in a cookie recipe. (Makes about ½ cup)

2 cinnamon sticks	2 tsp. ground cloves
2 tbsp. allspice berries	1½ tbsp. ground ginger
2 tbsp. coriander seeds	1 tsp. freshly ground nutmeg

Break up the cinnamon sticks and add to the allspice, coriander, and cloves. Grind to a fine powder. Blend in the ginger and nutmeg. Pack the mixture into a sterilized jar, seal, and label.

....

THE HERBS AND SPICES OF INDIA
by Carolyn Moss

There are so many books, magazine articles, and television programs around today about herbs that most of us are aware the Italians use a lot of basil and oregano and the French favor tarragon and thyme. However, when it comes to experimenting with Indian food many of us just reach for a jar of curry powder without considering what goes into it.

But in fact it is easy, and very rewarding, to make your own curry powders and other fresh spice mixes from fresh ingredients. I'd like to encourage you by talking about some of the flavorings used commonly in India, Pakistan, and in the wonderful but troubled island off India's southern tip, Sri Lanka, to take a plunge of your own and learn more about some of the herbs and spices of this region.

You will find that many of the herbs and spices in the following list are familiar friends—though a few will likely be new to you. Although supermarkets are getting better and better in their range of exotic spices, some of you may have to use the internet to locate some ethnic markets (try Chinese as well as Indian, Sri Lankan, or Pakistani; in parentheses I have included the Indian name of the item). If you live in a more remote location and are unable to find Asian markets, you will want to explore mail order and online stores—a good place to locate such suppliers are the back pages of food magazines.

And just one more thing—if you don't like hot food and have an impulse to skip over this article, then please don't. Much food from the subcontinent is fragrant and spicy rather than just plain hot. The use of such foods has also been found to do wonders for the immune system, so perhaps all of our lives could all use a little spicing up from time to time.

Asafoetida *(Heeng)*

This is one herb that you will only find in specialist stores. I have to admit to including this item for interest value possibly more than for practical use. It is found in Asian cooking from Afghanistan and Kashmir in the north to Sri Lanka in the south. It is to be found in the form of a block of resin and has, to the average Western nose, the most appalling smell. The irreplaceable doyen of American cookery writers, James Beard, likened it to truffles, although I would say he was being charitable. However, a pinch thrown into recipes when spices are being fried in oil adds a certain depth and authenticity to the food. It also has the property of relieving gas and flatulence and aiding digestion.

Bay *(Tej Patta)*

An aromatic leaf from a tree which will grow to 20 or more feet in the right conditions, bay is used in many cuisines of the world. It is normally used whole and, unlike many herbs, dries well, Occasionally recipes will call for ground bay, in which case pound it in a pestle and mortar or grind it in a spice grinder.

Cardamom *(Elachi)*

Cardamom is to be found in three forms: ground to a powder, in small pale-green pods, and less commonly, in larger rough dark brown pods (usually found only in ethnic stores). The two forms of pod are interchangeable in recipes. They must be pounded in a pestle and mortar (or with the bottom of a bottle) to extract the seeds, which should then be lightly crushed. The pod can be included in cooking for extra flavor but must be fished out before serving. Ideally if a recipe calls for ground cardamom you should pound up some seeds yourself. Spices purchased in powdered form never give as good a flavor and deteriorate very quickly.

Cardamom is used in savory meat, vegetable, and rice dishes on the subcontinent, and is also found in sweet preparations such as rice pudding or festive candy. Interestingly, cardamom also crops up in Scandinavian baking as a cake and cookie flavoring.

Cayenne Pepper (Pisi hui lal mirch)

This is one of the hottest preparations available and is made from powdered dried red chilies of the fieriest variety. It is freely available in supermarkets and should be used in great moderation. It will, of course, be familiar to those who enjoy Tex-Mex food as well as Asian cookery. It is a product where the powdered form is the norm and perfectly acceptable.

Fresh Green Chilies (Hari mirch)

It is the use of fresh chili which has given Asian food its reputation for fighting bacteria. These chilies also contain vitamins A and C, although one can't consume large quantities of chili. Although it is tempting to think that where a recipe calls for fresh chili, dried will do—surely it is only to add heat—there is a real difference in the freshness and vibrancy of a dish to which the fresh spice has been added. So do try to find them. There are, of course, many varieties of chili about, and in broad terms, the larger the variety, the milder it is—with the tiny red pea chilies and the little round habanero being the fiercest. If you aren't sure, proceed with caution. And always be vigilant in handling chili—do not touch your face, especially your eyes, while working with them and for a short time afterward. Just deal with the chili and then wash your hands well when you are done.

Red Dried Chili *(Sabut lal mirch)*

Again, one could use powder to get the kick into a dish, but dried whole chilies gives a different spicing effect in dishes. A tip: if you are concerned about heat, cut the pod open and throw away the seeds.

Cinnamon *(Dar cheeni)*

Cinnamon is a very familiar spice. It is a bit unusual, as it comes from the bark of the cinnamon tree. Most herbs and spices are leaves or seeds and pods. Cinnamon is often found in powdered form which is fine for sweet dishes. For Indian rice and curries one needs the actual small bits of bark, which look like small hollow sticks, to be included in cooking and fished out before eating.

Cloves *(Lavang)*

Cloves are another Asian spice which has settled itself well into Western baking. An English Christmas cake would certainly not be complete without a pinch of clove powder. Again, for Indian cooking we want to use the whole clove, which is actually the entire tiny dried bud of the clove flower. The cloves must be removed before eating as biting on a whole one is not too pleasant an experience for the inexperienced. Indians do, however, suck on them as breath fresheners. The concentrated essential oil of cloves has slightly anesthetic properties and is recommended (diluted and on a cotton pad) for treating toothaches.

Coriander *(Dhaniya)*

This lovely spice is used widely throughout the subcontinent and is found in recipes in three forms: the fresh leaves, the whole seeds, and a ground powder. The leaves are closely related to the cilantro used, of course, in Mexican food. In Asia, these are normally added near or at the end of cooking, almost like a parsley garnish but with a much more pungent effect. The whole seeds can be ground at home most easily in an electric coffee or spice grinder. Where a recipe calls for whole seeds, they need to be crushed lightly before using. I would mention that coriander is extremely easy to grow from seed. It is an annual and will grow outside in the summer months anywhere in the United States (other than Alaska), and all year round in the more southerly states.

Cumin *(Zeera)*

Cumin can be used as a whole seed or ground into a powder. Many recipes call for the seeds to be roasted before using. This is done by placing the seeds in a small dry pan over a medium heat. Do not use any fat, and do not leave the pan unattended. Stir the seeds until they start popping and emit a lovely, spicy fragrance. Remove them from the heat and continue with your recipe or store for future use.

Curry Leaf *(Kari Phulia, Kari Patta)*

The curry leaf is widely used in southern India and Sri Lanka to flavor everything from egg dishes to soups and rice. It gives a citrusy, and not, as you would expect, a curry flavor. Likely, you won't find this ingredient in the supermarket. Ethnic stores may have the dried leaf, and, on occasion, you will find the fresh leaf imported from Kenya rather than from the subcontinent.

Fennel *(Soonf)*

Whereas in Western cooking we enjoy the bulb and leaf of the fennel, Asian recipes require only the seed. Fennel tastes like its close relative the aniseed and is used in spice mixes as a garnish. It is also useful as a breath freshener chewed after a meal. Fennel has digestive qualities and is used in babies' "gripe water" to soothe and placate them.

Fenugreek *(Methi)*

With fenugreek, both the rather odd little seeds, which are almost like tiny cubes, and the fresh leaves, are called for in recipes. The leaves will probably only be found in ethnic stores, and so are out of the range of many of us. The seeds are easier to come by, and you may also come across the dried leaf—although I am not a fan of dried leaves. This ingredient, leaves or seeds, is found throughout Indian cookery and is a major ingredient in the Balti recipes which have been popular with some Indian restaurants in recent years. Balti is a strange phenomenon, which, like much Chinese food, has evolved in restaurants and has little to do with what is actually served in people's homes in India itself, although it is still rather delicious.

Garam Masala

I have included this item because you may well come across it while shopping for your other herbs and spices. The words simply mean "hot spices" and are a form of authentic curry powder used in India, Pakistan, and Sri Lanka. There is no fixed recipe and each manufacturer and family will have their own version. They will normally include cardamom, cinnamon, cumin, cloves, pepper, coriander, and possibly something extra such as nutmeg. As you will see from this list, and despite the translation of the name, the effect of garam masala is aromatic rather than hot. Garam masala is sometimes simply sprinkled onto a dish after cooking.

Fresh Ginger *(Adrak)*

Although the dried powder is sometimes called for in Eastern cooking, more common is the wide use of fresh ginger. Ginger is a wonderful knobbly root that is peeled and grated, sliced, or pounded to a paste. It adds a great pungency and freshness to recipes. Fresh ginger also has considerable medicinal properties and, made into a tea, sweetened to taste, has been found to cure chronic sickness and nausea, such as morning sickness during pregnancy, that will not respond to any other kind of treatments.

When you buy a lump of ginger root and only want to use a small piece, plant the rest in a small pot of sandy soil on your kitchen windowsill. Water from time to time. It will keep fresh—just dig up, wash, and cut off whatever you require each time. It will also sprout new knobs and may even send up leaves.

Mint *(Podina)*

Another ingredient which will need little introduction, mint is used occasionally as a fresh leaf. It is also used dried in many curry paste mixtures. Be sure only to use dried mint if the recipe specifically asks for it. It is generally not a good substitute for fresh. FYI—mint is one of the easiest herbs to grow in a garden or pot.

Mustard Seeds *(Sarson)*

We are all familiar with mustard, but here we are talking about the whole black, or dark or reddish brown, seeds of the mustard plant. They give off a marvelous flavor when fried in oil and used as directed in Indian recipes, and they are great just fried in some good oil and sprinkled over salads of mixed green leaves or grated carrot.

Nutmeg *(Jaiphat)*

Another friend from the bakery cupboard, whole nutmeg should always be used freshly grated in Asian food. You can even purchase darling little nutmeg graters with their own lidded box attached at the back for keeping the nutmegs in. Whole nutmegs look rather like tiny brains, particularly in cross section, and under the old Law of Similars, where the early medicinal herbalists thought plants cured that which they most resembled, nutmeg was recommended for head problems.

Paprika

This is the Hungarian name for a form of powdered chili that is used for depth of flavor and color rather than heat. However, you may find brands labeled mild or hot, in which case you'll have to experiment to determine your preference.

Saffron *(Kesar)*

Another unusual part of the plant is used here—saffron threads are the stamens of the saffron crocus which is grown widely in parts of northern India and Spain. It is the most expensive spice in the world by weight, although a tiny box should last for a good few recipes. It gives off a beautiful yellow coloring that can be replicated by turmeric (see below). However, its flavor cannot be reproduced, so do try to use whenever possible. Recipes will say how to use the spice, whether it is to be pounded first or soaked in water or milk. Just a pinch added to good basmati rice raises a simple dish to an altogether higher plane. Saffron is, of course, used in Western cooking—particularly in gourmet sauces and Italian risotto.

Sesame *(Til)*

Associated more with oriental food and burger buns, sesame seeds are readily available and are often found in sweet and savory Indian recipes, sometimes just dry roasted in a frying pan and added as a flavorful garnish at the end.

Turmeric *(Haldi)*

This spice is normally found preground and adds a bright yellow color to rice or curries. It has digestive properties, and although it brings a mild flavor it is mostly used for coloring. Fresh turmeric is a root and looks like a yellow, thin ginger root. It is rarely to be found in its fresh form in the West, so the powder will do just fine.

Recipes

Space forbids me giving you a lot of recipes with which to try out the above spices, but books abound in the stores and libraries, so you should easily be able to find something to suit you. Some people are put off Indian recipes by the long list of ingredients. What I will do, then, is give you a couple recipes that you can make up in advance and keep in your cupboard or refrigerator and then have the means to cook up something good and spicy at very short notice.

Garam Masala

½ whole nutmeg

1 tsp. cumin seeds

½ tsp. whole cloves

1 tbsp. cardamom seeds
(removed from pods)

½ tsp. coriander seed, grated

1 tsp. black peppercorns

1, 2-inch cinnamon stick

Put all the ingredients into an electric coffee grinder and whiz until everything is finely ground. Sieve if you wish, although it is not necessary if you have managed to grind things to a reasonably fine powder. Store in an airtight jar away from heat or light.

Curry (Balti) *Paste*

4 tbsp. coriander, ground	2 tbsp. cumin, ground
2 tbsp. fenugreek seeds	2 tbsp. garlic powder
2 tbsp. paprika	1 tsp. cinnamon, powder
5 tbsp. garam masala (see above)	1 tsp. bay leaf, ground
1 tsp. ginger, ground	1 tsp. chili powder
1 tsp. black pepper	Vinegar
1 tsp. asafetida (optional)	½ c. vegetable oil
2 tbsp. turmeric	

If all spices are already powdered, simply mix. Otherwise, mix and grind them finely. Add enough vinegar to make a thick paste. Heat the oil in a frying pan. Add the paste and fry, stirring continuously until the color has darkened and the oil separates. Store in a lidded jar making sure the paste is covered with oil. Simply use 1 or 2 tablespoons of the paste when you stir fry meat, chicken, or vegetables, or add when a recipe calls for curry paste or powder.

....

GARNISHES AND GREMOLATA
by K. D. Spitzer

If you are nervous about herbs and want to feel comfortable in using them in your daily life, a good tip is to grow them yourself. A strawberry jar by the back door, a window box on the deck railing, or a tiny plot by the kitchen door can make you comfortable with these plants, and in turn influence your cooking in many ways. When fresh herbs are just a step away from your kitchen counter, you're more likely to pause to grab a handful to throw into any dish. Tossed on takeout or dusted over frozen dinners, fresh herbs add a special flavor and a personal touch.

Don't worry about the particulars in using herbs. They don't need to be minced finely just because the recipe calls for it—all you really need to go is pinch the leaves off with your fingers and drop them in whole. There are no set rules—just do what works for you.

Some Herbal Ideas

It is fairly common now to find fresh herbs in the grocery store, which is a great boon in the winter months. When you bring them home, pick them over and rinse in cold water. Shake or spin dry, wrap loosely in a paper towel, and then secure with plastic wrap or aluminum foil. They should keep for a couple weeks preserved in this fashion. If you are new to growing herbs in pots, you need to be aware that plants in pots dry out very quickly. Here in New England, I often have to water every day in July and August. It's best to water in the morning. The reward, of course, is fresh herbs, practically at my fingertips.

There are too many varieties of herbs to count, so perhaps this is a stumbling block for many people. But do not be worried—the key is just to make a start, trying various herbs and making notes on what you do and do not enjoy. Experiment a little! If you find you like thyme, then try lemon thyme or other varieties of the herb. Put whole sprigs of herbs you think you might like under the skin on the chicken you're roasting. Sprinkle the fresh leaves on goat cheese. Try it on sliced tomatoes.

Use it along with rosemary to infuse your olive oil. Wrap sliced sweet potatoes, thinly sliced onion, minced garlic, and whole sprigs of lemon thyme in aluminum foil; drizzle with olive oil and secure tightly. Bake at 350 degrees F for an hour or so—the time depends upon how large the packet is. See what happens. With herbs, the possibilities are just about endless.

Plant spearmint in a pot with a large diameter, and keep the pot on your doorstep. This will make it readily available and also prevent this invasive herb from taking over the garden. Pinch off a stem or two, and put the leaves in your salad. This is a wake-up flavor that will impress your family and guests. Put several sprigs in a water pitcher along with slices of lemon or lime, and let it sit in the fridge for an hour or two before serving. In the springtime, freeze yellow forsythia or red quince blossoms inside ice cubes and toss them into the pitcher along with the mint and lemon or lime before serving. The flowers are edible as well as showy. In winter months, substitute thin slices of fresh ginger for the mint.

Toss whole basil leaves in your salad. Chervil's feathery leaves have been ignored far too long in favor or the ubiquitous cilantro. Once you have tasted this versatile French-lineaged herb, you will happily add it to salads, eggs, and fish. Using it often will keep a pot of it pinched back and bushy. The more you use it, the happier it is. This is true of most herbs.

Don't overlook pungent herbs with fruit. Poach slightly underripe pears and peaches with bay leaves and peppercorns. Garnish with nasturtiums for additional peppery punch, and a touch of class. Spearmint or pineapple mint are delicious with mango or papaya; drizzle with fresh lime juice.

Gremolata

The Italians created a garnish for soups, stews, and roasts that elevates homely comfort foods to a real taste sensation. Ordinarily paired with osso buco, gremolata is very versatile and can be changed to include what's available. There are just three basic ingredients: garlic, parsley, and lemon zest. Sprinkle this mixture on your entrée just before serving. This can really wake up a pot roast or a slow-cooking stew. It's also delicious on grilled fish. Start with the following recipe, and choose the proportions to suit your own taste buds.

Basic Gremolata

2 tbsp. chopped, fresh flat-leaf parsley   3 garlic cloves, minced
1½ tsp. grated lemon zest

Mix together and drop a spoonful on each portion of what you're cooking. Flat-leaf parsley provides flavor and vitamin C; it's available year round and you should always have some in the vegetable crisper.

Note: Curly parsley is really only as good as a garnish. Don't waste your money on it.

Tomato Fennel Soup

Here's a simple and effortless soup that can be served anytime; most of the ingredients can be found in your pantry. Served to company, it has an impact that belies its simplicity. Fennel bulbs are sold in most grocery stores under the name "anise," which reflects its flavor but not its actual place in the vegetable kingdom. If you haven't discovered this herb/vegetable, do so soon. Remove the stalks and save for a vegetable broth. Add the feathery fronds to scrambled eggs, salad, or even gremolata. Cut the bulb in half vertically, remove the center core, and then thinly slice to add to salads for a burst of freshness on the tongue. Poach gently in chicken or vegetable broth to serve as a side dish.

2 tbsp. olive oil	3 c. chicken broth
1 fennel bulb, finely chopped or shredded	¼ c. lemon juice
1 garlic clove, minced	Sea salt
1, 28-oz. can whole tomatoes	Freshly ground pepper

Using a heavy kettle, drop in the olive oil and add the fennel bulb and garlic. Sauté for 10 minutes, but do not let the vegetables brown—they just need to sweat and become translucent. Drain the tomatoes (save the juice) and add them to the pot. Let warm for about 5 minutes, then add the rest of the ingredients, including the drained tomato juices; cover and simmer for 15 to 20 minutes. Remove the pan from the heat and purée the soup in a blender or food processor. Return to heat and season to taste with salt and pepper. At this point the soup can be refrigerated for 24 hours before serving. Add the feathery fennel fronds to the basic gremolata recipe above, and sprinkle a spoonful onto each serving of the hot soup. This recipe will serve four.

Note: Olive oil for cooking does not need to be extra virgin. A good quality pure olive oil is acceptable. Canned tomatoes are a great buy during the 10 months fresh tomatoes are out of season. Drain them well and slice for sandwiches and salad.

Hazelnut Gremolata
A nut gremolata can be dusted over grilled vegetables or portabella mushrooms, sprinkled on a baked potato, or spread on bruschetta to serve as an appetizer. Add some olive oil and serve on pasta.

1 c. hazelnuts, finely chopped	2 tbsp. fresh thyme leaves, chopped
2 tbsp. flat leaf parsley, chopped	1 c. extra virgin olive oil
Salt and pepper to taste	

Add a few tablespoons of water to the herbs and oil so that the mixture will blend into a paste.

Walnut Gremolata

Here's a less expensive version to use on pasta for a late-night supper with bread and wine.

1 c. walnuts, finely chopped	Juice and zest from one lemon
2 to 3 cloves garlic, minced	1 c. flat leaf parsley, chopped
¾ c. extra virgin olive oil	Salt and pepper to taste

Blend ingredients until a paste forms. This can be refrigerated and will keep for a couple weeks.

For a quick pasta supper, cook capellini to serve no more than four. Add ¼ to ½ cup water to thin the paste, and toss with the capellini.

Mint Gremolata

Getting tired of salsa and the whole chili pepper thing? To add a Greek or Moroccan flair to your meals of grilled lamb chops or leg of lamb, serve them with the following mint gremolata. Also, you may use this gremolata to season a sliced orange salad—just add the zest of one orange to the recipe. Or just sprinkle on a tabouli-stuffed tomato.

Zest from one lemon	¼ c. spearmint, chopped
2 tbsp. flat leaf parsley, chopped	3 garlic cloves, minced
½ c. Parmesan or Romano cheese	

Mix ingredients together. Follow serving suggestions above, or simply put it into a small dish to pass at the table.

Gremolata Salad Dressing

Salad dressing can be jazzed up with gremolata. Toss this recipe with fresh greens or pour over hot potatoes for a refreshingly different potato salad.

¼ c. flat-leaf parsley, chopped	1 clove garlic, minced
2 tbsp. extra virgin olive oil	2 tsp. Dijon mustard
Juice and zest, minced from one lemon	1 tbsp. cold water
Salt and freshly ground pepper to taste	

Mix ingredients and stir well. This will make about ½ cup of dressing. You may want to double it for potato salad.

....

COOKING WITH MAGICAL INTENT
by ShadowCat

Be careful what you ask for, said the wise man once, or you might get it.

Cooking is a sacred, magical art. To prepare and serve food is to nurture life, to actually feed that divine spark within us that sustains us. To serve others is to serve the gods. That said, it is clear why feasting is part of a vast array of religious holidays in almost every culture. Feasting is celebration of life and spirit. To be a cook is to be a priest or priestess—relegated to serving in the kitchen, but still serving up spirit, joy, and life.

Many years ago I talked to Scott Cunningham about a book he was writing, now published under the title *Cunningham's Encyclopedia of Wicca in the Kitchen*. At the time, I had two young children at home and a full-time job, so the cooking I did was mostly the easy kind—processed food that could be usually be warmed up and put on the table in 15 minutes. I had no time for the magical aspects of cooking, or so I thought.

Scott told me of his culinary experiments in turning food preparation into spell work. He was excited about the magical properties of food and spices, and that one could cook and bake with magical intent. Nice idea, I thought, but I was too busy to use such magic in my kitchen.

Now, the children are grown and raising families of their own, and recently I picked up Scott's book again. Suddenly something magical happened—I could now relate to his basic idea. Now that I had the time to really throw myself into learning cooking techniques and trying new recipes, I began to wonder: Is it possible to make magic in the kitchen? Since then, I have started paying more attention to my cooking, and I find I am now infused with magical intent when I am preparing food. Here is how you can be too.

Magic in the Kitchen

The first thing to do in making your kitchen more magical is ritual cleansing. To do so, sweep your kitchen floor of any unwanted presences. Put your hair up and out of the way if it is long. Wash your hands well and make sure that all of your utensils are spotlessly clean. Wipe your countertops, focusing on cleansing them to prepare for magical work. Now don your magical apron, which like a magical robe changes you from a mundane individual into a magical cook. You might even purchase a new apron, perhaps with symbolism special to you, particularly for the purpose of magical cooking.

One of the most important things I discovered as a cook is to be sure I use the correct utensils for the receipt at hand. For example, for years I made stew in a stainless-steel pot, cursing it for sticking and burning on the bottom. One day I was watching a chef on a cooking show make stew in a cast-iron, enameled Dutch oven, and it struck me that I might try one. I went to the store and found one by Martha Stewart (much cheaper than the French kind), and of course, the next batch of stew didn't stick or burn.

The lesson? Arm your magical pantry accordingly. Get rid of old pots and pans and habits. Throw out old flour and spices and start fresh. Buy only what you need, but exactly what you need. If you are making a stir fry, get a real wok and season it well. The wok is one of the oldest and most versatile cooking utensils on earth. I use mine for making a stir fry, making an omelet, cooking noodles and corn on the cob, and for stirring up sauces and gravy. Seasoned regularly, the wok is the perfect non-stick surface on the range.

Now, examine the magical properties of the herbs and spices you use on a regular basis. You might want to eliminate some or make some changes in what you use to change your magical intent. Be daring with herbs and spices. More is not necessarily better, but being willing to try new herbs is a key to good cooking. You might even consider having your own organic herb garden. Mine grows right outside my kitchen door. Herbs don't need much space to flourish, and fresh herbs add fresh life to your food. Here are a couple examples of recipes useful for preparing food with magical intent.

Peace and Prosperity Pizza

1 prepackaged pizza
  dough *(for prosperity)*
1 tsp. oregano *(for peace)*
1 tsp. marjoram *(for peace)*
1 jar pizza sauce *(for prosperity)*
½ c. Parmesan cheese *(for personal power)*

1 c. sliced mushrooms
  (for psychic awareness)
1 tsp. basil *(for prosperity)*
1 small can black olives *(for peace)*
1 lb. mozzarella cheese *(for love)*

Altogether these elements create a peace and prosperity pizza, which may be prepared and consumed with magical intent. You might want to have a salad on the side, so try this one for peace and protection.

Peace and Protection Salad

Lettuce, any variety *(for peace)*
Sliced black olives *(for peace)*
Cucumber slices *(for peace)*

Tomato slices *(for love and protection)*
Chopped green onions *(for protection)*
Various herbs of your choice: basil, mint, etc . . .

Dressing

½ c. olive oil *(for peace)*
½ tsp. paprika *(for protection)*
2 cloves garlic, finely chopped *(for protection)*

⅓ c. vinegar *(for protection)*
1 tsp. salt *(for protection)*
½ tsp. sugar *(for love)*

Combine dressing ingredients in a covered container and shake to blend. Pour over salad and toss. Sprinkle with coarse ground black pepper *(protection)* and grated Parmesan cheese *(personal power)*.

When you have completed your food preparation, it is important to clean up your kitchen and put everything away. Wash the dishes, wipe down countertops, sweep the floor, and put your magical apron in the laundry. I encourage you to look at your favorite recipes to discover what you are really cooking up. Try new recipes. Invent your own. Cooking is magic.

....

THE HERBAL FLAVORS OF GREECE

by James Kambos

I was introduced to Greek cuisine, and its many flavorful herbs, in my grandmother's garden at an early age. Greece was my grandmother's homeland. After settling in America in the earlier part of the last century, she continued to follow her native eastern Mediterranean cooking traditions. She was very different from many of the other women around her.

For one, gardening was my grandmother's passion. Early in May each year she would prepare her kitchen garden for planting. As the tiller churned the soil, I'd watch with excitement as the scent of earth rose in brown waves. It smelled of spring and life renewed. Soon, she would plant, in her plot, the vegetables that are essential to Greek cooking. This included slender green-speckled zucchinis, shiny purple-black eggplants, and an endless array of summer squash, bell peppers, and, of course, garlic.

The plants that captured my imagination the most were the herbs. These give Greek cooking its robust flavor. My grandmother planted these along the edge of the garden's border or in terra cotta pots on the patio. I remember the feathery plumes of dill, rising in the back of the border and capped with their brilliant yellow-green seed heads. Basil, considered by Greeks to be one of the most sacred of all herbs, would overflow in the pots on the patio. And the varieties of mint—I'll never forget the fragrant clumps of mint, tucked here and there in a shady corner of the garden. Their crinkled foliage would release a heady fragrance each time I rubbed them—and I did this often.

That was many years ago, but I carry on the same tradition and try to preserve my heritage. On hot and dry July mornings, as I tend my own herb garden, I find I am again surrounded by many of the same herbs I loved in my grandmother's garden. In the early morning stillness, I'm greeted by the perfume of oregano, thyme, savory, dill, and mint. And I think how important these plants are to Greek cooking.

As my hoe unearths a rock, I smile because it reminds me of the folk story about how Greece was created. The tale goes something like this: After the council of gods and goddesses created the earth and all of the other great nations, they noticed that a few rocks remained unused. These last rocks were tossed into the Mediterranean Ocean, and as the legend goes, became Greece. This is only a folktale, but like most folktales it does contain a kernel of truth.

A Brief History of Greek Cooking

Greece is indeed a dry, rocky country with little fertile soil. It is sun-drenched and has very little good farm or grazing land. Despite all these shortcomings, Greece has produced such an abundance of flavorings in its cuisines that the country has influenced cooks and bakers for centuries.

The inspiration for Greek food has always come from the East. Greece is located in the southeastern corner of Europe. It is surrounded by the aquamarine waters of the Ionian Sea to the west, the Aegean Sea to the east, and the Mediterranean Sea to the south. To the north, Greece is cut off from the rest of Europe by remote rugged mountains. This unique geographic position has influenced Greek cooking since ancient times.

Being more accessible by sea, Greece has always looked to eastern and southern trade routes for goods, food, and spices. This left Greece open to the herbs and spices from the Middle East and North Africa. Also, Greece has always fallen under the influence of Eastern empires. Briefly, the Persians ruled. Then, the Byzantine Empire, based in Constantinople (present-day Istanbul), controlled Greece for about eleven centuries. When the Byzantine Empire fell to the Ottoman Turks, Greece became part of the Ottoman Empire, and it stayed so for nearly four hundred years until independence in 1830.

As empires were won and lost, the cuisine of Greece took shape. The herbs and spices used in the Greek kitchen today have ancient beginnings. Some may have been brought to Greece by invaders, others may have been discovered by the conquerors in Greece and then taken back to their homeland. The Ottoman Turks were a good example. The rulers of the Ottoman Empire had great respect for the cuisines they encountered as their empire spread. Some of the Greek flavorings were discovered by the Turks and then spread throughout their great empire. Then again, some of the Turkish herbs and foods were later incorporated into the native Hellenic cooking style. No matter how it occurred, the flavor of Greek food will always be linked to the culinary pool of the Middle East.

Taste of Greece

Greece is an herbalist's delight. Blue skies, even bluer seas, and wind-swept rocky hillsides impress even the most jaded traveler. Many of the herbs I struggle to grow in my American garden grow wild or can be cultivated year-round in Greece's dry, healthy climate. In Greece, meat is a luxury food and is seldom the primary focus of a meal. So to expand the flavor of any recipe, or to add extra zip to vegetarian dishes, Greek cooks rely heavily on the use of herbs.

The following is a list of herbs, spices, seeds, and other flavorings used in Greek cooking. Some of these ingredients are not herbs at all, but are included in case you are interested in some of the non-herb natural flavorings from Greek cuisine. Many of these herbs and spices are well-known to you, but others may be new. All items listed can be found at any Greek or Middle Eastern grocer in your town. Where possible, I have also included magical uses and folklore information along with the culinary uses of these herbs.

Anise

The seeds, extract, and oil of this herb are sometimes used in Greek pastries such as paxemathia, a sort of Greek biscotti that are great to dunk in coffee. Anise is also used to flavor the national drink of Greece, ouzo. Ouzo is a clear, powerful aperitif and should be drunk with mezze, an appetizer. It is a strong drink but may be drunk straight or poured over ice. Mixed with water, it becomes cloudy, hence its nickname "lion's milk." If you travel in Greece, you may come across homemade ouzo. Watch out; it just might knock your socks off. During a trip to Greece, I was invited to take part in a village celebration. The gentlemen in the town square handed me a bottle of the bootleg stuff. All eyes were on me as I took a sip. It burned all the way down, but I managed to choke out in Greek, *na kalo*—meaning "it is good." Their eyes sparkled and they slapped me on the back. Just remember, ouzo deserves respect.

Basil

This beautiful herb is held in great esteem by the Greeks. It is the traditional flower of the Orthodox church. As a food element, basil is delicious combined with tomatoes and in tomato-based sauces. It may have been used in the earliest forms of aroma-therapy. Greek men would frequently carry a sprig tucked behind their ear or in a shirt pocket, taking it out occasionally to savor its scent. Traditional Greek basil is a small annual plant and grows nicely in pots or a window box. In folk magic, use basil to clear and protect a sacred space.

Cinnamon

Greeks use cinnamon in many pastries. However, unlike in America, cinnamon is used in Greece as a subtle flavor for some white sauces and meat dishes. It adds an extra depth of flavor.

Clove

Cloves are used in sweets and in Greek folk magic. The flavor of cloves is frequently added to the famous Middle Eastern pastry, baklava. Near the Christmas holiday, Greek bakers will garnish certain pastries with whole cloves. This has a deep religious meaning because the clove symbolizes spices brought to the Christ child as gifts. In Greek folk magic, the scent of clove aids in purification.

Dill

Dill grows all over Greece. Magically it is used to protect a home against evil. Dill is used in meatballs, in filling for stuffed grape leaves, and in salads and some bean dishes.

Garlic

People around the world use garlic to protect against evil. In Greece, garlic is used to repel the dreaded evil eye. The word for garlic in Greek is *skortha,* and people frequently whisper this word as magic to protect themselves from the evil. In the Greek kitchen, garlic finds its way into many sauces and dips. To impart a subtle garlic flavor to an old standard dish, try tucking a clove or two into a roast or leg of lamb prior to cooking it. This is simply delicious.

Lemon

Lemons grow in Greece, and the cooks of Greece would be lost without them. The juice of lemons is frequently combines with olive oil and oregano to make a zesty marinade for chicken. Straight lemon juice can also be sprinkled over meatballs, before and after baking or broiling. The best known Greek soup, avgolemono, receives much of its flavor from lemon juice. Also, if you are preparing lamb, try rubbing the meat first with half a lemon. This removes any of the strong gamey flavor that some people find objectionable in lamb.

Mahlepi (mahleb in *Arabic*)

This unusual flavoring was brought to Greece by the Persians. It is ground seed of a tree that is similar to a cherry tree. It is used in making breads. I have used it to make Orthodox Easter bread.

Mastic (mastika in *Greek*)

Mastic is not an herb but a dried sap. Few Americans have ever heard of it, and the stories surrounding it are fascinating. First of all, mastic is derived from the sap of the mastic tree. The only place in the world where mastic trees grow are on the Greek island of Chios, my ancestral home. The trees are small and planted in groves. Late each summer the bark is cut and the trees then "cry." The sap drips, then hardens after the harvest into yellowish amber-like crystals. These crystals may be pulverized into a powder and used to flavor liqueurs, candies, puddings, and gum. At confectioner shops in Athens, I have seen mouth-watering displays of the mastic-flavored Greek candy called lokum (or more commonly Turkish Delight), piled high on fancy trays. Much of the mastic is exported around the Middle East. Some of the mastic is left in its crystal form as a natural chewing gum. Above the sink in my grandmother's kitchen, we always kept a terra cotta jar filled with natural mastic. I was encouraged to chew it as a child because it was an oral cleanser and teeth whitener. Westerners probably wouldn't care for it in its natural form, but I learned to like it. During the Ottoman Empire, much mastic was sent to Topkopi Palace, the sultan's home in Istanbul. There is was used as an aphrodisiac by the ladies in the sultan's harem. At sunset they would chew a bit of mastic to sweeten their breath in case they were chosen for a night of passion with the sultan. If you are magically inclined, a pinch of mastic added to a love charm can add an extra punch. Modern science, it seems, has recently discovered mastic. I learned in my research that mastic taken in capsule form can aid in the treatment of stomach ulcers. You should check with a licensed health care professional before you try this.

Mint

Mint is actually used a great deal in the cuisines of the eastern Mediterranean. Unlike the Western world, where mint is relegated to the role of garnish, tea, or jelly, cooks from Greece eastward love the fresh taste it adds to salads, stuffings, and meatballs. For a quick sauce, combine ½ teaspoon crushed dried mint to one cup cold plain yogurt. Spoon over plain rice pilaf for a touch of Greek flavor.

Olives and Olive Oil

According to Greek mythology, the goddess Athena created the first olive tree. No Greek kitchen is complete without olives and golden olive oil. Olive oil was so cherished by the ancients it was given as prizes to athletes. The modern medical community has proved what the ancient Greeks may have knows: Olive oil, used in moderation, is healthy. It helps lower bad blood cholesterol levels. One of my favorite olive varieties available in America is the kalamata olive. The olives are dark purple and oblong. They are packed in vinegar and olive oil and are the best all-purpose Greek olive. Kalamatas can add a splash of Mediterranean color and flavor to salads or a plate of appetizers.

Oregano

This mountain-grown herb is indispensable to Mediterranean food. I like it fresh or dried in chicken, pasta sauces, or lentils. It is slightly bitter and earthy.

Rosemary

Instead of adding this herb directly to food, on many occasions Greeks add rosemary to hot cooking coals, which lets the smoke penetrate the meat—usually lamb—with a supremely delicate flavor. I have prepared a Turkish chicken stew that calls for rosemary and found that the flavor marries quite well with poultry also.

Savory

Savory is one of the finest, but one of the least used, herbs this region of the world offers. Winter savory thrives in my garden and air-dries beautifully for winter use. I add it to lentils and other bean soups. It also blends well with eggplant and is great sprinkled on pizza. When you use it, and I hope you do, combine it with a pinch of dried oregano.

Sesame Seeds

In Greece, sesame seeds are used to garnish numerous breads and cookies. More than just a garnish, sesame seeds are a high-energy food. They are frequently combined with honey to make a crispy and light health food bar. Such bars are easily found in American health food stores.

Other Herbs

Parsley, sage, and thyme must also be mentioned on this list. Parsley grows year-round and is blended into cheese and used as fillings for appetizers. Sage, as in America, is added to pork dishes. Thyme grows wild in the region. I like to combine thyme with chopped parsley and add it to boiling water or broth before preparing rice. Combined they blend to make an easy herbal rice pilaf.

Flower Waters

Among the most exotic flavorings used in the Greek kitchen are the flower waters. There are two kinds: rose water and orange blossom water. These fragrant waters are made by distilling water over rose petals or orange blossoms. They are mostly used in syrups and sweets, and they are exquisite. You can purchase them bottled from Middle Eastern grocers or some health food stores. I always refrigerate them after opening. Flower waters are delicate and should never be added to boiling syrup. Always let the syrup cool slightly, then add the flower water. (Later in this article I have included a recipe containing flower water, so you will better understand this.) Flower waters were probably developed by the Persians, whose sophisticated cuisine dates back a bit earlier than the Greeks.

Greek Herbal Recipes

I don't have the space to share with you all the recipes I'd like to. What follows are three recipes that can be put together to form a meal, and that will allow you to try some of the herbs and flavors I have explained above.

Greek Tomato Sauce

I have not mentioned that the Greeks love tomatoes and pasta. Traveling in Greece, I encountered a tomato sauce similar to the following and, after much trial and error, eventually duplicated it at home. The tomatoes should be left chunky. This dish freezes well.

1 small onion, finely chopped	2 cloves garlic, minced
1 tbsp. olive oil	¼ c. fresh parsley, finely chopped
Salt and pepper to taste	1 tsp. dried oregano
8 Roma tomatoes, peeled and coarsely chopped	1 tbsp. fresh basil, chopped or 1 tsp. dried basil
1 tbsp. tomato paste	1 tsp. brown sugar
1, 8-oz. can tomato sauce	

In a medium saucepan, sauté the onion in oil until soft. Add the rest of the ingredients, stirring to break up the tomatoes.

Bring to a boil; turn down the heat and simmer, uncovered, for 30 minutes. Stir occasionally. Serve by tossing with cooked spaghetti or penne pasta. Serves 4.

Greek Salad

The Greek salad served in America rarely exists in Greece. If you order a salad in a Greek village café, you'll likely be served sliced tomatoes and a few slices of cucumber splashed with a little olive oil. Simple but delicious. Here's a recipe for a more traditional Greek salad.

1 head curly endive	1 small thinly sliced red onion
1 head iceberg lettuce	¼ lb. feta cheese, cubed
1 cucumber, peeled and sliced	½ tsp. dried oregano
2 tomatoes, sliced into wedges	6 to 8 anchovy filets
12 Kalamata olives	

DRESSING

½ c. olive oil	3 tbsp. red wine vinegar
Dash fresh ground pepper	

Tear the endive and lettuce into small pieces and place them into a salad bowl. Add the cucumber, tomatoes, olives, and onion. Separately, roll the cubed feta in the oregano and set aside. Whisk together the dressing ingredients in a small bowl until foamy. Pour over salad ingredients and toss. Garnish salad with feta and anchovy filets. Serve this pasta and salad with hard rolls or garlic bread and red wine. The dessert that follows can be made a day or two ahead.

Walnut-Honey Cookies

This walnut-honey cookie recipe is not well-known outside of Greece, but my guests always love them. In Greek they are called Phoenekia [Fe-neek-ya]. As a boy, I remember them always being on the table at parties.

½ c. butter or margarine	½ tsp. cinnamon
¼ c. olive oil	2½ c. flour
¼ c. sugar	1½ tsp. baking powder
1 egg	Dash of salt
¼ c. orange juice	½ c. cream of wheat cereal
½ tsp. grated orange peel	½ c. ground walnuts (reserve ¼ c. for garnish)

Beat the butter until creamy. Add olive oil and sugar, and beat until smooth. Blend in egg, juice, orange peel, and cinnamon. In a separate bowl, stir together the flour, baking powder, and salt, and add gradually to the batter. Mix until smooth. With your hands, knead in cream of wheat cereal and ¼ cup of the walnuts. Pinch off walnut-sized pieces of dough and shape into ovals. Place on a greased cookie tray, one inch apart. Bake at 350 degrees F for 20 minutes or until golden. Let cool. Make the syrup below.

SYRUP

¼ c. sugar	¼ c. water
¾ c. honey	1 tbsp. orange blossom water (optional)

In a small saucepan, boil together the sugar and water until clear. Remove from heat and cool slightly. Stir in honey and orange blossom water. Place a few cookies at a time in the saucepan and coat with syrup. Transfer the cookies, using a slotted spoon, to a clean tray. Garnish with the remaining ¼ cup walnuts. To serve, place each cookie in a paper baking cup to catch any excess syrup; arrange on a platter. Or, pack in an airtight container until ready to serve. They keep well. Yields about 30 cookies.

Learning More About Greek Food

Many people embrace a more wholesome lifestyle and are discovering the simple and healthy food of Greece. This article has served as a short introduction to the herbs and flavorings used to enhance this very ancient cuisine. Remember, Greek cooking is just one segment of the much larger realm of Middle Eastern food. And it is my wish that your interest in Greek food will open the door, leading you to explore the other fascinating cooking traditions of the region—including Arabian, Armenian, Iranian, Jewish, Kurdish, North African, and Turkish.

In general, most of the ingredients and herbs used in Greek recipes will be found in the spice and gourmet food sections of major supermarkets. To obtain the more exotic ingredients, try health food stores, Greek, or Middle Eastern grocers.

....

GREAT HERBAL SNACKS
by Dallas Jennifer Cobb

Have you ever tried to feed a bunch of kinds and been met by a chorus of protests? Are you constantly challenged to feed the children in your life healthy snacks that they will actually like? Do you live with picky and impossible-to-please eaters? Then this article is for you.

The Child/Food Conundrum

It is difficult to get children to eat well, and almost impossible to get them to eat healthy foods. As a mother, I have had lots of experience feeding children healthy snacks. I have also had first-hand experience with several extremely picky eaters. Through it all, I have learned how to shape snacks and meals into yummy adventures that kids will dig into. In particular, I have used herbs to flavor otherwise nose-turning foods, and well I know their culinary and therapeutic value.

In order to stay focused and on topic, this article focuses primarily on the culinary use of herbs to entice and enchant the finicky eaters in your life. The recipes included below have been tested by a small herd of two- and three-year-olds and given a grubby thumbs up. My daughter's playmates return often to our house clamoring for treats. And believe it or not, my partner even looks forward to leftovers when he arrives home from work.

Feeding Pitfalls

While herbs are nutritional and therapeutic, kids won't eat them unless they are incorporated into foods that look good and taste great. When you are introducing new foods, avoid the most common pitfalls—those statements that signal a warning to picky eaters. That is, try not to say any of these statements: "it's good for you"; "it won't kill you if you eat it"; or the dreaded, "just try it, you'll like it."

Yes, you know that herbs are good for us, but it won't help to tell your children that. You see, kids have a kind of radar that is constantly scanning for the devious tricks adults use to con them into eating yucky stuff. In the unique language of children "good for you" and "healthy" translate to "yucky" and "tastes bad."

Instead of telling children that the food is good for them, focus instead on making the food look, smell, and taste good. These are the big sellers for the picky palate of children. As sensual creatures, children judge food by look and smell. And if it passes those tests, it may get to their mouth so long as it doesn't feel "funny."

Pleasing Picky Eaters

Here are some food tips for pleasing picky eaters. Present foods in colorful and creative ways. Kids love a meal they can play with, so encourage them with fun food. For instance, try using animal-shaped cookie cutters to shape sandwiches. Offer sauces for dipping in small, brightly colored tubs. Arrange food in patterns (a clown's face, perhaps?) or geometric shapes on the plate. Serve a variety of brightly colored foods that appeal to children (apples, carrots, blue corn chips, tomato wedges, zucchini sticks) and let them choose. Make eating fun by creating a meal or snack around a theme—such as wagon train foods that cowboys used to eat, hiking provisions for a trip to the top of a mountain, a tropical rain forest treat that monkeys and toucans would love to be served, or a tea party for dollies and the March Hare, who of course is running late and due to arrive at any moment.

In particular, fun is appealing to children at eating time, and laughter and games take a child's mind away from the uncertainty of new foods. New foods are often a hard sell with children because they are unfamiliar with them, and therefore suspicious. It is probably linked to a self-preservation instinct handed down through evolution, so don't bother fighting with it.

Choice makes a child feel powerful and safely in control of his or her own feeding. And even if a child only eats two or three of the offered food, if you serve only healthy things then you know at least he or she has eaten something healthy.

On the other hand, when you tell your child that some food "won't kill you," rather than reassuring him or her instead you will create a deep fear in them—the fear of eating something healthy and yucky. So do yourself a favor and don't ever catch yourself saying this (even if it's what your mother used to say to you).

Herbs for Kids

Be aware, there are many herbs that aren't safe for children's consumption. Just because something is a herb doesn't mean it is good for all. Here's a list of herbs safe for children to consume:

Anise *(Pimpinella anisum)*

Basil *(Ocimum basilicum)*

Borage *(Borago officinalis)*

Calendula *(Calendula officinalis)*

Caraway *(Carum carvi)*

Catnip *(Nepeta cataria)*

Chamomile *(Chamaemelum nobile)*

Chives *(Allium schoenoprasum)*

Coriander *(Corandrum satibum)*

Cumin *(Cuminum cyminum)*

Dandelion *(Taraxacum officinale)*

Dill *(Anethum graveolens)*

Fennel *(Foeniculum vulgore)*

Garlic *(Allium sativum)*

Hyssop *(Hysoppus officinalis)*

Lavender *(Lavendula angustifolia)*

Lemon balm *(Melissa officinalis)*

Lovage *(Levisticum officinale)*

Marjoram *(Origanum majorana)*

Meadowsweet *(Filipendula ulmaria)*

Nasturtium *(Tropaeolum majus)*

Oregano *(Origanum vulgare)*

Parsley *(Petroselinum crispa)*

Peppermint *(Mentha x piperita)*

Rooibos *(Aspalathus linearis)*

Rosemary *(Rosmarinus officinalis)*

Sage *(Salvia officinalis)*

Sorrel *(Rumex scutatus)*

Spearmint *(Mentha spicata)*

Stevia *(Stevia rebaudiana)*

Sweet Basil *(Ocimum basilicum)*

Tarragon *(Artemesia dracunculus)*

Thyme *(Thymus vulgaris)*

Yarrow *(Achillea millefolium)*

In general, try to make foods familiar by having them at the table frequently, consuming them yourself, and offering them as one of the choices that children can select from on their plates. Sometimes getting a child to try a new food is simply a matter of letting him or her see someone else eat it.

Another trick is to involve your children in making food with you so that they see the ordinary process of preparation. It often helps to demystify the individual ingredients.

The Kid-Friendly Kitchen

There are a few herbs that are so versatile and tasty they are common in many child-friendly recipes. Keep these handy in your kitchen: calendula, catnip, chamomile, lavender, peppermint, and stevia. While not always considered herbs, the spices cinnamon, ginger, and cocoa are also very popular with my ragamuffin herd of experts.

Children love to help in the kitchen, so get them involved in your cooking and baking. You can teach them measurement and mixing, baking and tasting, and have fun at the same time. Children feel a great sense of accomplishment following a simple recipe and truly enjoy making a treat for the whole family.

Herbal treats can be as simple as adding suitable herbs to an already successful recipe, or creating new treats based on the herbs your family likes. And great herbal snacks don't have to be complicated. Try adding a little fresh cilantro to your favorite salsa, some mint jelly to your toast, or lavender to Christmas shortbread cookies.

Generally I try to avoid having a lot of refined sugar. It seems to set the kids off and that makes for a difficult time for everyone. I have successfully used maple syrup and honey as sweeteners for many years, and I only recently discovered stevia. This herb tastes great, is easy to bake with, and brings with it no sugar highs and lows.

Herbalicious Snacks

Below are a few recipes for snacks that will please even the pickiest eaters. Try them and keep a little list of what works and what doesn't. Soon you will have neighborhood children clamoring to come to your house at snack time.

Beverages

LAVENDER LEMONADE

¼ c. dried lavender blossoms	4 large lemons
2 c. boiling water	1 c. sugar

Steep lavender for 10 minutes in the boiling water, then strain. Let the lavender water cool a bit, then combine it with the juice from the lemons and sugar in a pitcher. Fill with ice and with water, and serve cold.

BABY BUNNY'S TUMMY TEA

Boil some water. Place 3 tablespoons of dried chamomile flowers and 1 tablespoon each of dried lemon balm and catnip in a teapot. Pour the boiling water over them. Cover the teapot and let it steep for 10 minutes. Strain the tea and sweeten it with honey or stevia. Chamomile has a soothing effect on the nervous system, and lemon balm and catnip will calm an upset tummy very quickly.

Fruity Mint Punch

5 c. strongly brewed Red or
   Lemon Zinger tea (available
   from Celestial Seasonings)

2 c. fresh orange juice

¼ c. fresh lemon juice

½ c. boiling water

½ c. mint leaves, finely chopped

Honey or stevia to taste

Brew and cool the tea, then mix it with the orange juice and lemon juice in a big pitcher. Boil a half cup of water and pour it over the mint leaves. Steep the leaves for 5 minutes. Strain the leaves and add the tea to the juice. Sweeten the pitcher with honey or stevia to taste. Cool and serve.

Herbal Popsicles

At my house, we make our own popsicles out of juices and teas. Buy a plastic popsicle mold at the dollar store and try making your own popsicles. For toddlers, I recommend tea-popsicles from rooibos or Sleepy Time tea (from Celestial Seasonings), or ones made from watered down juices. For bigger kids, just pour the juice in the mold and freeze.

When we make lemonade popsicles we often put a little bit of chopped lemon balm, lavender, or mint in the mold and then pour the lemonade in. The kids love to squeal at the results, "Yuck, a bug," and eat them anyway.

Sweet Treats
Ginger Snaps

These delicious cookies are clamored for in my household. They are a little spicier than ordinary ginger snaps, so kids eat a little less (but adults eat a little more).

1 c. butter	½ tsp. baking soda
1 c. sugar	½ tsp. powdered ginger
¼ c. blackstrap molasses	2 c. flour
1 egg	1 tsp. cinnamon
1 tsp. vanilla extract	½ tsp. powdered cloves
¼ tsp. salt	

Preheat oven to 350 degrees F. Cream the butter and sugar, then add the molasses, egg, and vanilla and mix well. In a separate bowl sift the dry ingredients together, then add the mixture to the creamed mix slowly. Drop the resulting dough by tablespoons onto a nonstick cookie sheet and bake for 15 minutes or until golden brown.

Luscious Lavender Shortbread

Shortbread is a favorite in my house because it is so easy to make and easy to eat. We used to make shortbread traditionally at Christmas, but a few years ago we started to make summer short-bread when the lavender was in bloom. We have also created successful rosemary and lemon balm shortbreads using this recipe.

1 c. butter (do not use margarine)	3 to 4 tbsp. fresh lavender, finely chopped
½ c. powdered sugar	2 c. flour

Preheat the oven to 300 degrees F. Take the butter from the fridge—it needs to be cold. Cut the butter into small pieces and place them into a large bowl, then thoroughly cream the sugar and lavender into the butter. Add the flour quickly, using your hands to mix if you have to. Refrigerate the dough for about 20 minutes. Turn the cookie dough out on a board that is lightly floured. Roll it until it is about ¼ inch thick, then cut into shapes. Kids love shapes—use your imagination. Bake the shortbread on a nonstick cookie sheet for 50 minutes, or until golden brown. Shortbread keeps well in sealed containers, so make lots to have on hand.

Natural Licorice Candy

Licorice helps alleviate cold and flu symptoms, is a natural (yet gentle) laxative, and kids love it.

1 c. blackstrap molasses	Whole wheat and all purpose flour, mixed (two parts all purpose to one part whole wheat)
1 tsp. ground licorice root	
1 tsp. ground anise root	

Warm the molasses in a large saucepan on low heat. Add the licorice and anise root. Add flour until you have a dense consistency that you can roll into tubes. Cut the tubes to a desired length. The candy hardens as it cools, and it will keep for a long time in the refrigerator.

Fragrant Apple Crumble

½ c. butter	¼ tsp. salt
1½ c. rolled oats	1 tsp. nutmeg
1 c. brown sugar (or ½ c. maple syrup in ¼ c. flour)	¼ c. dried rose petals (or ⅛ c. lavender)
1 c. spelt or whole wheat flour	1 tsp. cinnamon
5 large apples, cored and sliced	1 c. apple sauce

Combine dry ingredients. Melt the butter and mix into the dry ingredients. Press half of the mixture into the bottom of a baking dish. Layer apples and herbs and spices and cover with applesauce. Cover all with the remaining dry ingredients. Bake at 375 degrees F for 30 minutes, then turn up to 450 degrees F to brown the top.

BALMY LEMON MADELEINES

½ c. butter (plus extra for greasing the pan)

2 large eggs

½ c. sugar

¼ c. plain yogurt

1 tbsp. lemon juice

Dash of vanilla extract

¼ c. molasses

1 c. unbleached flour

½ tsp. freshly grated nutmeg

3 tbsp. ground lemon balm leaves

¼ tsp. salt

Grated zest of ½ lemon

Grated zest of 1 orange

Preheat oven to 400 degrees F. Generously butter a madeleine pan. Melt the butter and cool it. In a mixing bowl, mix eggs, sugar, yogurt, lemon juice, and extract, the slowly add the remaining ingredients. Spoon a tablespoon of batter into each madeleine shell and bake for 12 minutes or until the tiny cakes are golden brown.

HERB TEA LOAF

This recipe is so easy and satisfying. Make it on a rainy day and play tea party all afternoon. Kids love to have this cake cut into small cubes. It fits on small tea set plates and they can brag later about how many pieces they ate.

2 c. unbleached flour

1 tsp. baking powder

¼ tsp. salt

1½ to 2 tsp. fresh lavender or anise hyssop blossoms

2 to 3 tbsp. mint or lemon balm leaves, minced

½ c. milk

½ c. (1 stick) unsalted butter, softened

1 c. sugar

3 eggs, extra large

1 tsp. vanilla extract

Preheat the oven to 350 degrees F. Combine the dry ingredients and set them aside. Mix the herbs into the milk and set aside. Cream the butter and sugar and beat in the eggs, one at a time, and add the vanilla. Alternately add dry and wet ingredients to the sugar and butter mixture. Mix well. Pour the batter into a nonstick cake pan and bake for 45 minutes or until golden brown.

LIGHTEST LEMONY SCONES

This is a great winter morning recipe. Get the children to help, and then in the few minutes it takes to clean up the kitchen, the scones are baked. Eat with jelly or jam and butter.

3 c. flour	¾ c. butter, cut into pieces
2½ tsp. baking powder	1 c. buttermilk or yogurt
⅓ c. sugar	1 tbsp. grated lemon zest
½ tsp. baking soda	1 tbsp. lemon balm, finely chopped
¾ tsp. salt	

Mix all the dry ingredients together and cut in the butter (do not use margarine) with two knives. Keep the mixture cool. Mix with your hands for only a short time. Add the milk, zest, and herbs and mix. Roll the dough into a ½ inch thickness and cut into interesting shapes. Bake at 425 degrees F to 10 to 12 minutes on a nonstick cookie sheet.

Savory Treats
WAGON TRAIN BISCUITS

My mother used to make these biscuits for my brother and me when we were little. She called them Wooster biscuits, after Charlie Wooster, the cook on the TV show *Wagon Train*. I included variations in my recipe so I renamed them. The tomato paste variations in my recipe results in biscuits that are tinged red-pink and flecked with green. The cheese ones are chewy and a little salty. The garlic-oregano ones are a bit like garlic bread.

Base

2 c. flour	3 tsp. baking powder
⅔ to ¾ c. milk, yogurt, or buttermilk	½ c. butter, cut with knives to pea-size pieces
1 tsp. salt	

Variations (try adding one at a time to base recipe)

1 large clove garlic and ¼ c. finely minced fresh oregano (1 tbsp. dried)	¾ c. shredded cheddar cheese and ¼ c. minced fresh sage (1 tbsp. dried)
¼ c. tomato paste and ½ c. finely minced fresh basil (2 tbsp. dried)	

Preheat the oven to 450 degrees F. Combine the flour, baking powder, and salt in a large bowl and blend thoroughly. Cut in the butter until the mixture resembles a coarse meal. Then mix in one of the savory flavorings of your choice: herbs, tomato paste, or cheese. Roll out the dough to ½ inch thickness and cut it into interesting shapes. Bake for 12 to 15 minutes. Eat these with soups, stews, or gobble them down slathered with butter.

PRESTO PESTO

1 c. fresh basil leaves, removed from stem	¼ c. fresh grated Parmesan or asiago cheese
¼ c. roasted pine nuts	Olive oil
Salt and freshly ground pepper to taste	3 large garlic cloves, peeled

Purée the ingredients in a food processor, adding just enough olive oil to make a smooth paste. Pesto is great on pasta, vegetables, or on bread. It is easily stored in the freezer. Just thaw it and make your own Presto Pasta dish.

Oven-Roasted Vegetables with Herbs

Kids love comfort foods, and this is a great cold-day treat. It is easy to prepare and has many variations. Use any combination of potatoes, sweet potatoes, acorn squash, carrots, and parsnips.

3 large potatoes	3 sweet potatoes
1 head of garlic, separated into cloves and peeled	2 onions, peeled and cut into wedges
6 carrots	¼ c. minced rosemary
¼ c. minced thyme	3 tbsp. olive oil

Cut all the vegetables into bite-sized chunks. Heat the oven to 400 degrees F. In a large bowl, toss all the ingredients together until the herbs are evenly spread. Place the mixture on a large baking sheet and bake, stirring occasionally, for one hour, or until golden brown. Add salt and pepper to taste.

Herbal Garlic Butter

Garlic seems to be a taste that is often overpowering for children. I have modified garlic recipes so that the kids will eat them, but I usually set some minced garlic aside for adults who want more.

2 cloves garlic, finely minced	1 tbsp. minced basil
1 tsp. minced oregano	1 tbsp. minced marjoram
1 tsp. minced sage	1 c. butter, softened

Finely chop the garlic and herbs. In a large bowl, combine the herbs with the butter and let the kids mash it up until it is creamy. Spread it generously on bread, rolls, or crackers. Pop them into the oven on a moderate setting until golden brown. This butter keeps well, but it makes plastic containers smell like garlic.

Monster Mash

Let's face it. Sometimes food seems slimy. Guacamole is easy to make and great for kids—as it is rich in essential fatty acids—but, because it looks yucky, it is often hard to get kids to eat it. Why not get them to make it and learn to associate the weird looking food with lots of kitchen fun?

2 ripe avocados	1½ c. mild salsa
1 clove garlic, chopped	Juice from 1 lime
½ c. finely chopped cilantro	⅛ c. finely diced red onion

Mash the avocados in a large bowl, add all other ingredients, and mix well. Serve with veggies, corn chips, or pita bread.

Cream Cheese Please

There are a thousand variations to this cream cheese recipe. Try one of these below or make up your own. Get the kids to squish all the ingredients together until the cream cheese has a smooth consistency. Spread it on bread and bagels, or serve as a dip with sliced veggies and crackers.

In a mixing bowl, combine cream cheese and desired herbs or fruits (see below for suggestions). Mix well. Spread two tablespoons on each piece of bread. Sprinkle with paprika (savory) or calendula petals (sweet). Use a cookie cutter to make shaped sandwiches. As fancy decoration, spread a little cream cheese on the edge of the sandwiches and then roll the edges in a mixture of chopped herbs or flower petals.

Pizza Style Cream Cheese

To one 8 oz. package of cream cheese, add:

½ c. sun-dried tomatoes, finely chopped   1 tsp. minced oregano

1 tsp. minced basil   1 tsp. minced chives

Salt and pepper to taste

Lemony Orange Cream Cheese

To one 8 oz. package of cream cheese, add:

⅛ tsp. stevia   Grated zest from 2 oranges

½ c. fresh lemon balm   Calendula petals

Herbed Cream Cheese

To one 8 oz. package of cream cheese, add:

1 tbsp. fresh   ½ c. lightly packed, finely chopped
  lemon juice   fresh herbs (parsley, watercress,
                      basil, chives—in any combination)
Paprika

Cucumber Mint Sandwiches

Every tea party needs a special sandwich. When we got tired of
peanut butter and banana, we turned to this British tea party
standard.

½ stick butter   8 thin slices whole wheat bread, crusts removed

1 tbsp. fresh mint leaves   2 small cucumbers, peeled and thinly sliced

In a small bowl combine the butter and mint and mix well.
Spread the mint butter on the bread slices. Lay the cucumber
on four of the slices and top with the remaining bread to make
four sandwiches. Slice them in half diagonally.

A Great Herbal Snack Life

Fortified with these great herbal snack recipes, you can start trying them out on the children in your life. Be sneaky, and be silent. Don't say a word about what you are making. Don't even whisper that you are trying something new.

Bake some Wagon Train Biscuits and put them out when you next serve soup. Or pack some Lavender Shortbread into tomorrow's lunches. I bet the worry will disappear and all you will hear from your children is "Can I have some more?"

BEVERAGES

······················

HAVE A HOMEBREW

by David L. Murray

Do you drink beer? Do you enjoy the flavor or a quality brewed beer? Are you disgusted with the high price of quality beer? If the answer is yes to any of these questions, consider brewing your own beer. Nearly anyone can brew beer. The only requirements are a sincere interest in homebrewing and a little patience. The rewards are:

Economy: With practice, you can brew world-class beer like those you can buy for a fraction of the cost.

Quality: You can take pride in knowing you've brewed a superior, all-natural beer. Homebrewed beer lacks the chemicals and artificial coloring in national brand beer.

Variety: The homebrewer can produce any style of beer he or she wishes by varying brewing ingredients. The modern homebrewer may choose from a vast selection of ingredients.

Homebrewing is by no means new. Mankind has been brewing fermented beverages for thousands of years. The first recorded practice of homebrewing was by the ancient Sumerians. They discovered that wetting and germinating grain preserved the grain for breadmaking. By combining the germinated grain with water and leaving the mixture in the open air they were amazed to find that drinking the resulting bubbling concoction caused a euphoric state of mind. Evidence of early beer brewing has also been found in many other ancient societies. The use of fermented beverages in ceremonial rituals was a common practice among the early Egyptians, Aztecs, and Incas.

The practice of beer brewing quickly spread through Europe and Asia by the wars of conquest and was carried to the New World during early exploration. The traditional styles of beer we enjoy today were brought to the United States by early European immigrants.

Prior to the Prohibition era of 1920 to 1933, homebrewing was a widespread practice. Many small house-breweries existed in cities and villages, usually limiting their beer production to their particular region. With the passing of the Volstead Act in 1920, nearly all breweries were closed with the exception of a few covert brewing operations using questionable ingredients. After Prohibition was repealed in 1933, home wine-making became legal again, but the term "and/or beer" was inadvertently excluded from the Federal Register by a court stenographer. Homebrewing remained illegal.

It wasn't until February 1979, during the Carter administration, that Congress repealed the restriction on homebrewing beer. The new law permits adults of legal drinking age to brew 100 gallons of beer annually, 200 gallons in households having two or more adults. The homebrewed beer must be produced for personal consumption only, and not for resale or distribution.

Legalization of homebrewing has already attracted a sizeable number of homebrewers and their numbers are increasing annually. The number of homebrewing clubs across the United States increased by 35 percent from 1991 to 1992, jumping from 230 clubs to 311 clubs. The number of microbreweries, micropubs, and contract brewers in the United States increased by 834 percent since 1985, from 29 brewpubs and micros to 242 in 1992, a 21 percent increase in 1992 alone.

What is Beer?

In essence, beer is a carbonated alcoholic beverage resulting from the fermentation of cereal grains, usually malted barley, and flavored with hops. Barley is a plant of the grass family *(Gramineae)* yielding kernels, or seeds, which contain large amounts of enzymes needed to convert the seed's starch to fermentable sugar. The malting of barley is the process of steeping the barley kernels in water until they germinate or sprout.

Next, the sprouted kernels are kiln-dried to reduce their water content, leaving behind the fermentable sugar and starch necessary for beer brewing. Barley has been a favorite source of fermentable sugar throughout history because of its ability to grow in varying climatic conditions.

Hops are the conical female flowers of the vining *Humulus Lupulus* plant. Each flower bears tiny glandular sacs at its base containing resin, or hop oil, which is used to impart bitterness and aroma. The addition of hops is a recent practice, started by brewers in the late nineteenth century to prevent contamination by air-borne or water-borne bacteria. The English are attributed with the first widespread use of hops. They included hop-boiling in the brewing process to preserve the beer for long voyages to their colonies.

Yeasts are living organisms, considerably larger than bacteria, responsible for converting soluble sugars and hops into beer. Wild yeasts are present in nearly everything we come in contact with, usually recognizable in the form of mold or fungus. Specific strains of yeast called Brewer's Yeast, or *Saccharomyces*, are cultures for the fermentation of beer.

The living yeast cells, when introduced into unfermented beer, absorb dissolved sugars and minerals through metabolic enzyme reaction. By obtaining oxygen from the surrounding liquid, the yeast cells convert the absorbed sugars to alcohol and carbon dioxide. This conversion of sugar to alcohol is known as the fermentation process.

There are two types of beer yeast used in homebrewing, lager yeast and ale yeast. Lager yeasts are bottom-fermenting yeasts which produce optimum fermentation at cold temperatures, usually from 32 to 55 degrees F. Ale yeasts are best used for brewing ales, stouts, porters, and wheat beers. The term top-fermenting or bottom-fermenting refers to the tendency of the yeast to flocculate, or gather, at the surface or the bottom of the fermentation vessel.

Another ingredient, and possibly the most important, is water. Water constitutes over 90 percent of beer. Most tap water in the United States is suitable for brewing, but if your tap water contains high levels of sulfur, iron, or bicarbonates, you may wish to use filtered or bottled water. Water anaylsis reports can be obtained from your local water company usually free of charge. A good rule of thumb in selecting your brewing water is if the water tastes bad, the beer will taste worse.

Lastly, the addition of fruits, vegetables, and adjuncts is quickly gaining popularity among homebrewers. With these extras, the homebrewer can impart a specific flavor or texture to his or her beer. Flavored-beer recipes are available in most homebrewing books, ranging from oatmeal-flavored to garlic-flavored beer. Taste is in the mouth of the beholder.

Ready to start brewing? Not quite. You will need to collect some essential homebrewing equipment first. You may already have some of the necessary items in your kitchen. Normally, the new homebrewer can expect an initial investment of $50 to $100 for equipment and ingredients. An important thought to remember is the money you save brewing your own beer will compensate your initial investment after seven or eight batches. Most homebrewed beer is produced at one-fourth the cost of the store-bought equivalent.

Homebrewing Equipment List

The following list of equipment will be necessary to brew five-gallon batches of beer at a time.

One 3 to 5 gallon pot (enameled or stainless). Stainless is best for sanitation. Available in most restaurant supply stores.

Sixty returnable 12 oz. bottles, or 25 champagne bottles. Bottles must be re-cappable, not twist-off. Available through most beverage suppliers, usually for the cost of the deposit.

One 5 to 7½ gallon plastic bucket (yes; another).

One large plastic funnel.

One 6-foot-long ⅜-inch inner diameter clear plastic tubing. Available in hardware stores.

One 3-foot-long ⅜ outer diameter (⁵⁄₁₆ inch inner diameter) clear plastic tubing. Available in hardware stores.

One fermentation lock with #6½ rubber stopper. Available through homebrewing supply stores.

One gross unused bottlecaps.

One thermometer, preferably 0 to 220 degrees F. Probe-type thermometers are available through restaurant supply stores.

One beer or one beer/wine hydrometer. Available through homebrewing supply stores.

One bottle washer (optional, jet-type brass model is best). Available through homebrewing supply stores.

One 5 to 7½ gallon glass Carboy (big bottles in water coolers) or same size food-grade plastic bucket. Food-grade refers to anything able to withstand boiling temperatures (212 degrees F). Carboys are available through hardware stores and drinking water supply companies. Plastic buckets are available through supermarket bakeries or hardware stores.

Note: Many homebrew suppliers have homebrew kits available which contain all or most of the equipment aforementioned and ingredients for the first batch of beer.

Making a Basic Ale

Upon acquiring the brewing hardware, you are almost ready to brew your first batch. The first step in brewing is deciding what type of beer you wish to brew.

The type of beer intended will aid your selection of ingredients. For the amateur brewer, a basic ale recipe follows which will produce, if property brewed, a medium-bodied ale. The new brewer should maintain a brewing record of each brewing session, including ingredients used, boiling times, specific gravities, and fermentation events. Your brewing records will assist you in duplicating or troubleshooting a previously brewed batch of beer. Ingredients for brewing basic ale:

Two 6.6 lbs. cans of hop-flavored malt extract syrup or a beer kit with the same quantities

Five gallons of clear, fresh water

¾ cup corn sugar (used during bottling)

One package dry ale yeast

The second and most critical step is sanitation. Contamination of unfermented beer by wild yeast or airborne bacteria is the most prevalent menace to homebrewing, usually resulting in an unpleasant-tasting, foul-smelling beer. There are many sanitizing agents available through homebrew suppliers, but a simple household bleach and water solution is inexpensive and very effective. Combine 2 ounces of bleach with 5 gallons of water and thoroughly rinse your primary fermenter *(carboy or bucket)* with the solution. Rinse the primary fermenter again with hot water until the bleach odor is gone.

Note: You will need to repeat this procedure with your plastic bucket, hoses, bottles, and rubber stopper prior to bottling the beer. Keep in mind that anything that comes in contact with your beer needs to be sanitized first.

The third step in brewing is boiling the wort (pronounced wert).

Wort is the mixture of water, malt, hops, and adjuncts, boiled together in your brewpot to release the fermentable sugars. Malt extract is malted barley which has been evaporated down to a thick, sticky syrup. It is very difficult to work with in its natural state. The best results are achieved by placing the cans of extract in a sink full of hot water for 30 minutes prior to boiling. The warmed extract flows from the can quickly and is readily dissolved into the wort.

Now you're ready to brew. Add 1½ gallons of water to your brewpot. Add the malt extract and stir thoroughly. Heat the wort and watch closely while the heat increases to a rolling boil. Many wort mixtures will become very foamy prior to boiling and attempt to spill over the sides of the brewpot. If you see the mixture is about to spill over, reduce the burner heat or remove the brewpot from the burner. It may take some experimentation in heat settings to attain a boil. After you have achieved a rolling boil, stir occasionally and continue to boil for 60 minutes.

After boiling for 60 minutes, it will be necessary to cool the wort below 78 degrees F to add, or pitch, the yeast. At this point your wort is highly susceptible to contamination from airborne bacteria. Keep it covered until you are ready to add it to the fermenter. Remove the covered brewpot from the burner and let cool. Many advanced brewers use wort-chillers to rapidly cool their hot wort, but for simplicity fill your sink or bathtub with cold water and ice. Place the hot brewpot in the ice bath (not above the rim), and replace the water whenever it gets warm. Cooling in this method usually takes one or two hours to drop the temperature below 78 degrees F.

While you are waiting for the wort to cool, fill your sanitized carboy or fermenter bucket with three gallons of cold water. Fill a measuring cup with ½ cup of warm water and add the dry yeast to the measuring cup. Let the yeast sit in the warm water for at least 15 minutes to activate.

The fourth step in brewing is pitching the yeast.

After verifying that your wort is below 78 degrees F, carefully funnel the wort into the carboy or bucket. Plug or seal the tap of your fermenter and thoroughly mix the wort with the cold water. Siphon off ¾ cup of the wort mixture from the fermenter to the flask that came with the hydrometer. An oven baster works well for this purpose. Cool the flask sample (in the freezer) to 60 degrees F and take a hydrometer reading. Record this reading. This is your original gravity (O.G.). Add the yeast mixture from the fermenting. Install the holed rubber stopper with the 3-foot length of plastic tubing stuck in the stopper. Place the opposite end of the tubing in a large cup or jar. Place the fermenter in a closet or dark corner out of direct sunlight.

The yeast you have added to the fermenter will multiply and slowly convert the wort/water mixture to alcohol. Signs of fermentation won't be visible right away. In 8 to 12 hours, a ring of foam should be visible on the surface of the mixture. This is the start of the fermentation process, called blow-off. After a day or two, foam will be expelled through the plastic tube. During blow-off, the fermentation process will blow off excessive oils and particle matter that would otherwise bitter the taste of your beer.

After three to four days, blow-off should subside and the normal fermentation process will continue. Remove the plastic hose from the rubber stopper and install the fermentation lock. Verify that the fermentation lock is filled with water to the half-full mark. The fermentation lock allows the carbon dioxide gas to escape during fermentation but restricts air from reentering the fermenter. Full fermentation should take two to three weeks. Watch the fermentation lock for the frequency of bubbles. When the bubbles occur less than one bubble per minute, it's time to bottle or keg.

The fifth step is bottling.

Prior to bottling your beer you should sanitize the second plastic bucket, bottles, and 6-foot-long plastic tubing with a bleach and water solution. Rinse well with fresh water. Elevate the fermenter on a tabletop or chair and place the plastic bucket on the floor. Siphon the beer from the fermenter to the plastic bucket with the 6-foot hose. This process is called racking. A good siphon flow can be attained by filling the plastic hose with water. Keeping thumbs over both ends, quickly slide one end into the fermenter and the other into the bucket. The weight of the water will start a siphon flow. Try to keep the hose end in the fermenter about a ½ inch from the bottom. By siphoning all but the last ½ inch of beer from the fermenter, you will avoid siphoning the sediment or trub *(pronounced troob)* into the bottling mixture.

Next, take another hydrometer reading and record it. The hydrometer should read lower than your O.G. This is called the final gravity (F.G.). To calculate the alcohol content of your beer, subtract the F.G. alcohol content from the O.G. content. Example: F.G. = 2 percent; O.G. = 6 percent; your alcohol content is $6 - 2 = 4$ percent. Most brewers record their original gravity and final gravity from the specific gravity scale on the hydrometer, i.e. O.G. = 1.062, F.G. = 1.012

Add ¾ cup of corn sugar to the beer in the plastic bucket and stir slowly. This is called priming the beer. Priming restarts the fermentation process by introducing a new sugar source for the existing yeast cells to digest. The unprimed beer in the plastic bucket lacks the appropriate carbonation for drinking. By restarting the fermentation process in the bottle, the carbon dioxide given off by the yeast is trapped in the bottle and forced back into the beer.

Lastly, you will bottle your beer. Boil your bottle caps in two cups of water for 15 minutes. Elevate your racking bucket on a table or chair and place your empty bottles on the floor. Start a siphon from the bucket to the bottles. The water method works well, but drain the water into a cup prior to filling the bottles. You will find that kinking the filler hose near the bottle end will enable you to control the flow into the bottles. Fill the bottles within two inches of the top and cap. If you are kegging, siphon to the keg, seal it, and pressurize with five psi of carbon dioxide.

The sixth step, and the longest, is conditioning.

You must allow the bottled or kegged beer to condition for a minimum of 10 days. During conditioning, the beer is being carbonated by the reactivation of fermentation. Conditioning mellows the bitterness and acidity of new beer and allows any residue yeast to settle to the bottom of the bottle or keg. While conditioning, store the bottles or keg in an upright position. Storage in a dark closet or corner is preferred. Do not store your beer in direct sunlight. The ultraviolet rays of the sun will sour or "skunk" your beer. To verify that your beer is done conditioning after 10 days, hold a bottle up to a light. If the beer looks clear through the light, it's probably ready to drink.

Now comes the payoff. If the brewing went well, you should be enjoying the fruits of your labor. Don't be discouraged if your first beer hasn't lived up to your expectations. Most homebrewers rely on trial and error to perfect a style of beer to their own tastes. Brewing the perfect beer comes with practice.

Once you've mastered basic brewing techniques, you will want to expand your expertise through different recipes. There are numerous beer recipes available through homebrewing books, extract can labels, online forums, and other homebrewers.

Many homebrewers turn their brewing hobby into a profession. They expand their brewing scale in the form of microbreweries, micropubs, and contract brewing, from hundreds of gallons per year to thousands of barrels per year. The brewing methods are identical.

Homebrewing can be a fun and rewarding hobby. Like a gourmet chef, you can take pride in brewing a quality beer. You'll also be amazed at the number of friends you make when they've tried one of your homebrews. The neighbors will use any excuse to get in your door to see what type of homebrew you've got in the refrigerator. You'll find that any style of beer is only a brewpot away.

Well, you're on your own. Remember, your beer is only as good as you make it. Homebrewers are their own worst critics. When you're able to drink and wholeheartedly enjoy the beer you have brewed, you have mastered the art of homebrewing. Good luck and happy fermentations.

·····················

HERBAL SYRUPS FOR BEVERAGES
by Carly Wall

What did people do before the invention of bottled soft drinks? They made their own instant drinks from fruits and herbs. It's so easy and economical, you have to wonder why these home-made "time-savers" have fallen to the wayside. I wondered this myself, and decided to drag out some of grandma's favorite old syrup recipes, which I share with you here. She liked using lemon syrup for her famous icy lemonade, to be sipped on the porch on hot summer days. She liked mint, so that was a regular around her household too.

How did these syrups originate? There was a need for fast drinks on hot days. On top of that, kitchens were pretty busy in summers during canning season, so these drinks were easy to make; all the kids had to do was mix a couple tablespoons of the flavored syrup with water and they were ready.

Syrups are bases of flavored sugars in liquid form that are easy to mix with either hot or ice water, or sparkling water or ginger ale for that little fizz on special occasions.

Some syrups were reserved for cold and flu season if the right herbs were used, and honey was used as the base for the syrup. In this case, the syrup was taken from the spoon, or added to hot water to help with coughs and sore throats. Lemon-flavored herbs, as well as horehound, hyssop, or wild cherry bark, were a few that were particularly favored for these concoctions. Since I've made cough syrups plenty of times over the years, I was interested in the drinks for pleasure that old-timers created to have on hand.

I discovered there were two types; the regular-flavored syrup and something called shrub, which was a flavored syrup made with vinegar. The vinegar gives a little tang to the taste (this mix was also good for cold and flu season). Both these syrup drink bases were versatile, meaning that not only could you use them for instant drinks, but you could pour the syrups over ice cream, add them to yogurt or hot cereals, or drizzle them over pancakes or biscuits. Try a few different flavors and combinations and see if you and your family don't find them enjoyable. They're an easy way to use herbs, and it's much more healthy than guzzling tons of soda. At least you know that in these drinks the herbal additions will give you a boost of vitamins as well as other added benefits. For an even healthier drink, you can make the syrup from honey to avoid refined sugar altogether. Have fun!

Basic Base Syrup Recipe

2 c. water (or fruit juice)   2 c. sugar
½ c. dried herb of choice

Bring water or juice to boil. Add herbs. Remove from heat and cover. Steep 20 minutes. Strain and squeeze out the herbs. Discard the plant material. Place the liquid back on the heat and bring to a boil again, adding the sugar. Boil 15 minutes. Pour into sterilized jars and seal. After opening, keep refrigerated up to one year. To use, add 2 tablespoons to 8 ounces iced or hot water, sparkling water, or ginger ale.

Basic Honey Syrup Recipe

1 c. water (or fruit juice)   3 c. honey
½ c. dried herb of choice

Place the herb into the water or juice and bring to a boil. Let steep covered for about 20 minutes. Strain. Return to heat and bring to a boil again, then turn down to simmer. Add the honey and mix well. Pour into sterilized jars and seal. After opening, keep refrigerated up to a year. For drinks, add 2 tablespoons to iced or hot water, sparkling water, or ginger ale.

Basic Shrub Recipe

1½ c. fruit juice   1 lb. sugar
½ c. dried herb of choice   ½ c. apple cider vinegar

Bring fruit juice to boil. Remove from heat and add the herbs. Cover and steep 20 minutes. Strain herbs out and return liquid to heat, bringing to a boil again. Add sugar and vinegar and boil for 15 minutes. Pour into sterilized jars and seal tightly with fresh, sterilized canning lids. Invert for five minutes. Lids should seal. If not, place in a boiling water bath for 10 minutes. Refrigerate after opening. It keeps up to a year. To use, add two tablespoons to iced or hot water or sparkling water or ginger ale.

Here are a few old-time recipes to get you started. Note that you can turn any of these drinks into creamy coolers by adding 2 tablespoons of syrup of your choice. Orange flavors are especially delicious this way.

Mint Syrup

3 c. boiling water   1 tbsp. mint extract

4 c. chopped mint leaves   Green food coloring, optional

4 c. sugar

Cover the chopped mint with boiling water. Cover and let steep 30 minutes. Strain. Bring liquid to a boil with the sugar; boil 10 to 15 minutes. Add mint extract and food coloring. Pour into sterilized bottles.

Floral Syrup

2½ c. water

1 lb. clean, pesticide-free,
    edible flowers (lavender, rose,
    jasmine, chamomile, etc ...)

1¾ c. sugar

Bring the water to a boil and add the flowers. Remove from heat and cover to steep 15 to 20 minutes. Strain. Return liquid to heat and bring to boil again, adding sugar. Stir.

Lemonade Syrup

2 c. sugar

1 c. water

1 lemon verbena
  (or spearmint leaves)

Juice of 6 lemons

Combine all together except for the lemon juice. Boil for 5 minutes. Strain out the lemon peel and herbs. Add the lemon juice and mix well. Pour into sterile jars. If you want the mix more yellow, add yellow food coloring or a few drops of red if you want pink lemonade. You can also purchase different flavoring oils to add to the syrup. Add them just before pouring into sterile jars, mixing well.

Strawberry-Mint Syrup

Fresh, cleaned strawberries

3 mint tea bags

2 c. sugar per every 2 c. juice

5 whole cloves

Place strawberries in a pan and add a bit of water. With a potato masher, mash the strawberries and warm on low heat. Strain the juice. For every 2 cups of juice add 2 cups of sugar. Place the juice and sugar in the pan and return to heat. Add mint tea bags and cloves, and bring all this to a boil for 15 minutes. Take out the cloves and tea bags and pour the syrup into sterilized jars.

Lavender-Cherry Syrup

1 lb. cherries, pitted

2 lbs. sugar

½ c. lavender buds

1 tsp. almond extract

2½ c. water

Bring cherries, lavender, and water to boil to 20 minutes. Strain. Add sugar to the cherry/lavender juice, and return to boil for 15 minutes. Add almond extract. Pour into sterilized jars.

Homemade Root Beer Syrup

2 c. water
1 tbsp. sassafras
3 tbsp. sarsaparilla
½ tsp. coriander
2 c. sugar (or 1 c. blackstrap molasses)

Bring flavorings and water to boil; boil for 20 minutes. Strain. Add the sugar and bring to a boil again for 15 minutes. Pour into sterilized jars. Add several tablespoons to ginger ale for a refreshing summer drink.

Jasmine-Almond Syrup

4½ c. water
1 c. jasmine flowers
Juice of 2 oranges
1½ c. fresh almonds, ground
3 tbsp. almond extract
6½ c. sugar

Bring water to boil and add almonds and jasmine flower. Cover and cool, then use muslin to strain and squeeze out the ground almonds and spent flowers. Return liquid to pan and add almond extract, orange juice, and sugar. Cook until the consistency is a thick syrup. Let cool. Pour into sterilized bottles.

Cinnamon-Bee Balm Syrup

2 c. water
½ c. bee balm
2 cinnamon sticks
2 c. sugar
Juice of 1 lemon

Bring water to boil. Add cinnamon sticks and bee balm and boil 5 minutes. Strain. Return to heat; add lemon juice and sugar. Boil 15 minutes or until syrup is thick. Bottle.

HERBAL TEA PARTIES

by Cindy Parker

When I was a child, my grandmother often made tea for me. As soon as the kettle whistled, she poured boiling water over the Lipton tea bag nestled in my cup. After a few dunkings, the brew would turn a beautiful amber color—almost ready to drink but not quite; it still needed Grandma's special touch—a red-and-white-striped hard peppermint candy. I'd wait for her to drop it into the hot liquid, then I'd watch as it dissolved into nothingness. This is my earliest and fondest memory of taking tea with my grandma.

Most of us, if we glance into the past, have some memory of taking tea. Maybe it's a favorite cup that comes to mind or the aroma of the brew itself. It might be a simple sweetcake that we remember eating with tea—perhaps cinnamon toast lovingly prepared by Dad or a scone baked by Mother. Cradling a warm cup of tea between your hands while inhaling the fragrant steam conjures feelings of comfort whether alone or in the company of others.

History of Tea

Tea itself is steeped in history and tradition. Legend credits the first liquid consumption of tea to Emperor Shen Nung in 2737 BCE. This health-conscious ruler of China was reputed to always boil his water before drinking it. One day a gentle freeze deposited a brand of the *Camellia sinensis* plant into his cauldron of hot water. He was so delighted with the heady aroma that he couldn't resist tasting the resulting infusion. He was most impressed and thus began the drinking of tea.

In the Orient, tea has long been popular among the monks as an aid to meditation. The ceremony that accompanied its use became a respected ritual among not only the spiritually inspired, but also among dignitaries and common people. Taking tea was time for participants to enter a peaceful space. Its ability to heighten alertness was scientifically validated with the discovery of the plant's stimulating constituents.

When tea traveled to Europe, it was used from a slightly different point of view. After its arrival in England, it took on a more culturally elite role with greater emphasis on proper etiquette and manners as the means of showing gratitude and respect. Anne, the Duchess of Bedford, was founder of the afternoon tea party tradition. At that time, it was customary to hold dinner until the men returned from hunting. The hunger pangs that stemmed from such a long wait between meals led this royal maiden to request finger foods during the later afternoon. She soon began inviting other women friends to join her. In time, tea became a prized commodity in England. Of course, this was true in early America as well, though because of the symbolic protest known as the Boston Tea Party—wherein rebels dumped crates of tea in Boston Harbor to protest high taxes—the colonists began drinking liberty tea that was brewed from local herbs. Today in America, herbal brews are again gaining popularity. Their delicate flavors and medicinal properties enhance the ancient ritual of taking tea in an atmosphere of peace and tranquility.

Herbal Tea Time

In general, tea time is the perfect opportunity to escape from the daily grind and renew our bodies, sharpen our minds, and honor our spirit. This may be done in solitude, or it may prompt invitations for others to join the party. Either way, herbs can make perfect brews for modern tea time. Their use began as an act of rebellion, but today their inclusion is a conscious choice. They not only provide tasty beverages but may also be used to flavor foods and add interesting garnishes.

There are various elements associated with the traditional tea party that may be adapted to modern-day schedules and time restraints. It's okay to make scones from a mix or even purchase them from a local bakery. A picnic can be spread out on a blanket rather than served on a coffee table or in a formal dining room. If you don't have enough matching dishes to serve all your guests, celebrate the fact that mixed cups and saucers reflect the unique-ness of each individual. Have fun, be creative, and always emit a calm presence, as peace is essential to any tea party.

Making Herbal Tea

The most obvious way to incorporate herbs in a tea party is in the tea itself. I like to serve a hot tea that contains some *Camellia sinensis*, either black, green, or oolong tea, along with a herbal blend that is completely caffeine free. It's also nice to include a cold beverage such as iced tea or lemonade. There are many plants to choose from when brewing an herbal tea, but for beverage blends, the more mild, fruity, or minty plants are best.

When mixing tea blends, I use volume to define parts. That is, each part is whatever measure is chosen depending upon the quantity desired. Simply combine the various herbs in a bowl, toss together to distribute evenly, and store in a glass jar. To brew, use 1 teaspoon of the blend for every 6 ounces of water. You can place the herbs loose in a cup to strain later or use a tea ball. Bring the water to a boil and pour over the herbs. Cover and steep 15 to 20 minutes. Remove spent herbs and serve. Here are a few of my favorite blends; common garden herb mixtures are usually best served hot.

GARDEN WISDOM TEA

3 parts chamomile	2 parts peppermint or spearmint
1 part rosemary	½ part sage
½ part thyme	

TRANQUILITY

This tea calms and relaxes both children and adults.

3 parts each of chamomile and lemon balm	2 parts each of linden flowers and rose petals
1½ part lavender	1 part hops

INDIAN SUMMER

This can be served as a refreshing iced delight.

1 part each of spearmint, hibiscus, and rose hips	½ part mixture of lemon and orange peel
3 parts of a mixture of lemon balm, lemon verbena, and/or lemongrass	2 parts chamomile

Tea Breads and Munchies

Munchies are always better when served with tea. A buttery English muffin oozing with raspberry mint jam makes a satisfying dish with tea. Quick breads such as zucchini spice or the favorite family nut bread become absolutely delicious. And there is no more perfect food with tea than the famous scone.

The scone is a biscuit that uses simple ingredients, requires no special equipment, and is easy to make. It also lends itself to infinite possibilities. Cheese, bits of smoked ham or bacon, or culinary herbs like sage or even pesto may be added to make a more hearty, savory scone. The traditional sweet scone may include fruit, nuts, or chocolate chips. The diversity is endless; they are best served fresh from the oven.

LAVENDER SCONES

⅔ c. milk	1 tsp. salt
1 tbsp. dried lavender buds	1 stick butter
2½ c. flour	½ c. sugar
1 tbsp. baking powder	

Heat milk and lavender almost to a boil. Allow to steep and cool. Strain and add enough milk to make a full ⅔ cup. Sift together flour, baking powder, and salt. Cut in butter with a pastry blender. Toss in sugar and stir in milk with a fork to form a soft dough. Knead 10 to 12 times on a lightly floured board. Roll out fairly thick and cut into rounds. Bake at 425 degrees F until lightly browned, about 12 minutes.

Savories

The healthiest, least fattening foods at a tea party are the savories. Dainty sandwiches are the standard fare but just about any main course food falls into this category—appetizers, soups, salads, pasta, casseroles, meat pies, and veggies. The dainty cucumber sandwich is probably the most traditional savory selection. But the sandwich provides much room for creativity. Open-face sandwiches may be garnished with fresh slivers of veggies or sprigs of herbs. Egg salad is perfect with dill or salmon paté with fennel. The bread may be cut into shapes with cookie cutters or cut diagonally into triangles, or horizontally and vertically into small squares. If one slice of white bread and one slice of whole wheat is used for each sandwich, they may be served with alternate sides showing, creating a checkerboard effect.

Some sandwiches may be made ahead of time, wrapped in plastic, and chilled. To make striped sandwiches, stack and fill several layers of bread and wrap. When ready to serve, simply slice and serve sideways to display the multiple layers. I also make pinwheels several hours in advance. After removing the crust from two pieces of bread, zap them in the microwave for 10 seconds to moisten. Immediately overlap them along one edge and use a rolling pin to press them together into one long piece of bread. After spreading this with filling, roll it up, wrap it tightly in plastic wrap, and chill. To serve, cut into rounds.

There are many fun things to do with sandwiches. You may want to apply a thin layer of mayonnaise to the sides and dip them in finely chopped green herbs or crunchy nuts and seeds. When hosting a children's tea party, it's fun to set out a variety of cookie cutters, peanut butter and cheese spread, and a variety of cut-up fruits and veggies so they may create their own artistic sandwich. The following are some recipe ideas for savory tea snacks.

Herbed Cucumber Sandwiches

2 cucumbers, seeded (or use the English variety)   8 oz. cream cheese

2 tbsp. sour cream   1 tbsp. lemon juice

2 tbsp. herb mix (I suggest 4 parts dried basil,
   2 parts dried onion flakes, 1 part dried thyme)

Slice cucumbers very thin, either peeled or unpeeled depending on your preference. Some people soak them in salt water, but I don't find this necessary. Mix the rest of the ingredients to make a filling. Spread bread with filling and top with a thin layer of cucumbers. Another piece of bread may be added or they may be served open-faced. For a wild food version, a layer of tender chickweed or dandelion leaves may be added.

Flower Sandwiches

Spread bread with strawberry cream cheese. Serve open faced garnished with edible flowers such as Johnny-jump-ups, dianthus, violets, or borage. These may also be made into pinwheels or stripes and can be quite colorful.

Chutney Pear Sandwiches

8 oz. cream cheese	2 fresh pears
½ c. peach or mango chutney	Lemon juice
Dark rye bread	

Spread cream cheese and chutney on dark rye bread. Brush pear slices with lemon juice and place on filling.

Nettle Quiche

1 c. fresh nettles	½ c. grated cheese of choice
½ c. chopped onion	3 eggs, beaten
1 clove fresh garlic, minced	1 c. milk
1 premade pie crust	

Place nettles in a pot of boiling water. Cook several minutes, strain, and chop. Sauté cooked nettles with onion and garlic. In a pie crust, layer cooked veggies with grated cheese. Mix eggs and milk and pour over pie. Sprinkle with calendula petals. Bake at 375 degrees F for 35 to 40 minutes, or until golden brown and firm.

Desserts

What would an herbal tea party be without a dessert dish to add a finishing touch? Confections are capable of etching luscious memories in the mind, especially when chocolate is involved. Biting into a juicy strawberry covered in chocolate never fails to stimulate the senses, just as a rich chocolate cake with raspberry filling soothes and comforts the soul.

Offering several desserts allows guests to choose what satisfies them. Simple fruit parfaits layered with yogurt and granola are obviously more healthy than ones made with ice cream and gooey fudge, marshmallow, or caramel. A tray of cookies allows your visitors to take pleasure in a tiny piece of sweetness.

Ma Parker's Coriander Cookies

½ c. butter	1 tsp. vanilla
2 c. flour	1 egg, slightly beaten
1 c. sugar	1 tbsp. milk
3 tbsp. ground coriander seeds	

Cut butter into flour with a pastry blender till crumbly. Add sugar and ground coriander seeds. Mix remaining ingredients and add to flour mixture. Mix until a soft dough forms. Roll dough into ½ inch balls and place on a cookie sheet. Flatten with a cookie stamp or the bottom of a glass. Bake at 400 degrees F for 6 to 8 minutes.

Trifle

Trifle is historically served at tea time. It is made by arranging several layers of cake, filling, and fruit, though variations come from different geographical area. Regardless of the choice of ingredients, a trifle should always be visually appealing. It is usually made in a clear glass bowl or in parfait glasses.

Pound cake, angel food cake, or ladyfingers may be drenched with a bit of liquor such as brandy or schnapps for added zip, with alternating layers of a filling such as Jell-O, pudding, or yogurt followed by a layer of fruit. I like to stack berries in between pillars of cake on the outer side of the bowl. Top with whipped cream and garnish with fruit and mint leaves.

Pawpaw Trifle and Other Cake Suggestions

Pawpaws are a Midwestern fruit that tastes something like a banana but looks like a small mango. I cut them open and squeeze out the flesh, which simultaneously mashes the fruit while removing the skin and seeds.

Cut a pound cake into squares. Mash pawpaw fruit and mix with vanilla yogurt. Combine fresh raspberries with sliced peaches. Layer all of the above in a clear glass bowl at least twice. Top with whipped cream.

A very simple dessert suggestion is gingerbread topped with cream or a lemon sauce. Use herbs to flavor desserts—peppermint with chocolate, pineapple sage with peaches, rosemary with fruit, and scented geraniums with cake. A very simple, healthy dessert may be made by drizzling round slices of fresh oranges with honey and sprinkling with cinnamon.

Serving Suggestions

Now that we've covered what to serve at a tea party, let's discuss how they should be served. Foremost, the most important element of a tea party is an air of calm tranquility. You should never appear to be hurried or hassled. Always respect proper etiquette and manners at your tea parties. Take care that everyone is polite and on their best behavior. This ambience will be enhanced through the harmony of people present, through the food, the dishes, the table setting, and so on. When hosting a tea party, select a focus to build the event around and make it sparkle with purity.

The traditional afternoon tea party, steeped in formal elegance and propriety, occurs usually in the dining room, at a large and beautifully arranged, linen covered table. Cups and saucers with matching plates are laid out along with linen napkins and appropriate eating utensils. The centerpiece usually embodies artistic elements from nature—blooming daffodils in the spring, a bouquet of colorful garden flowers in the summer, a cornucopia of gourds in the fall, or an arrangement of dried flowers and grasses in the winter. The food should be attractively served in a way that displays a variety of offerings at different eye levels. Having tiered plates is the key here. Each level may contain a sampling of the various types of food—desserts on the top, savories in the middle, and breads on the bottom. Larger platters are then used to serve the bulk of the entrées. Special serving dishes such as trifle bowls and cake stands provide different heights that further enhance eye appeal and visual interest.

If these dishes are not part of your kitchen cupboards, don't panic. Maintain that air of calm tranquility by creatively utilizing whatever you already have in accordance with the occasion. If it's an outdoor tea, a simple checkered tablecloth with paper napkins will do just fine. Don't get hung up on rules but rather celebrate adaptability. One of my favorite ways to solve the problem of supplying enough teacups when I do classes is to ask everyone to bring their own favorite cup and saucer. This adds another dimension to the festivities as participants are encouraged to share stories about the cups they brought.

Tea may be experienced in so many ways. The possibilities are endless and require little more than hot water and the plant material to pour it over. Of course, it may be embellished as extravagantly as one desires. This simple ritual is rich in tradition but also provides a medium for unique expression. May the information provided here be your springboard to many wonderful encounters not only with tea, but with fellow human beings as well.

·····················

BHANG: THE SACRED DRINK OF SHIVA
by Magenta Griffith

On the night of Maha Shivratri, the major holiday of Shiva worship, devotees prepare and drink an intoxicating beverage called bhang. Traditionally, this is made from cannabis, almonds, and milk; devotees sing songs in praise of their god and dance to drums. Offerings of bhang are poured out before or on statues of Shiva. This celebration would be incomplete without this herbal beverage.

Shiva, the Destroyer

Shiva is one of the three great gods of India—which include Brahma, the Creator; Vishnu, the Preserver; and Shiva, the Destroyer. He is considered by many to be the most powerful god of the Hindu pantheon. Known also by many other names—Mahadeva *(the Great God)*, Mahayogi *(the Great Yogi)*, Nataraja *(Lord of the Dance)*—Shiva is perhaps the most complex of Hindu deities. Shiva is the patron god of mystics, ascetics, and yogis. To some of his devotees, Shiva is both creator and destroyer. In one story, he opens his third eye and his gaze destroys the world. He then dances the world back into being. One mystical doctrine states that he has done this innumerable times, but since he recreates the world perfectly, no one knows it has been destroyed and recreated.

Shiva is also called the Bhole Shankar, one who is oblivious of the world. By this name, he is worshipped by yogis and other ascetics, including wandering holy men called sadhus. Bhang is certainly part of the practices of some sadhus, and sharing bhang with a holy man is considered obligatory if offered, even if one does not otherwise use cannabis.

Bhang

Bhang refers to the lower leaves of the cannabis plant, which is considered the mildest of the three grades of the plant. Ganja is the flowering tops only and is usually smoked, and charas refers to the resin, which is also called hashish. Botanically, cannabis is considered to be a member of the same family as hops, which is used in making beer. In India, it was used extensively in folk medicine. It was believed to lower fevers, induce sleep, improve appetite, and cure dysentery. India is not the only place it was used medicinally; Chinese herbalists prescribed it to treat, among other things, malaria, rheumatic pains, and "female disorders," likely menstrual cramps. The use of cannabis preparations goes back at least several hundred years in India, to as early, to as early as 1000 BCE. At one time it was theorized that soma, the ancient sacred drink mentioned in the Rig-Veda, was bhang, though the descriptions of soma ultimately differ from contemporary bhang in appearance. It is possible that bhang was later substituted for soma in rituals, and soma was made from a now-extinct plant.

Bhang is thought by some in India to bestow supernatural powers on the users. Cannabis preparations may have been used as part of Tantric rituals; one of the properties ascribed to it is as an aphrodisiac. As such, it makes sense that this herb is sacred to Shiva, since he is the patron of Tantra, and often is worshipped in the form of a stone lingam, or phallus. Offerings are made to the Shiva lingam, which can be anywhere from a few inches to a few feet high, by pouring milk, bhang, or other sacred drinks over it; flowers are left at the base, usually in the form of a wreath encircling the lingam.

According to legend, bhang originated when Shiva was dancing the destruction of the world. Since all the other gods were afraid he would completely destroy the world, they went to his wife, Parvati, and begged her to do something. She thought for a while, then told the various gods, "You, bring me milk; you, bring me the leaves of this plant; you, bring me the bark of that tree; you, bring me almonds," and on through all the needed ingredients. She put them together, cooked them, and strained them with her sari, and put the first batch of bhang in a jar. She took the jar to Shiva and said, "Here, destroying the world is thirsty work, have some of this." So he drank it, and continued to dance, but more slowly, and then he drank some more, and stopped altogether, and told Parvati, "That was good, do you have any more?" So she gave him more bhang, and he said, "I'll destroy the world some other time." This is why we don't drink bhang every day, just on special occasions.

The following recipes is one version used in India. Since cannabis is illegal in most of the United States, I cannot recommend using this recipe, as authentic as it is.

Original Recipe for Bhang

4 c. whole milk
½ oz. cannabis, finely chopped
¼ tsp. cinnamon
1 dash cardamom
2 tbsp. almonds, blanched
  and finely chopped

¼ c. sugar
⅛ tsp. cloves
¼ tsp. powdered ginger
½ tsp. rosewater (optional)

Put milk in a pan, add cannabis, and stir while heating over a low fire. Gradually add other ingredients, continuing to stir. Heat until it begins to steam, and keep simmering, never allowing it to come to a boil. Keep stirring, if not continuously, fairly often, chanting "Om nama Shivaya" while stirring. Cook for about a half hour. Strain through fine strainer or cheesecloth and chill.

American Recipe for Bhang

4 c. milk, whole or 2 percent
¼ tsp. powdered ginger
½ tsp. rosewater (optional)
2 tbsp. almonds, blanched
  and finely chopped

⅛ tsp. cloves, dried
¼ tsp. cinnamon
1 dash cardamom
¼ c. sugar

Put milk in a pan and heat over a low fire until it begins to steam. Gradually add the rest of the ingredients, continuing to stir. Keep stirring continuously, chanting "Om nama Shivaya" while stirring. Cook for about 10 minutes. Strain through fine strainer or cheesecloth and chill. If you wish to use this preparation for another deity, be sure to use an appropriate chant.

YARROW BEER

by Chandra Moira Beal

Years before hops became the predominant flavoring and bittering agent in beer, yarrow was often used by brewers. The herb provided pleasant flavors and acted as a preservative, and medicinally it had astringent and pungent qualities that drinkers found pleasant. In fact, during the Middle Ages, adding herbs such as rosemary, valerian, and yarrow to beer was quite popular. Such concoctions were called "gruit," and the herbs were believed to increase beer's intoxicating effects.

Yarrow Today

Yarrow today lives on as a hardy, prolific herb with many applications. It grows wild in many parts of the world and is easy to grow in the garden. The plant is a perennial that usually grows in bushy clusters. The stalks can grow as high as two feet and have white or pink flowers that bloom from summer to fall.

White-flowered yarrow has the most potent flavor of all the varieties of the plant. Its leaves are rich in vitamins and minerals. In general, yarrow has a strong aromatic fragrance reminiscent of sage. If you are gathering your own, the leaves are most pungent in the spring. Dried yarrow flowers are fairly common at health food stores and can be used in place of the fresh flowers.

Ruled by Venus, yarrow promotes love and courage and enhances psychic powers. The Navajos used yarrow as an aphrodisiac, so you may want to explore the herb's potential uses in this realm with your loved one.

Yarrow beer makes a good summertime brew with its light, herbal flavors, but it is also delicious any time of the year.

How to Make Yarrow Beer

Homebrewing is a fun hobby. There are many volumes of books devoted to its crafting. The beer recipe included below is designed for the beginning homebrewer and uses a minimum of specialized equipment. You'll find many of these implements in your kitchen, though you should visit a homebrewing supply store for specialized equipment.

Homebrewing supplies are now available online too. It is worth investing in a few timesaving brewing devices if you plan to brew more than once. You will also find malt extract and cane sugar at brewing supply stores as well as at gourmet grocery stores.

EQUIPMENT

A large stainless-steel cooking pot

A long-handled spoon or paddle

Five-gallon glass jug

Optional: outdoor propane
   cooker, wort chiller, ice

48 glass beer bottles and caps

Airlock and rubber cork

Measuring spoons and cups

A cooking thermometer

Plastic siphon tubing

Sanitizing agent
   (idophor or bleach)

Bottle capper

INGREDIENTS

5 gallons cold fresh water

2 lbs. sugar

1 pkg. liquid ale yeast or dry bread yeast

2 oz. dried chamomile flowers

2 oz. dried raspberry leaf

2 oz. dried yarrow leaves or flowers

1 oz. dried agrimony leaf

½ oz. crushed fennel seed

½ lb. malt extract

1 oz. cane sugar

Juice of 2 lemons

134   Beverages

To brew your own beer, you need to set aside several hours to devote to the process. Before you begin, be sure that you have all the equipment and ingredients you need.

If you're using liquid yeast, the package must be brought to room temperature before you begin brewing. If you're using dry yeast, make a starter just before you begin to brew. Using a starter gives the yeast a head start and helps prevent weak fermentation.

Put 1 cup of water (90 degrees F) that has been boiled for at least 15 minutes into a sterile jar and stir in the yeast. Cover with plastic wrap and wait 10 minutes. Stir in 1 teaspoon of sugar. Cover and place in a warm area out of direct sunlight. After about 30 minutes or so, the yeast should be actively churning and foaming. It will now be ready to pitch.

Sanitizing

The next thing you need to do is sanitize everything that will come in contact with your unfermented beer. To do this you'll need a sanitizer such as idophor or chlorine bleach. Immerse everything in a solution of 1 tablespoon bleach to 5 gallons of water, or follow the directions that come with your sanitizer. A large plastic bucket makes a good container for this, or a large kitchen sink. It takes time for the sanitizer to do its job, so allow your equipment to soak in the sanitizing solution for at least 30 minutes. If you use bleach, you must next rinse everything thoroughly to remove the odor. A solution of idophor does not need to be rinsed away.

Note on Water

The water you use is very important to this process. After all, beer is mostly water. If your tap water tastes good at room temperature, it should make good beer. It will just need to be boiled for a few minutes to remove the chlorine and kill any bacteria. Do not use water from a salt-based water softener, and don't use distilled (deionized) water. Beer needs the minerals for proper growth. A good bet is the bottled water sold in most supermarkets as "drinking water." Real spring or aquifer water is even better if you can get it.

Add 5 gallons of cold water to your brew pot and bring it to a boil.

Note: If you're using a five-gallon pot on the stove, it may cover two burners and take a while to heat. If you have an outdoor propane cooker, it can save you a lot of time.

While the water is boiling, mix together the dried herbs and fennel seeds. You can add them loose when you add the malt, or tie them in a muslin bag for easier cleanup.

The Wort

When the water boils, add your malt syrup and the sugar. Stir it well, making sure the syrup and sugar dissolves and does not stick to the bottom of the pot. (You don't want your beer to taste like burnt sugar.) Now you've got what is called "wort." Make sure the wort keeps up a good rolling boil, and that it does not boil over onto the stove. Not only is it a mess, but this boil-over can negatively affect the flavor of your beer as certain compounds turn bitter when overheated. Set your timer to 1 hour and let the wort boil.

After an hour has passed, turn off the heat and stir in the lemon juice.

Let the wort cool to less than 80 degrees F. While it is above 130 degrees F, bacterial and wild yeasts are inhibited, which is good. However, it is very susceptible to oxygen damage as it cools, which is bad. There are also sulfur compounds that evolve while the wort is hot. If the wort is cooled slowly, these can dissolve back into the wort, causing cabbage or cooked vegetable flavors in the final beer. The objective is to rapidly cool the wort before oxidation or contamination can occur. Also, if the liquid is too hot it will kill the yeast.

If you have a wort chiller (usually a copper coil with connection to a garden hose on either end so cool water flows through), use it now. To cool the wort quickly without a wort chiller, place the pot in a sink or tub filled with ice water that can be circulated around the hot pot. Take great care because wort is heavy and very hot. While the cold water is flowing around the pot, gently stir the wort in a circular pattern so the maximum amount of wort is moving against the sides of the pot. If the water gets warm, replace it with cold water. The wort will cool in about 20 minutes. Do not add commercial ice to the wort itself. Commercial ice harbors a lot of dormant bacteria that would love a chance to work on the new beer.

When the wort is cool enough, transfer it from the cooking pot to the glass jug using the siphon tube. Put the jug on the floor so it is lower than the cooking pot. Sanitize the siphon first, then place one end of the tube in the cool wort and the other in the jug. Gravity will start the flow, and the beer will follow the water into the new vessel. Monitor the transfer closely, and when you see the thick, sludgy sediment at the bottom, pull the end of the siphon out of the jug. This is mostly dead yeast. You should try to leave this behind by not allowing the suction end of the tubing to touch it, as it can add undesirable flavors to your beer. The sediment, or "trub," can be composted or thrown away.

Pinching the Yeast and Waiting

Now, open your sanitized yeast package or yeast starter, and add the contents to the jug. This is called "pitching" the yeast. Gently rock the jug to aerate the wort, splashing it around. This provides oxygen to the yeast so it will do its job.

Now assemble your airlock and cork, fill the jug with water, and insert it into the top of your jug.

In about 12 to 24 hours, some signs of yeast activity should be present. That is, you should see bubbles rising through your airlock, and if you sniff the gas coming from the airlock it should smell yeasty or beer-like.

After a few days, the vigorous fermentation should subside. The surface of the beer will become clear of foam. When the bubbles in your airlock appear only once a minute or so, their production will have stopped. Your beer is now ready to move to the next stage. Reaching this stage takes about a week.

Conditioning with Sugar

Dissolve the cane sugar in 1 quart of water and bring it to a boil. Add this mixture to the contents of the jug. The yeast will feed on this new sugar and continue to produce carbon dioxide, causing carbonation and pressurization in the bottles. This is a process called "conditioning."

You could drink your beer at this stage when it's still "green," or weaker than it will be in a couple weeks. But most people prefer the stronger alcohol content and the carbonation that comes with conditioning.

Bottling

You will need at least 48 bottles (two cases) and the same number of caps to bottle a five-gallon batch of beer. Don't use the screw-top kind of bottle, as the caps will not adhere properly. It is fine to reuse pop-top bottles that have been thoroughly washed and sanitized. If you want to avoid capping altogether, the flip-top Grolsch-style bottles work well. Again, be sure that anything you use has been fully cleaned and sterilized.

Using the siphon process again, fill each bottle, leaving about an inch of headroom. The headroom allows the carbon dioxide to expand and create a proper seal. When your bottles are filled, cap them, and place them in a cool, dark place for at least 10 days to condition, or become carbonated. The flavor of your beer will be best after about three weeks.

Chill and Enjoy

When it's time to enjoy your first homemade beer, chill it upright for several hours. There will be some sediment at the bottom of each bottle. This is mostly spent yeast, and you should avoid mixing it into your beer as it will cloud it and add a bitter, yeasty flavor. Pour your beer slowly, in one smooth motion, and stop before you pour any of the yeasty dregs into your glass.

Say a toast to your fresh yarrow beer before you drink it.

Kegging

If you prefer, you may keg your beer instead of bottling it. Kegging does require additional equipment, but it offers added convenience over bottling.

You must, of course, sanitize your keg and anything else that will come in contact with your beer. If you are using a plastic keg, then follow the sanitizing procedures outlined above. If you are using a metal keg, use iodine to sterilize your keg as bleach and other oxidizing sanitizers may react with the metal. This is extra work, of course, but it is better to be safe than sorry.

Prepare your priming sugar as before by dissolving it in water and bringing it to a boil. Siphon your beer into the keg and add the dissolved sugar as you go. Seal the keg and place it in a cool place for two weeks.

When it seems ready, tap your keg and enjoy a few glasses of your homebrew.

....

Herbal Wines and Liqueurs
by Chandra Moira Beal

Grape growers don't have a monopoly on winemaking. Herbs, fruits, flowers, and even vegetables can be made into delectable wines and liqueurs.

Making your own herbal wines and liqueurs is fun and easy, and a great way to continue an ancient tradition. Wines and liqueurs can be used socially or medicinally, or can be incorporated into your magic rituals. These time-tested recipes are simple and economical, using ingredients found in gardens and field. There is no end to the possible combinations of wines and herbs. Let your imagination lead you into new realms.

Getting Started

Before you attempt your first recipe, gather all the equipment you need to make wine. This includes one-gallon glass jugs, corks or screw-tops, strainers, large stainless-steel cooking pots, funnels, wooden spoons, and fermentation locks. A fermentation lock is a device that fits into the top of your jug and is filled with water. It allows the gases produced by the yeast to escape, but it prevents contaminants from sneaking into your wine. They are inexpensive and readily available at brewing supply stores. I highly recommend this simple but effective device.

Some Basic Starter Tips

When filling your bottles, leave as little headroom between the liquid and the cork as possible. This minimizes the chances of a sharp flavor invading your wine.

Sanitation is the key to successful brewing, so wash anything and everything that will come in contact with your wine in hot, soapy water. Do not use bleach as it can leave an odor behind that will be absorbed by your wine. Other odor-free sanitizers such as idophor are available at homebrew shops.

Start with fresh, cool water in your brew pot. Use only the freshest ingredients available. More than anything, your wines will be as good as the ingredients that go into them. Use exact measurements, and follow instruction carefully. Always pick through your herbs, and remove any green stalks, leaves, or stems. These plant elements tend to contain bitter oils not welcome in your wine.

Because high temperatures will kill the yeast, it is important to let the hot liquid cool completely, to at least 75 degrees F, before adding yeast to it.

Most of these wines will tend to improve with age. Let them sit for at least six months before tasting. Wines will also clarify as they age, so when you can read a sheet of paper help up to the glass through the liquid, your wines are probably ready.

Racking is another way to clarify your wine, but this is more time-consuming. It involves repeatedly pouring the liquid off the settled yeast wastes at the bottom of the jug into a clean jug.

You can also taste along the way and adjust the sweetness to your personal tastes.

The Basic Procedure

The procedure is basically the same for each of the following wines. First, heat the water to just below boiling so it will extract the herbs' essential oils but not their bitterness. Pour the hot water over the herbs and allow them to steep (the duration of steeping will vary by recipe). Strain out the herbs and add the sugar, any citrus element called for, and the yeast. Stir to dissolve the sugar. Stirring aerates the yeast and activates it. As the yeast bacteria eat the sugar, they produce carbon dioxide—thus causing the beverage to ferment.

You should see bubbles in your liquid within 24 hours as evidence of yeast activity. If fermentation is slow to start, shake your jug vigorously to aerate again. Make sure the ambient temperature where you are keeping your incipient wine is not too hot or cold. Yeast prefers a temperature around 60 to 65 degrees F to ferment—such temperatures are typical of a basement or garage. Place a fermentation lock over the top of the bottle and place the bottle in a dark, cool place to age. It will keep for years until opened.

Herbal Wine Recipes

Coltsfoot Wine

Coltsfoot is best known for its expectorant qualities. A glass of this wine may help quiet a cough.

2 qts. coltsfoot flowers	½ lb. raisins
1 gal. boiling water	½ oz. yeast
1 lemon, cut into thin slices	3 lbs. sugar

Pick the flowers on a sunny day and wash them to remove any insects. Place the flowers in a large bowl and pour the boiling water over the top. Cover the bowl with a clean tea towel and let it sit for 4 days. Strain the liquid into a large saucepan over medium heat and add the lemon slices and raisins. When the mixture begins to boil, turn off the heat. Pour the liquid into a large bowl and let it cool. Stir in the yeast and sugar and stir to completely dissolve these into the liquid. Cover the bowl again with a towel and stir it once a day for 3 days. The wine is then ready to strain and bottle. Cork it loosely or use a fermentation lock. Let it age for 6 months.

Cowslip Wine

Cowslip flowers are said to help cure jaundice. The plant itself is associated with the Norse goddess of beauty and love, Freya. It is a good herb for protection, and it has strong maternal qualities.

2 qts. cowslip flowers	3 lbs. sugar
1 gal. boiling water	½ oz. yeast
1 lemon, thinly sliced	

Pick the flowers on a sunny day and wash them well to remove any insects. Use only the heads of the flowers. Place the flowers in a large bowl and pour the boiling water over the top. Cover the bowl with a clean tea towel and let it sit for 4 days. Strain the liquid into a large saucepan and add the lemon slices. When the mixture begins to boil, turn off the heat. Pour it into a large bowl and let it cool. Add the sugar and stir to dissolve. Spread the yeast on a piece of toast and float the toast on top of the liquid.

Cover the bowl again with a towel and stir it once a day for 3 days. Remove the toast, strain the liquid, and bottle. Cork it loosely or use a fermentation lock. Let this wine age for at least 6 months. This wine may need to be sweetened with more sugar after a few weeks of aging.

Dandelion Wine

The dandelion is unfairly criticized as a weed. Dandelions are actually very rich in vitamins and minerals, and they are good for indigestion and kidney trouble. The plant also makes a very mean bottle of wine.

2 qts. fresh dandelion flowers	1 gal. boiling water
1 lemon, sliced thin	3 lbs. sugar
1 orange, sliced thin	½ oz. yeast

Pick the flowers on a sunny day when the flowers are fully open. Remove all green stems and stalks and measure 2 quarts of loose, fresh flowers. Wash the flowers in cold water to remove any insects. Place the blossoms in a large bowl. Add the sliced lemon and orange and pour the boiling water over the top. Cover the bowl with a clean tea towel and let it sit for 10 days. Strain the liquid into another bowl and add the sugar. Stir to completely dissolve the sugar into the liquid. Spread the yeast on a piece of toast and float the toast on top of the liquid. Cover the bowl and let it sit for another 3 days. Remove the toast and strain again. Bottle the wine with a loose cork or fermentation lock.

Elderflower Wine

Elder has long been associated with protection against disease, lightning, and it can assist in divination.

1 gal. elderflowers	1 gal. boiling water
Zest from 1 lemon	3 lbs. granulated sugar
Zest from 1 orange	1 oz. yeast

Cut the stalks from the flowers and measure out a gallon of flowers. Wash them and remove any insects. Place the elderflowers in a large bowl with the lemon and orange zest. Pour the boiling water over the top. Cover the bowl with a clean tea towel and let it sit for 4 days. Strain the liquid into a large saucepan and bring it to a boil. Add the sugar and stir well until it is dissolved in the liquid. Let the mixture cool and add the yeast. Cover the bowl again and let sit for 6 days, stirring every day. Then strain and bottle with a fermentation lock. Age for 6 months.

Ginger Wine

Ginger is excellent for indigestion, and this wine will warm you during cold winter nights.

2½ oz. ginger root	Juice of 3 lemons
2 gal. water	2 tbsp. honey
3½ lbs. granulated sugar	

Bruise the ginger and put it in a saucepan with 3 pints of water. Bring the water to a boil, turn down the heat, and simmer for 30 minutes. Pour sugar into a large bowl. Add the lemon juice and honey. Pour the ginger and the hot liquid into the bowl and stir well to dissolve the sugar. Boil the remaining water and add it to the bowl. Let it sit for 24 hours. Strain and bottle.

Rosehips Wine

| 3½ lbs. rosehips | 3½ lbs. sugar |
| 1 gal. boiling water | |

This is an easy to make recipe that doesn't involve yeast. Wash the rosehips and cut them in half. Place them in a large bowl and pour the boiling water over the top. Cover the bowl with a clean tea towel and let it sit for 2 weeks. Strain the liquid into a bowl and add sugar. Stir until dissolved, then cover and let it sit for another 5 days, stirring daily. The wine is ready to bottle at this stage.

Marigold Wine

In Mexico, marigolds are used as visionary herbs and can be found in recipes for love divination.

4 qts. marigold flowers	1 gal. boiling water
1 orange	3 lbs. granulated sugar
1 lemon	½ oz. yeast

Pick the flowers on a sunny day and wash them clean of insects. Place the flowers in a large bowl. Grate the orange and lemon rinds and squeeze out the juice. Add the rind and juice to the flowers. Pour the boiling water over the top. Cover the bowl with a clean tea towel and let it sit for 4 days. Strain the liquid into a large saucepan and bring the mixture to boil. Pour sugar into a bowl and pour the hot liquid over the top. Stir the liquid until the sugar is dissolved and then allow it to cool. Stir in the yeast. Cover the bowl again and stir it for the first 3 days. Strain and bottle. Age for 6 months.

Herbal Liqueurs

Making your own liqueurs is somewhat easier than making wine or beer, and the results are rewarding. Liqueurs make dazzling gifts with their bright colors and decadent spirits. They are also great for personal and ritual use, or medicinally in small sips.

Don't limit yourself to just sipping these concoctions, though. Liqueurs are also delicious drizzled over ice cream, added to coffee, or brushed on foods as a glaze.

These recipes can all be adjusted to your tastes by adding more or less sugar. To sweeten, the general ratio is 1 ounce of sugar to 4 ounces of base liquid. If the liqueur is too sweet, add a bit of lemon juice and let it steep before using. If you like a more syrupy drink, add 1 or 2 teaspoons of glycerin.

Always let liqueurs mature for at least a week, and preferably for a month. Maturing mellows and balances the flavor. The process of steeping is what blends the base alcohol with the flavor of your additions. When straining to separate the liquid from the solids, press as much liquid as you can from the fruit, as this liquid holds all the flavor. You may need to strain some things such as nuts more than once. To clarify the liquid even further, strain it through a paper filter, such as for making coffee. Be sure to taste your recipe at this stage and adjust the sugar or steep it longer if necessary. The shelf life for most liqueurs is about six months. It is helpful to keep a log of what you made and when, and to label all your creations.

When working with fruit, fresh is always best. Fresh fruit has the most potent flavor, though dried, canned, or frozen fruits will work in a pinch. Nuts and herbs should always be crushed first to release volatile oils. In recipes calling for herbs or spice, start with the minimum amount of ingredient listed. Herbs and spices are potent and can always be adjusted up for a stronger flavor, but not down.

You'll need a few piece of equipment to start, most of which can be found in the common kitchen. Gather some glass jars (dark colors and quart-sized are best), a cooking pot, funnels, a blender or food processor, a strainer, cheesecloth, a hammer or rolling pin, a paring knife, and coffee filters.

Look for pretty bottles at garage sales and thrift stores, or at hobby supply shops. Decorative labels are easy to find, or you can make your own. You can find corks at homebrew shops, or seal your bottles with foil and brightly colored yarn or melted beeswax.

Before you begin, mix a batch of sugar syrup to use it in many of the recipes to follow. Each recipe below yields 1 quart of liqueur.

Base Recipe for Sugar Syrup

1 c. granulated white sugar   ½ c. water

When making sugar syrup, the ratio is 1 part water to 2 parts sugar. Boil for 5 minutes and be sure the sugar is dissolved. Cool completely before proceeding.

Licorice Liqueur

This liqueur is tasty iced or hot, and can help soothe sore throats and other upper respiratory ailments.

2½ tbsp. licorice root, chopped   ½ c. sugar syrup
1½ c. vodka

Wash the licorice root and chop it into small pieces. Add to the vodka and steep for 1 week. Strain and filter. Add sugar syrup and steep another week. Adjust to taste.

Cinnamon Liqueur

This liqueur is a stimulant and a popular ingredient in love potions.

1 cinnamon stick	1 c. vodka
1 tsp. ground coriander seed	½ c. sugar syrup
2 cloves	

Steep all of the herbs in vodka for 2 weeks. Strain and filter until very clear. Add sugar syrup to taste. Let stand another week. Makes a nice hot toddy when added to hot water.

Peppermint Liqueur

Peppermint's menthol oil makes this liqueur a mild anodyne that anesthetizes nerve endings. The liqueur can quiet a nervous stomach as a tonic, help any nausea, and stimulate appetite. It is also quite tasty.

2 to 3 tsp. peppermint extract	3 c. vodka
1 c. sugar syrup	

Combine all the ingredients and stir. Let stand for 2 weeks. If you don't want too strong a mint taste, use just 2 teaspoons of extract. Add more sugar syrup for a thicker liqueur.

·····················

MAKING MAGICAL HERBAL TEAS
by Jonathan Keyes

Around the summer solstice, I often travel to a secluded spot on the Sandy River very near Portland, Oregon. There I begin my hunt for the elusive native herb known as mugwort. This beautiful plant can be difficult to find, even if you look quite carefully. I am able, however, to draw on years of experience to find mugwort's silver leaves ruffling gently in the breeze.

After locating some small stands, I usually ask permission to collect a few stalks of this gentle, yet powerful herb. I listen carefully to what messages the mugwort offers. It almost always will say what's on its mind. Before harvesting, I pull a little tobacco out of a pouch and give an offering. I always try to give back to the mugwort that I harvest, thus fostering a good relationship for future harvesting in my favorite secluded and hard to find harvesting spots.

A few hours later, I am home and brewing up a cup of mugwort in my kitchen. I can smell its stimulating, pungent, distinct aroma as the tea brews. The steam envelops me, and I begin to fall into the dreamy state that mugwort often elicits.

I then take a few sips and take in a little of mugwort's essence. It is bitter and strong. I can feel my taste buds and insides start to come alive. The mugwort starts to stir things up, get things moving. A knot of tension in my stomach starts to shift and turn, slowly untying itself and releasing the strain. A few more sips and I can feel my blood moving as a trickle of sweat forms on my brow. A half a cup later and the anxiety and stress in my system dissipates under a calm and even flow of energy that circulates through my body.

With each sip, mugwort draws me into her spell, magically soothing and uplifting me. I can hear her messages to "be still" and "unwind." I fell more receptive, more attuned, more open, and more myself. This simple tea has magically helped me transform and become fully present to the moment and the subtle vibrations around me.

Tea-Crafting and the Four Elements

Herbal teas, when we make them with good intention and a good heart, have the ability to transform us. Each aspect of making a tea, from collecting or buying the herb to how we prepare it and drink it, is vital to whether it is a magical experience or just another activity in our day. Taking the time to truly craft a tea helps us to become wiser, healthier, and more attuned to the world around us.

Crafting tea is a time-honored tradition in places such as China and Japan where rituals are often performed in conjunction with tea making. Timing, presentation, and proper brewing methods are all coordinated to augment a sense of peace and tranquility and to come into harmony with the flow of the natural world.

Making magical teas starts with an understanding of the four basic elements that comprise the natural world—earth, water, fire, and air. Each of these elements is associated with particular aspects and the processes of the natural world. Earth is associated with the trees, mountains, hills, valleys, and fields. Water is associated with the rivers, lakes, and oceans. Fire is associated with the sun and the flame. Air is associated with the currents of wind and the sky.

When we make a magical herbal tea, we are communing with these natural elements and replicating the natural processes of the planet earth at a basic level. In so doing, we are creating a relationship and harmonizing with the forces of nature through the simple practice of making herbal tea.

The Earth Element

The first step in making herbal tea is to collect or find the best herbal material possible to put in your brew. This first step is vital because it is our initiation into creating a relationship with a particular herb. The best way we can do this is the way I described above with my mugwort: collect it in its natural state in the wild. Gathering herbs can take some practice and a small amount of botanical knowledge of the plants in your native region. The reason wild plants are the best to work with is that they have evolved and adapted to find the perfect niche to grow and thrive in. This is where they feel most comfortable and at home. Because of this, they resonate with the greatest strength and vibrancy. The soil conditions and the amount of light, heat, and moisture are in perfect harmony to allow the plant to grow.

Approaching an herb in its natural environment is similar to approaching any wild creature. It should be done with care and respect. If you can, take the time to learn the ways of the herb you are gathering. Read about it in herbal and botanical books. Get to know its shape, color, fragrance, and appearance.

After developing an alliance with a particular herb, learn what are its best parts to pick. For some herbs you may want to collect the leaves, the roots, or just the root bark. Herb books will give you guidance on this matter.

Before gathering the herb, spend some time in contemplation and appreciate of the powers of the plant. Knowing what it is good for and how you will use it will help the plant give its life more easily. You may want to make prayers, offer tobacco or a strand of hair, or just speak words of appreciation and thanks. Make sure you do not overharvest. Try to limit your gathering to no more than 25 percent of a stand. Leave no trace of yourself behind.

If you are a novice at gathering herbs in the wild, ask an herbalist friend to take you on collecting expedition. Herbalists have years of experience identifying herbs in the wild and will show you the best methods of collecting each individual herb. They'll also help you avoid poisonous plants when collecting.

Though it can be wonderful to collect a herb in the wild, cultivating and gathering herbs in your own backyard is also rewarding. May herbs—such as lavender, chamomile, angelica, and peppermint—can be easily grown in the area around your house. Growing your own medicinal plants helps you to have a year-round relationship with them that helps in magical tea making. You can watch as each herb grows day by day, and you can give energy to the herbs through regular watering, pruning, composting, and mulching. Whether cultivated or gathered in the wild, try to harvest the herb before it gets too hot and sun starts to wilt the plant. Gather flowers and leaves in the spring or summertime. Gather roots after the energy of the plan has turned inward in the fall or very early spring.

Finally, the next best way to make a magical herbal tea is to buy the loose dried herbs from a reputable source—one that gives tender care to each herb they harvest. Check around and make sure the dried herb looks fresh and full of vital essence. Avoid leaves that have turned brown or yellow or have splotches on them. Dried herbs should have retained their fragrance and color. You should be able to breathe in their essence.

Get to know the farmers and wildcrafters who gather herbs for you. Make sure they are doing their work in a positive, giving way. The better the herb is cared for, the better will be its effect. Store-bought herbs can sometimes be collected in a machine-like manner with little care and consideration. This diminishes the magical and healing properties of the herbs.

If you have collected a herb in the wild, I highly recommend making a fresh tea soon after you get home. Most herbal teas we drink are from dried plants, but I find that herbs give their most vital essence and best magical qualities when they are prepared fresh as soon after harvesting as possible. It is useful to have a patch of your favorite herbs growing in your backyard.

HERBAL TEA MAKING AND ASTROLOGY

To make the herb collection experience more magical, you can pick days that are astrologically associated with the herb. By following the movement of the moon through the zodiac, one can choose the best day for collecting. Many pocket astrological calendars will tell you what sign the moon is in each day so you can plan your gathering days accordingly.

Moon in	Ruler	Herbs to Collect
Aries, Scorpio	Mars	Basil, cayenne, garlic, gentian, ginger, ginseng, hops, juniper, nettle, pine, sarsaparilla, tobacco
Taurus, Libra	Venus	Burdock, catnip, feverfew, elder, western red cedar, licorice, mugwort, rose, thyme, vervain, violet, yarrow
Gemini, Virgo	Mercury	Caraway, coltsfoot, dill, elder, fennel, lavender, oats, parsley, peppermint, red clover, valerian

Moon in	Ruler	Herbs to Collect
Cancer	Moon	Aloe, cleavers, lemon balm, marshmallow, willow
Leo	Sun	Calendula, chamomile, cinnamon, eyebright, goldenseal, hawthorn, rosemary, St. John's wort, sunflower
Sagittarius, Pisces	Jupiter	Borage, chicory, dandelion, dock, echinacea, hyssop, maple, Oregon grape, rosemary, sage
Capricorn, Aquarius	Saturn	Comfrey, horsetail, mullein, oak, plantain

Along with knowing what astrological sign the moon is in, it is also helpful to know the phase of the moon. In general, waxing moons are helpful for gathering the aerial parts of plants, such as the leaves and flowers. It is better to gather the underground portion when the moon is waning.

I find that full moons are a particularly magical time for gathering herbs, as the energies on the planet are intensely vibrant and full of power. Collecting herbs at the full moon can help augment the strength and potency of the herb that is being gathered.

The Water Element

After you have collected the best herb for your magical tea, make sure you have the best quality water as well. Though it may sound strange, not all water is the same. Yes, water may all contain the same one hydrogen and two oxygen molecules, but there is a lot more going on than meets the eye.

Water is the key medium for interacting between the human and the plant world. It is the mediator for helping there to be communication. The plants communicate through their complex chemistry of resins, alkaloids, minerals, and oils. Water helps deliver this message to the human body so that is can assimilate the information in the best possible way.

Water from wild places such as streams and rivers will be highly charged and carry the wildness of the land that it comes from. Often this type of water is more invigorating and helpful for those people who are weak or feeble.

Water that is from deep below the ground, such as from artesian wells, has an earthy quality that is very grounding and healing. This water can be helpful for calming and relaxing people. Oftentimes water contains minerals (this is known as hard water). Mineralized water will be healing in its own right, but will not extract as much nutrients and active constituents from an herb as will soft, or demineralized, water.

Choosing water for a magical tea is a very important part of the process. We wouldn't want to go to all the trouble of getting the freshest herbs and then use tap water that is rife with pollutants. Either collect your water from a fresh source or use water that is purified in the best possible manner.

Once you have gathered good water, make sure to find a good pot to boil the water and a good vessel to pour the tea into. Cast-iron pots will leach iron into the tea, which can help heal those people who are more anemic and "blood deficient" in nature. Stainless-steel pots work great as well, but avoid anything that is aluminum or has a layer than can peel off.

Finding that right herbal teapot is an important part of the tea-making process. Beautifully designed and colorful pots add to the sense of sensual enjoyment. The best teapots are made of clay and are hand-sculpted by an artisan. The love and care that goes into making the teapot helps make the tea-drinking process more uplifting and magical.

The Fire Element

Fire is the key alchemical tool for helping the herb deliver its medicinal and healing contents to the water. In traditional Europe, alchemy was known as the science that would transmute baser elements such as lead into precious metals such as gold. On a symbolic level, fire is associated with the spiritual effort and heat required to overcome baser instincts and to develop a mind and heart associated with God. This form of spiritual alchemy is at the root of practices such as t'ai chi and yoga. Heat generated from postures and movements helps to train the heart toward a goal of "attainment" or oneness with the divine.

In making herbal teas, using the right amount and source of heat is essential for drawing the best qualities from a plant and delivering it to the water. The fire element is instrumental in helping the plant communicate its magical gift to human beings.

In traditional times, tea would be made over a true flame. The type of wood used to make the flame would be important to the process. Cedar wood has different properties from maple, fir, or cherry. Unless you have a wood-burning stove that you can make tea on, it is unlikely you can consider these things. Flame from a gas-burning stove is the next best choice for making a good tea because it burns efficiently and you can adjust it very easily. Electric stoves are also a good source of the fire element.

When working with the fire element, remember that it is very powerful and has an intelligence of its own. Fire will talk to you if you listen. If the fire gets too hot, the vibration emanating from your stove will seem angry or overly excited. If the heat from the stove it not enough, you will sense that it feels lacking. The proper amount of heat is essential to the process of making tea.

We should always think about the amount of heat we are using in our home environment, and this is especially true of heat for magical teas. Too much heat is wasteful. By connecting with the fire element, we start to be mindful of how much heat we use each day. Using the proper amount of heat helps us to develop a considerate and mindful heart. The process of making tea can then become a meditation for developing integrity when working with the fire element.

The Air Element

To start the process of making tea, pour a quart of water into a pot and bring it to a boil. Then place an ounce of dried herbs into your teapot. Once the water has boiled, pour the water in to the teapot and allow it to steep. While doing this, direct your intention to honoring the herbs and their properties. Give thanks and make prayers of gratitude for their healing powers.

After the water has been completely poured, take a moment to breathe in the aroma of the herbs now that they have been mixed with the water. This is the air element associated with magical tea-making. Breathe in the herb's essence as it gently coats your mouth, throat, and bronchial passages. The uplifting qualities found in the essential oils in herbs can be tremendously beneficial to the respiratory tract, nerves, and immunological system.

After breathing in the infusion for 10 or 20 seconds, make sure to cap the pot so the essential oils don't evaporate. Then let the tea sit for about 10 to 60 minutes. Delicate, flowery herbs such as chamomile and elder flower should be consumed sooner as their properties can fade more quickly. Rooty teas can sit for up to an hour, as it takes a long time for their properties to completely dissolve into the water. The longer a tea sits, the more bitter it tends to become.

Sun and Moon Tea

Aside from making teas over the stove, there are a couple of other magical ways to make tea. Making a sun tea is a way of connecting with the original source of the fire element, the sun. Sun tea is made simply by placing your herbs and water in a quart glass jar that sits out under the sun. The water heats up with the sun's rays. The herb delivers its medicinal and healing properties to the water, though it usually takes a little longer than making tea on a stove. You should generally wait about four to six hours before you drink this brew. Sun tea is especially helpful for those people who tend to be fatigued, cold, and depressed.

One of my other favorite ways of making tea is to utilize the magical power of the moon. On the night of a full moon, follow the same directions for sun tea except place the glass jar out under the moon. If you can, choose a time when the moon is in the same sign that rules the herb (see table on page 154).

Steep the tea for an entire night and drink it in the morning. The tea will be cold but will have taken in some of the essence of the moon's energies. This is especially helpful for people who run too hot and tend to be anxious and "wired." Moon tea helps you become more relaxed.

Drink Your Tea!

After making tea, pour yourself a delicious cup. Use a strainer to strain out the herbs and allow the tea to come through. Take some time to enjoy this sensuous and sumptuous experience. Find a favorite chair or relax into a bath and breathe in the aroma of the tea. Sip slowly and delicately. Never hurry your tea!

Taste the flavor of the tea and feel how it affects you as you drink in its essence. Notice your change in mood. Allow the tea-drinking process to be slow and relaxing. This is not something to be rushed. After sipping a couple cups of tea, notice how you feel. The tea should have imparted its best medicinal qualities to you, and the alchemical process of harmonizing with the elements will have helped to transform and harmonize your spirit.

Making magical tea is simply the process of bringing mindfulness and good intention to every part of the tea-making process. It involves attention to detail along with respect for the herb. Through care and consideration, tea-making becomes a full body and full spirit experience that helps us to transform and become more fully alive and present.

Compare steeping a store-bought tea bag to going through the more involved process of crafting a magical cup of tea. See if you notice a difference. I know I have!

....

DANDELION AND CHICORY COFFEE
by Tammy Sullivan

Believe it or not, the humble dandelion, especially mixed with a bit of chicory, makes a nice and healthy substitute to your daily cup of joe. These two plant items can be brewed singly, blended together, or added to coffee for medicinal benefits and a gourmet flavor.

The Story of Two Misfits

While both dandelion and chicory are generally thought to be troublesome weeds, they in fact have quite a pedigree in medicinal and culinary use.

The Dandelion

The dandelion is known as *taraxacum officinale*, lion's tooth, piss-a-bed, monk's head, puffball, priest's crown, and swine's snout. The dandelion grows in fields, meadows, roadsides, and waste places.

As to vital statistics, the dandelion is a perennial that grows between two and twelve inches in height. Its flower is a golden yellow, one to two inches in diameter, and solitary atop a smooth, hollow stem. It opens in full daylight and closes at dusk. The leaves form a rosette on the soil surface and are between one to eighteen inches in length, jagged, and grooved and emerge directly from the root. The dandelion flowers from June to October.

In general, the dandelion's leaves are used to make a magenta dye, and its flowers are used to make a yellow dye. Once the flower matures, the petals wither and it forms a puffball seed head that disperses with the wind.

The dandelion has an auspicious history in the medical field and was classified as a drug for more than one hundred years in the United States. Ancient Egyptians knew and used the plant, but it was Arabian physicians of the Middle Ages who first officially recognized the healing properties of the dandelion. It is used for cleansing purposes, to treat obstructions of the liver, gallbladder, and spleen, and as a diuretic.

European woman have rinsed their faces in dandelion water for centuries, due to its ability to fade freckles and its refreshing effects. Dandelion water has been used to treat eczema, scurvy, and other skin problems. Today a tonic made from dandelion is a common ingredient in European herbal baths. Dandelion, if rubbed about a person's body, is said to have the ability to make one feel welcome wherever one goes. It is also thought to grant wishes. Dandelion does have the ability to predict the weather to a degree. If rain is coming, the flowers close up tight.

Surprisingly, dandelion leaves are edible and delicious. They are often added raw to spring and summer salads. They are also boiled and steamed with seasonings for a side dish. The leaves and flowers are commonly brewed into wine.

Chicory

Chickory, also spelled chicory, is known as *Cichorium intybus*, succor, wild endive, and blue sailors. Like the dandelion, it is also a perennial. The name "blue sailors" stems from a legend about a beautiful young girl whose true love abandoned her and went off to sea. Left alone, she waited by the roadside for his return. The gods took pity on her and turned her into the chicory flower, so she may forever be a delight for all to see.

The chicory grows from two and five feet in height. The leaves are jagged, groovy, and hairy, and they grow directly from the root, forming a rosette on the soil surface up to twelve inches in length. The flowers are generally blue, but also sometimes pink or white, and they look similar to those of the dandelion.

The greens of the chicory are not only edible, but highly desirable and marketed in many supermarkets as endive. Radicchio is a curly leafed, reddish type of chicory. The chicory root may be treated as a vegetable and boiled and eaten with butter. This plant grows wild on roadsides and waste places, and flowers from June to October. If you boil the leaves of the chicory plant a vivid blue dye is produced.

Chicory roots were used for making a hot beverage similar to coffee in France long before coffee was introduced there. The French have used a mixture of chicory and coffee for hundreds of years. Chicory is said to be a counter-stimulant for caffeine and is used to decrease the bitterness of coffee.

Magically known as an herb of love, chicory, when used in secret, is said to enflame the lover of your choice with passion. For a thriving romantic life, wear a chicory flower on your person. Be sure to replace it every fifteen days or so. Like its counterpart the dandelion, chicory has a long history in medicine. It is used to treat digestive disorders as a cleansing agent, and Culpeper recommended it for swooning of the heart. Bach lists it as a corrective for those who love selfishly.

Legend states that chicory, when eaten in certain ceremonies, has the power to render one invisible. It is also thought to have the ability to open locks, and if gathered on the night of July 25 at midnight, holds special power. Both the dandelion and chicory are endowed with a long taproot. The root is used for the coffee-making process. If a piece of root is left when harvesting, a new plant will grow.

Harvesting Tips

Harvesting chicory roots should be undertaken in late spring or early summer, before the roots become too hard. It is best to cultivate the plants in your own garden, as chicory roots become increasingly bitter after two years, but be prepared for a battle.

Left on its own, chicory sets itself firmly in place. The taproots of these plants are long-reaching and strong. It is much easier to harvest this plant after a heavy rain. Pulling chicory from your garden, on the other hand, tends to be simpler due to the looser, cultivated soil.

Dandelion roots are best harvested in the fall of the year. They should be harvested before the plant flowers. Because they are very juicy you need to take extra steps with dandelion to improve the drying procedure. Begin by scrubbing and peeling the root, then slicing it, being very careful not to bruise the root. You should steam the root pieces until the milky juice no longer seeps from them. Alternately you may choose to use a dehydrator before the roasting process.

Roasting Tips

To roast these herbs, the roasting process is the same for dandelion as it is for chicory. Gather the roots and scrub them vigorously with a stiff brush. Slice and roast slowly at 200 degrees F. When they are a dark brown color all the way through, set them aside to cool, then store in a tightly closed container. You might wish to grind the roots fresh each time you use them, for premium taste.

Dandelion coffee, on its own, has a slight chocolate taste, while chicory alone may have a bit of a caramel taste. At the last third of the roasting process, pay special attention to the smaller pieces. If they seem to be getting a bit too brown, spray them with cool water to stop the roast. Be careful not to char the roots.

The benefits of using chicory and dandelion as a substitute for coffee are that you are reducing your caffeine intake and cleansing your system. Chicory is known to lower blood sugar. Both dandelion and chicory are known for curing digestive disorders, and both are known for being helpful to the liver and digestive system. Adding chicory and dandelion to traditional coffee, however, is a flavor explosion, and a good way to stretch your coffee supply.

Brewing Tips

You will want to use whatever measurements suit your palate, but a good rule to follow is to use one level teaspoon of total ingredients per cup of boiling water. If you grind the roots finely you can use the mixture as you would use an instant coffee. For more coarsely ground roots, you may use any traditional coffee brewing method. It is important to use only fresh, clear water when brewing your coffee. Coffee is 98 percent water, therefore bad water means bad coffee.

My favorite recipes is to use three parts dandelion, two parts chicory, and two parts coffee. Since chicory has a tendency to darken the color of coffee, many people mistakenly assume that the resulting flavor will be stronger. You can sweeten your brew, no matter the proportions, with sugar and cream as you would traditional coffee, or you may wish to use flavored syrups. The addition of chicory and dandelion enhances the flavor of espresso and other coffee drinks.

Another recipe is to take twelve ounces of cold, leftover chicory and coffee and place it in your blender. Add about one-half cup of whole milk, a good dollop of flavored syrup, and blend. You may also add a few chocolate chips or fresh fruit to the mixture.

Chicory Café au Lait

This beverage requires no more than a cup of warm milk and a small piece of roasted chicory root. Combine the two in a small saucepan and heat on low, stirring constantly, until it is heated thoroughly. Pour into a cup and enjoy. The great thing about this drink is since there is no caffeine, you may drink it any time of the day or night with no worry of losing sleep.

The Absolute Best Cup of Coffee Recipe

Coarsely grind 2 parts coffee, 2 parts chicory, and 3 parts dandelion. Boil 4 cups of water in a pan. When the water is boiling, turn off the heat and add 8 tablespoons of your coffee mixture. Add 8 tablespoons of sugar and stir slowly until the sugar is dissolved. Let it rest for about 5 minutes. Strain the mixture into cups using a fine strainer or sieve.

This coffee will have some grit in the bottom, so don't stir it and don't drink the last sip. The coarser the grind, the less grit. If you wish to add milk, heat it separately to the point of boiling. Take the strained cup of coffee and pour it and the hot milk into another cup at the same time, allowing it to bubble and mix itself perfectly. One sip and you will see why I call it the Absolute Best Cup of Coffee.

Iced Coffee

Whisk together two tablespoons of your brewed coffee mixture and one cup of cold milk. Pour this mixture over ice cubes. You may garnish with whipped cream and sprinkles if desired.

Note: Any and all of these recipes can be made using only chicory and dandelion if your goal is to eliminate coffee completely from your diet.

MAIN DISHES

·······················

A GALA HERBAL BREAKFAST
by Caroline Moss

A "gala" herbal breakfast can be as grand or intimate as you like. You can set up a romantic anniversary breakfast or a family celebration. The only limit is your own imagination.

The ideas below can be served as an entire menu or picked from as you wish to add a different touch to an everyday offering of toast and cereal. Also pay attention to the various décor ideas I have suggested, as herbs can add simply by their presence at the table or in a decorative vase. You will develop your own ideas once you become more familiar with the versatility of herbs.

Decorative Ideas

A sprig of pressed herb could be used on the invitations to start things off in the right spirit.

Decorate with small pots of herbs instead of conventional flowers on the table. These are simple, though care must be taken when using strongly scented plants.

Give guests an herb memento of the occasion such as a small potted herb plant, herb posies decorated with ribbons or lace, or a pot of herb jelly (recipe below).

Offer herb-decorated menus with pressed leaves or a sprig of something fairly robust that won't wilt too quickly, tied with ribbon, raffia, or twine. Lavender or rosemary should hold up well for this.

Food and Drink Ideas

These are some basic recipes and ideas to get you started.

Melissa Fizz

Serving a delicious, sparkling drink, slightly alcoholic if you wish, in your best glasses, is one way to get any breakfast off to a festive start. A traditional drink in Europe would be a Buck's Fizz, which is equal quantities of freshly squeezed orange juice and champagne. For this alternative, infuse chopped lemon balm leaves overnight in orange juice (use a tablespoonful of leaves per cup of juice). In the morning, strain and mix with equal quantities of any sparkling white wine or lemonade.

Herb Teas

It has to be acknowledged that not everyone likes herb tea. For a larger affair, it is probably necessary to serve a choice of coffee or ordinary tea. It is appropriate, however, to offer one of more herb teas as befits the event's theme. That certain herbs have health benefits is now well known. Some are meant only to be taken for medicinal purposes. The following is a selection of those herbs that make delightful drinks: spearmint, lemon balm, bee balm/bergamot/oswego tea, chamomile, lemon verbena, and thyme.

A few points on herb teas in general: 1. They have the added benefit of being caffeine and tannin free. 2. They can be taken hot or iced. 3. The different herbs listed above can be mixed in whatever combination you wish. 4. Always try to use fresh herbs for tea, even if you use dried in cooking. It makes a huge difference. 5. Sweeten to taste—even if you don't take sugar in coffee or standard tea you may find a little honey in herb tea helps the flavor. 6. As with all culinary herbs, be sure to use leaves that have not been sprayed with artificial or poisonous garden fertilizers.

Minted Strawberries

This refreshing combination of strawberries and mint always adds a touch of fun to the simplest repast. You may also, however, want to experiment in combining your favorite fruit with finely chopped herbs. Try mint, lemon balm, lemon verbena, and hyssop.

For this recipe, slice 6 or 7 strawberries per person. Sprinkle with a little sugar to taste, and add a teaspoonful of orange juice and ¼ teaspoon of finely chopped mint per portion. Let sit for an hour before serving.

It is nice to serve this in frosted glasses. To do so, lightly beat an egg white in a shallow saucer. Put some white sugar into another saucer. Dip the rim of your serving glasses first into the egg white, drain well, and then into the sugar. Leave to dry.

Eggs en Cocotte

For something a little more substantial and sustaining, eggs en cocotte is a dish of French origin. A cocotte is a small pot. Should you not have such a receptacle on hand, a small teacup does very well. The joys of this dish are twofold: unlike most egg dishes, it does not need any last minute attention and will look after itself, and each person to be served can very easily be given a choice of flavorings to make their own customized little egg.

For the basic recipe, simply butter your cocottes or cups. Add a large, fresh egg. Add whatever additions, if any, are required (see below). Add a small knob of butter. Top with a couple teaspoons of heavy cream. Season with salt and freshly ground black pepper. Place all the prepared cups in a roasting tin full of warm water in a hot oven for 10 minutes. Check after 5 minutes as you want to be sure the yolk stays slightly runny. For flavorings, use any of the following: chopped bacon; grated cheese; chopped herbs such as chives, parsley, chervil, or marjoram; chopped tomato; crumbled, browned sausage; fried onion; and chopped bell pepper.

Oregano and Chive Sausage Patties

These patties add a meat element to the breakfast table, should you want such a thing, while they continue to introduce more fresh herbs. To make them, simply take some of your favorite sausages, remove the skins by cutting each sausage through lengthwise and peeling, and combine the resulting pile of sausage meat with a good quantity of finely chopped fresh herbs. I use about ½ teaspoon of herbs per sausage. Oregano and chive is a nice mixture, but you can experiment according to your taste.

Form the flavored sausage meat back into sausages or, as I normally do, small patties, and fry in a small amount of hot oil. Broiling will, of course, give a less fatty result.

Herb Bread with Soft Cheese

Rather than serving plain bread and butter with your herbal feast, you can add another layer of flavor. To your favorite bread recipe, simply add some freshly chopped herbs. You can also do this with bread mixes. Both thyme and chives work well, as well as rosemary and marjoram, if used in moderation. Whatever you decide on, simply add a teaspoon per cup of flour. These herbed breads can also benefit from a tablespoon of finely grated Parmesan or similar cheese per cup of flour.

To serve with your herb bread, or with plain bread if you prefer, mix a tablespoon of chopped fresh herbs (such as parsley, chives, chervil, or fennel) to a ½ cup of soft cheese. Serve the spread on small pieces of bread as canapés or pile into a dish alongside your sliced herb bread.

Herb Muffins

I favor the following muffin recipe when using fresh herbs.

1 egg	½ tsp. salt
¼ c. fat (oil, butter, margarine, peanut butter)	2 tsp. baking powder (3 if using a whole grain)
2 c. grain (flour, oats, cornmeal, oatmeal)	1 c. liquid (milk, buttermilk, yogurt, fruit juice)
2 tbsp. finely chopped fresh herbs (parsley, chives, marjoram, fennel, thyme, or tarragon)	½ c. optional extras (chopped nuts, grated apple, grated zucchini, grated carrot, grated cheese)
2 tbsp. sweetener (sugar or honey)	

Beat egg. Combine all ingredients taking care not to overmix. Put into muffin cups or a well-greased pan and bake at 400 degrees F for 20 minutes or until cooked through.

Toast with Herb Honey

For an easy way to add interest to honey, simply infuse a plain jar of honey with your own flavorings. Try to seek out local beekeepers or at least use organic honey. Most honey from supermarkets have been heat-treated to stabilize the product, which destroys valuable trace nutrients.

To make this treat, take a jar of runny honey. Poke in three or four 3-inch sprigs of an herb. Warm in a pan of water, taking great care not to bring to a boil. Cool the honey and put the lid back on. Leave for a couple of weeks, then fish out the herb. If giving a jar of flavored honey as a gift, put one fresh sprig into the jar. Try using common thyme, lemon thyme, and lavender.

You will have noticed that most of the above ideas for lovely breakfast dishes were not precise recipes but rather general formulas to be adjusted according to your own preferences and available ingredients. I do hope you have fun experimenting and that one day you serve a memorable gala herbal breakfast to your loved ones.

....

AN HERBAL THANKSGIVING CELEBRATION
by Lynn Smythe

You can make wonderful herb and spice infused dishes to serve at your next big traditional Thanksgiving dinner. Or you may choose to enjoy the recipes by hosting a Mabon celebration. Mabon is the time-honored witches' Thanksgiving feast, otherwise known as the fall equinox, occurring around September 21 each year.

To me, a Thanksgiving feast is all about the side dishes and other accompaniments, while the turkey is a bonus. This article features a variety of appetizers, salads, side dishes, and dessert recipes to add to your turkey.

Obtaining Herbs

I have the luxury of living in southeastern Florida where my Zone 10 organic garden provides me with fresh herbs year-round. If you have a garden and grow your own herbs, you could harvest extra and freeze or dry them so they are ready to use whenever you need them. Also, many grocery and health food stores now stock packages of fresh herbs on a continual basis in their produce section. Or you could start an indoor herb garden by growing herbs in containers, which will be available even through the cold winter months.

Although I prefer the taste of fresh herbs, dried herbs can be substituted for fresh if necessary. Use approximately one teaspoon of dried crushed herb to replace each tablespoon of fresh herb.

Herb and Spice Blends

I have included some classic herb and spice blends that work well to flavor many holiday recipes. You may be able to find some of these blends in the spice section of your local grocery store. You can also experiment and make your own blends to lend a unique flair to your own recipes.

Pepper Blend

Sprinkle this blend into soups, stews, sauces, and gravies as a nice change from regular black pepper. Place all the ingredients into a peppermill and grind as needed.

1 tsp. black peppercorns   1 tsp. white peppercorns

1 tsp. allspice berries   1 tsp. juniper berries

Pie Spice Blend

Add this mix to pumpkin, apple, or other types of pie. It can also be used in hot mulled apple cider. I use preground spices to put this blend together. This recipe makes approximately two and a half tablespoons of pie spice blend.

2 tsp. cinnamon   1 tsp. cloves

1 tsp. ginger   1 tsp. nutmeg

1 tsp. allspice

Poultry Seasoning

Use this seasoning blend to flavor chicken, turkey, duck, or Cornish game hen. It also makes a great addition to any kind of stuffing that is served along with your poultry dishes.

1 tsp. celery seed	1 tbsp. fresh marjoram, minced
1 tbsp. fresh sage, minced	1 tbsp. fresh savory, minced
1 tbsp. fresh thyme leaves	

Thanksgiving Recipes

Depending on the actual number of guests coming to your Thanksgiving dinner, you may choose to make all or just a few of these dishes. A variety of appetizer, side dish, entrée, and dessert recipes have been included for you to choose from.

Pre-Meal Delights
HOT MULLED CIDER

This wonderful brew can be left on the stove throughout the duration of your holiday meal if desired. It imparts a wonderfully aromatic scent that permeates the house and adds to the festive mood. I like to serve this to my guests as soon as they arrive.

1, 1-inch piece fresh ginger root, peeled and sliced	2 whole cinnamon sticks, broken into pieces
2 star anise pods	1 tbsp. whole cloves
1 gal. apple cider	Peel from 1 orange
Unsalted butter	Ground nutmeg for garnishing

Pour the apple cider into a large stockpot and place the pot on the stove over medium heat. Place the broken cinnamon sticks, star anise pods, cloves, ginger, and orange peel onto a piece of cheesecloth. Fold the edges of the cloth over and tie it with a piece of string. Place the spice bundle into the pot of apple cider and let it come to a boil. Immediately reduce the heat to low and simmer for 30 minutes. To serve, fill a mug with the cider, add a teaspoon of butter, and sprinkle with a little bit of nutmeg.

POTATO LEEK TART WITH NUTMEG AND CHIVES

This tart is a wonderful dish to serve as either an appetizer or entrée depending upon what other foods are being served at your Thanksgiving celebration. Spreading the cheese onto the bottom of the tart shell after prebaking it helps prevent the crust from becoming soggy. For the crust:

1½ c. whole wheat flour	1 egg
½ tsp. nutmeg	2 tbsp. water
½ tsp. salt	1 c. Swiss cheese, shredded
½ c. (1 stick) butter, chilled	

Preheat your oven to 375 degrees F. Place the flour, nutmeg, and salt in a large mixing bowl. Mix the butter into the flour using a pastry knife or two knives until it has the texture of coarse cornmeal. In a small bowl, whisk together the egg and water, then add it to the flour mixture using your hands. Thoroughly mix all the ingredients together. Press the dough into the bottom and sides of a greased, 10-inch tart pan. Prick the bottom and sides of the crust a few times with a fork. Place the pan in the oven and bake for 10 minutes. Remove it from the oven and immediately spread the cheese over the bottom of the crust. For the filling:

1 tbsp. olive oil	½ c. heavy cream
1 c. potatoes, peeled and diced	½ tsp. ground nutmeg
2 c. leeks, chopped	⅓ c. fresh chives, chopped
3 eggs	½ tsp. salt
¼ c. milk	

Add the olive oil to a large frying pan set over medium heat. Add the potatoes and cook for 5 minutes. Add the leeks and cook for another 10 minutes. Place the potato and leek mixture onto the bottom of the prepared tart shell. In a mixing bowl, whisk together the eggs, milk, cream, nutmeg, chives, and salt. Pour the egg mixture into the tart shell. Place the tart pan in the oven and cook at 375 degrees F for 40 to 50 minutes until the eggs are set and no longer runny. Remove the tart from the oven and let it cool 5 to 10 minutes prior to cutting. Cut the tart into wedge-shaped pieces. This recipe makes approximately 16 appetizers or 8 dinner-size servings.

Breads and Rolls
BUTTERMILK SAGE BISCUITS

The sage in these biscuits makes a wonderful flavor enhancer to complement your Thanksgiving turkey.

1¼ c. all-purpose flour	1 tsp. granulated sugar
2 tsp. baking powder	6 tbsp. butter, chilled
½ tsp. baking soda	2 tbsp. fresh sage, finely chopped
½ tsp. salt	¼ c. buttermilk

Preheat your oven to 450 degrees F. In a large mixing bowl sift together the flour, baking powder, baking soda, salt, and sugar. Cut the chilled butter into the dry ingredients using a pastry blender or two knives until it has the appearance of coarse cornmeal. Add the sage and buttermilk and stir until well blended. Spray a twelve-compartment muffin pan with nonstick cooking spray. Fill each compartment approximately halfway. Place the pan in the oven and bake for 12 to 15 minutes until golden brown. This recipe makes 12 biscuits.

CRANBERRY BASIL MUFFINS

I like to eat these muffins along with turkey salad with sage (recipe below) the day after Thanksgiving.

1 c. all-purpose flour	1 c. cake flour
½ c. granulated sugar	1 tbsp. baking powder
1 tsp. baking soda	6 tbsp. butter, chilled
1 c. buttermilk	1 c. fresh sweet basil, minced
1 c. dried cranberries	

Preheat your oven to 400 degrees F. In a large bowl, sift together the all-purpose flour, cake flour, sugar, baking powder, and baking soda. Cut the butter into the flour mixture using a pastry knife or two knives until it has the texture of coarse cornmeal. Stir in the buttermilk, basil, and cranberries. Spray a muffin pan with nonstick cooking spray then evenly divide the dough into each compartment of the pan. Place the pan in the oven and bake for 12 to 15 minutes until golden brown. Makes 12 muffins.

POPOVERS

I remember the first time I experienced popover. I was eight years old and visiting my grandparents in Florida. We were waiting at a fancy steak house when the waiter brought out a basket of these delights. I've been a convert ever since. The savory version can be made as a dinner accompaniment, whereas the sweet version can be served as a dessert along with sweetened butter or whipped cream on the side. The directions are the same for either version, though the ingredients are slightly different.

Savory popover ingredients:

2 eggs	1 tbsp. fresh thyme leaves
1 c. milk	1 tbsp. melted butter
1 c. all-purpose flour	1 tsp. paprika
½ tsp. salt	

Sweet popover ingredients:

2 eggs	1 tbsp. granulated sugar
1 c. milk	1 tbsp. melted butter
1 c. all-purpose flour	1 tsp. ground cinnamon
1 tsp. ground allspice	

Preheat your oven to 450 degrees F. In a large bowl whisk together the eggs and milk. Sift in the flour and stir well. Stir in the remaining ingredients. Grease and flour a muffin pan. Fill nine of the muffin compartments half full with the batter. Bake for 20 minutes. Without opening the oven door, turn the heat down to 350 degrees F and continue to bake for another 20 minutes. Remove the popovers from the muffin pan and serve immediately. If they remain in the muffin pan for more than a minute or two they have a tendency to become soggy. Makes 9 popovers.

Sweet Butter

Whisk together a half stick of room temperature butter, one cup powdered sugar, and one teaspoon of vanilla extract. Serve with the sweet version of the popovers if desired.

Salads

Cranberry Clove Orange Salad

This dish is a cranberry salad variation served at Thanksgiving. My kids also like it as a delightfully fruity snack any time of the year.

2, 3-oz. pkgs. raspberry gelatin	1½ c. cold water
½ tsp. ground cloves	1, 11-oz. can mandarin oranges, drained
1 c. boiling water	1, 16-oz. can whole berry cranberry sauce

Place the gelatin and cloves into a medium mixing bowl. Pour the boiling water and stir until the gelatin is dissolved. Stir in the cold water and place the bowl in the refrigerator until the gelatin is partially set (about 1 hour). Remove the bowl from the refrigerator and stir in the mandarin oranges and cranberry sauce. Cover the bowl and return it to the refrigerator until the gelatin is fully set (about 4 hours).

CRANBERRY PECAN SALAD
WITH BASIL, MINT, AND ORANGE DRESSING

This makes a wonderful green salad which can be served as part of a Thanksgiving dinner. For the salad:

| 6 c. mixed greens (iceberg, romaine, butter greens, spinach, and so on) | 1 c. pecans, chopped |
| 1 c. dried cranberries | 1 c. carrots, peeled and shredded |

Tear the lettuce into bite-sized pieces and place them in a large salad bowl. Add the cranberries, pecans, and carrots, and toss well. Prior to serving, drizzle on some of the dressing and toss well. Offer additional dressing on the side, if desired. For the dressing:

1 c. sour cream	1 c. rice vinegar
½ c. orange juice	1 tbsp. fresh basil leaves, minced
1 tbsp. fresh mint leaves, minced	½ tsp. salt
1 c. vegetable oil	1 tbsp. Dijon-style mustard

Whisk together all the ingredients in a small bowl until well blended, or pour all the ingredients into a canning jar and shake well. Makes approximately 1½ cups dressing. Leftover dressing can be stored in the refrigerator for up to one week.

Side Dishes
CREAMED ONIONS WITH THYME AND NUTMEG
This recipe makes a wonderful side dish. Pearl onions are deliciously sweet and not at all pungent like regular onions.

1 lb. pearl onions	2 tbsp. butter
3 tbsp. all-purpose flour	½ tsp. ground nutmeg
½ tsp. salt	2 c. milk
2 tbsp. fresh thyme leaves	½ c. dry breadcrumbs
1 tbsp. freshly grated Parmesan cheese	1 tbsp. butter, melted

Slice the ends off the pearl onions. Add water to a small saucepan and bring it to a boil. Add the onions to the pan and blanch them for five minutes. Remove the pan from the heat, drain off the hot water, and cover the onions with cold water to slightly cool them. Drain off the cool water, peel off the onion skins, and place them in a 1½ quart, glass baking dish. Preheat your oven to 350 degrees F. Melt the butter in a small saucepan set over medium heat. Whisk in the flour, nutmeg, and salt, and cook for one minute. Whisk in the milk and continue heating while whisking until the sauce begins to thicken. Remove the pan from the heat and stir in the thyme. Pour the sauce over the onions. In a small bowl mix together the breadcrumbs, melted butter, and Parmesan cheese. Top the onions with the seasoned breadcrumbs, place the dish in the oven, and bake for 30 minutes. Let it cool slightly before serving, as this dish will be very hot.

Garlic and Parsley Mashed Potatoes

The amount of garlic that you add to these potatoes depends upon your personal preference. My husband and I love garlic so we always add at least 10 cloves of garlic making this recipe. You may want to use fewer cloves.

5 to 10 whole cloves garlic	½ tsp. salt
½ c. (1 stick) butter	1 tsp. white pepper
2 lbs. potatoes, peeled and cut into quarters	1 c. fresh parsley, finely chopped
½ c. milk	

Blanch the unpeeled garlic cloves in boiling water for three minutes. Drain the hot water, pour cold water over the cloves, then peel off the skins. Smash each garlic clove with the flat side of a large kitchen knife. Melt the butter in a small saucepan and add the smashed garlic, then simmer on low heat for 20 minutes. Fill a large stockpot with water and bring to a boil, then add the potatoes and cook for 20 minutes until the potatoes are tender. Drain off the water. Add the garlic/butter mixture, milk, salt, and white pepper to the potatoes and mash well. Add the parsley and serve immediately. Makes 6 to 8 servings.

Lemon Balm Stuffing with Fruit and Walnuts

Using vegetable broth in place of the chicken broth in this recipe makes it suitable for vegetarians.

2 tbsp. vegetable oil	⅓ c. fresh lemon balm, finely chopped
2 c. celery, diced	2 c. chicken broth
2 c. apples, peeled, cored, and chopped	1 c. (2 sticks) unsalted butter, melted
2 c. mushrooms, chopped	1 c. walnuts, chopped
1, 15-oz. pkg. unseasoned bread cubes	1 c. dried cranberries, chopped
2 tbsp. fresh sage, minced	

Preheat your oven to 375 degrees F. Add the oil to a large frying pan over medium heat. Cook the celery and apples in the oil for 5 minutes. Add the mushrooms and cook for another 5 minutes. Place the mixture in a large bowl. Add the breadcrumbs, sage, and lemon balm. Stir in the chicken broth and melted butter and mix well. Stir in the walnuts and cranberries. Place the prepared stuffing into a greased 3-quart baking dish. Place the dish in the oven and bake for 45 minutes, stirring occasionally to keep it from burning on the bottom.

Minty Carrot Bites

This is one of my favorite cooked-vegetable recipes, and I usually don't like the taste of cooked carrots. The mint and honey add a nice, refreshing flavor to these carrots.

2 tbsp. butter	4 c. carrots, peeled and sliced into ¼ inch pieces
½ c. honey	⅔ c. fresh spearmint leaves, finely chopped
2 tbsp. water	2 tbsp. lemon juice

Place the butter into a large frying pan on medium heat. Add the honey, water, and carrots, and bring to a boil. Reduce the heat to medium-low, cover the pan with a lid, and simmer for 5 minutes. Remove the lid, turn the heat up to medium, and cook for 5 to 10 minutes while stirring occasionally. When the carrots begin to caramelize and most of the liquid has evaporated from the pan, remove the pan from the heat and stir in the chopped mint and lemon juice. Serve this dish immediately.

Sweet Potato Cakes with Nutmeg

½ c. heavy cream

½ tsp. ground nutmeg

2 eggs

½ c. all-purpose flour

4 c. sweet potatoes, peeled and shredded

⅔ c. vegetable oil

Sour cream (optional)

Maple syrup (optional)

In a medium bowl, whisk together the cream, nutmeg, eggs, and flour. Stir in the sweet potatoes and mix well. Heat ⅓ cup of the oil in a large frying pan over medium heat. Make individual potato cakes by pouring in approximately ¼ cup of the batter and flattening each cake by pressing down with a spatula. Add the additional oil to the pan if needed. Cook until the cakes are well browned on both sides (approximately 3 minutes per side). Place the finished potato cakes on a paper towel-lined plate to absorb any excess oil. Serve with sour cream or maple syrup on the side if desired. Makes approximately 10 sweet potato cakes.

Entrées

Oven Roasted Turkey with Tarragon Orange Sauce

This recipe is a change from the traditional roasted turkey. This dish can also be made with a large roasting chicken or duck instead of turkey. For the turkey:

1 turkey

2 tbsp. olive oil

1 recipe Poultry Seasoning (see recipe on page 175)

Remove any giblets or other organs from inside the turkey. Rinse the turkey and pat it dry. Place the turkey on a rack in a large roasting pan. Rub the olive oil over the turkey using a pastry brush or paper towel. Spread the seasoning over the top of the turkey. Cook the turkey according to the package directions. For the sauce:

1 c. butter	½ c. white wine
1 c. all-purpose flour	1 tbsp. fresh tarragon, minced
2 tsp. orange zest	½ tsp. salt
2 c. orange juice	1 tbsp. heavy cream

In a small saucepan, melt the butter over low heat. Whisk in the flour and cook for 1 minute. Whisk in the orange zest, orange juice, wine, tarragon, and salt, and bring the sauce to a boil over medium heat. Turn the heat down to low and simmer until the sauce has thickened. Remove the pan from the heat and whisk in the cream. Serve this sauce along with the prepared roasted turkey.

TURKEY SALAD WITH SAGE

This is a tasty way to use up your leftover turkey. Serve it along with the Cranberry Basil Muffins (from page 178) if desired. This salad can also be made with leftover chicken.

2 c. leftover cooked turkey, chopped	½ c. celery, diced
½ c. walnuts, chopped	½ c. mayonnaise
1 tbsp. fresh sage, minced	½ tsp. salt
1 tsp. pepper blend	

Mix all the ingredients together in a bowl. Chill the salad in the refrigerator until ready to serve. This recipe makes three cups of salad.

And Last, But Certainly Not Least—Dessert

At our house, we are usually so full after eating such a large Thanksgiving meal that we have little room for dessert. For those of you still desiring a sweet treat after you've finished your big Thanksgiving meal, here is the recipe for one of my favorite desserts.

CARROT CAKE WITH CREAM CHEESE FROSTING

This is one of my favorite desserts to serve during the holidays. For the cake:

2 c. all-purpose flour	2 c. granulated sugar
2 tsp. baking soda	4 eggs
2 tsp. baking powder	2 tbsp. fresh cinnamon basil, minced
1½ tbsp. Pie Spice Blend *	3 c. grated carrots
½ tsp. salt	1 c. chopped walnuts
1⅓ c. vegetable oil	

*See recipe on page 174.

Preheat your oven to 325 degrees F. In a large mixing bowl sift together the flour, baking soda, and baking powder. Stir in the pie spice blend and salt. In another bowl mix together the oil, sugar, eggs, and cinnamon basil using an electric mixer.

Stir this mixture into the flour mixture. Add the carrots and walnuts and stir well. Place the batter into a greased and floured 9 × 13-inch baking pan. Place the pan into the oven and bake for one and a half hours or until a cake tester inserted into the middle comes out clean. Let the cake cool before frosting. For the frosting:

1, 8-oz. pkg. cream cheese, room temperature	2 tsp. vanilla extract
½ c. (1 stick) butter, room temperature	4 c. sifted powdered sugar

Mix together the cream cheese and butter in a bowl using an electric mixer. Stir in the vanilla extract. Mix in the powdered sugar one cup at a time until the frosting is well blended. Makes approximately 3 cups of frosting, a perfect amount for the carrot cake.

HERBAL COMFORT FOODS

by Dallas Jennifer Cobb

When I need comforting, I turn to food and drink. I am sure that I learned this from my mother and grandmother, both British. For them, tea was not just a drink, but a time of day and a medical intervention.

In my childhood home, tea time was both a ritual and a right. Midmorning we would gather in the kitchen for tea and toast, or tea and a bickie (biscuit). When body or feelings were hurt, a "cuppa" tea and a shortbread, or a warm bowl of soup with steaming bread, was a healing balm.

So now, when I am stressed and in need of comfort, I find myself turning to the very foods my mum and grandma gave me for comfort.

Like me, many people reach for particular foods to comfort and sustain them when they are stretched thin—foods that hold an emotional association or memory of good times. What are your comfort foods? When you are stressed, what do you reach for?

If you are like most people, you reach for stimulating substances like caffeine, chocolate, alcohol, and sugar. But even if you crave these foods and think that they will provide you with comfort, most of them provide very short-term positive effect, but can contribute to some really negative effects.

Choosing healthy foods to comfort us can help to counteract and reduce the negative biochemical and physiological effects of stress. Also note that when you eat is almost as important as what you consume. Having three to five small meals a day can help to reduce stress on the digestive tract and give us more stable blood-sugar levels throughout the day. Drinking lots of water will maintain an optimum level of hydration, counteracting stress by circulating the available nutrients within the system.

For the sake of this article, consider comfort foods to be those that are nutritious, nurturing, wholesome, and satisfying—foods that ease the stressors on mind, body, and spirit.

When I am stressed or overwhelmed, I often reach for foods associated with historic comfort. Whether it is a cup of warm herbal tea that reminds me of the nurturing feeling of my grandmother's kitchen, or the quick-to-whip-up dinner biscuits that satisfy my longing for a warm, full tummy, most of my satisfying comfort foods have herbs in them.

I want to welcome you to come and sit in my kitchen, and let me share some herbal comfort with you. Many of my tried-and-true recipes are included, plus a list of recommended herbs for uplifting you on a low day, and reminders of other simple practices you can use to wrap yourself in a warm blanket of comfort. Whether you are worn out, sad, or just need some loving care, these recipes will help you to reach for comfort foods that will truly uplift you, adding to your health.

The Uplifting Effect of Herbs

Herbs have generally high levels of antioxidants, compounds found naturally in foods that manage and remove damaging free radicals. Though oxygen is necessary for life, it also has a damaging quality. Just as oxygen can cause rust in metal or the browning of an exposed fruit, oxygen can also cause damage within our bodies. Similarly, oxidation within our bodies produces free radicals—molecules or parts of molecules caused by the metabolic process of oxygen.

Free radicals can damage cells and destroy their function, cause genetic damage, tissue degeneration, aging, and susceptibility to disease. An antioxidant is something that slows or prevents this damaging process within our bodies. Most natural antioxidants come from fruits, vegetables, and herbs.

The most powerful herbal antioxidants are green tea and grapeseed extract, closely followed in efficacy by rosemary, sage, lavender, clove, allspice, sweet marjoram, nutmeg, lemongrass, turmeric, and coriander.

Overcoming Stress

Stress is our internal reaction to our external environment, and can be physical, mental, emotional, or spiritual. For an internal stress response to be triggered, we must perceive the external stimuli as something as dangerous. Within our bodies, stress induces a complex biochemical and hormonal response.

This stress response stimulates our body to use nutrients more rapidly to meet the increased biochemical needs of metabolism. Stress can deplete us of essential nutrients, causing internal imbalance and greater susceptibility to illness or disease.

Common responses to stress include increasing adrenal production, suppressing the immune system, and stimulating the production of free radicals. Stress has also been shown to decrease the naturally occurring protective antibodies within our systems, and deplete nutrients and antioxidants.

Because stress depletes our bodies of nutrients, we need to choose foods that are nourishing and nurturing. Herbs that are nutrient rich and full of antioxidants help us overcome the effects of stress.

Herbal Comfort Food Recipes

When you reach for comfort foods, remember to honor your body and your health. Choose foods that hold both a psychological comfort value and a physical comfort value. Choose foods that uplift spiritually, emotionally, and physically, foods abundant with antioxidants. Let the comfort food be part of a solution to stress rather than contribute to further stressing your system. Junk food will not satisfy your nutritional needs, or your body.

I have included a few recipes that hold emotional resonance for me, and contain herbs with high antioxidant and micronutrient values.

Sweet Treats

GINGERSNAPS

Need some real quick uplifting? Take a pass on the caffeine and grab one of these. A little spicier than your usual gingersnap, these delicious cookies pack a stimulating boost. In addition to antioxidants, ginger, clove, and cinnamon are known for their stimulating qualities, plus have added immune boosters. They can aid circulation, help break up phlegm, and generally warm the body. Blackstrap molasses is high in iron in an easy-to-assimilate form, plus its complex sugars give us a boost without the big letdown that comes from highly refined sugar.

1 c. butter	½ tsp. baking soda
1 c. sugar	½ tsp. powdered ginger
¼ c. blackstrap molasses	2 c. all-purpose flour
1 egg	1 tsp. cinnamon
1 tsp. vanilla extract	½ tsp. powdered cloves
¼ tsp. salt	

Preheat oven to 350 degrees F. Cream the butter and sugar, then add molasses, egg, and vanilla and mix well.

Sift the dry ingredients together, then add these slowly to the creamed mix. Drop dough by tablespoons onto a nonstick cookie sheet. Bake 15 minutes or until golden brown.

LUXURIOUS LAVENDER SHORTBREAD

Because shortbread is a tradition in my home at Christmas, I associate it with good family times. When I need some serious comfort I often reach for this recipe. My healthy modifications include using whole grain flour for added fiber and complex carbohydrates, and adding beneficial herbs.

1 c. butter (do not use margarine)	3 or 4 heaping tbsp. fresh lavender flowers, finely chopped
½ c. powdered sugar	2 c. whole-grain flour (wheat or spelt)

Preheat oven to 300 degrees F. Take the butter from the fridge—it needs to be cold. Cut butter into pea-size chunks; place in a large bowl. Thoroughly cream lavender and sugar into it with a fork.

Add flour quickly, mixing thoroughly. Try not to use your hands because they heat the dough up and make it tough. Refrigerate the dough again for about 20 minutes.

Turn the cookie dough out on a floured board and roll to ¼ inch thickness. Cut into hearts or some other comforting shape. Bake at 300 degrees F on a nonstick cookie sheet for about 25 minutes or until golden brown. Other herbs to use in shortbread:

Ginger: substitute ¾ cup crystallized ginger, finely chopped	Rosemary: substitute 3 to 4 tablespoons fresh rosemary, finely chopped
Lemon balm: substitute 5 tablespoons fresh lemon balm, finely chopped.	

LOVELY LICORICE

Licorice root is known as a natural laxative, plus it helps alleviate colds and flu, and calms frazzled nerves. The blackstrap molasses is an easily absorbed source of iron that is sweet tasting.

1 c. blackstrap molasses	1 tsp. ground anise root
1 tsp. ground licorice root	Whole grain flour (wheat or spelt)

Warm molasses in a large saucepan on low heat. Add 1 teaspoon each licorice and anise root.

Use about 2 parts spelt to 1 part whole wheat flour. Too much whole wheat will give the licorice a bitter taste. Add flour until you have a dense consistency that you can roll into snakes. Cut snakes to desired length.

The licorice will harden as it cools, and keeps a long time in the refrigerator. Make a big batch, and stow some away for a rainy day when you will really need it.

Savory Treats

I heard a rumor that real estate agents will sometimes go to a home prior to an open house and bake bread in the oven to fill the home with the luscious scent of fresh baked bread. They do this because so many of us have deep, positive associations with the smell of fresh bread.

Whether it is bread or biscuits, cookies or cakes, the effect of fresh baking is universal. It warms the soul, and sometimes even warms a wintry house.

So if you need some comfort, heat the oven, let the kitchen warm up, and get to the task of baking. Metaphorically speaking, you may find yourself uplifted by the leavening bread.

WHOLE GRAIN HERB BREAD

⅔ c. water	3 tbsp. olive oil
2 tsp. sugar	1 tsp. salt
⅔ c. skim or soy milk	½ tsp. dried basil
2 tsp. dry active yeast	½ tsp. dried oregano
3 egg whites	4½ c. whole grain flour (wheat or spelt)

Bring the water to a boil in a small pot. Remove from heat, stir in sugar, milk, and yeast. Mix well. Let this stand for 10 minutes until it is slightly frothy.

Combine egg whites, oil, salt, basil, and oregano in a large bowl. Add yeast mixture to it and blend well. Add 4 cups of flour, ½ cup at a time, mixing well after each half cup.

Knead the dough on a floured board until it is smooth and elastic. Add more flour if it is too sticky. Form into a ball and cover with a cloth. Let dough rise in a warm place for about 1 hour. Divide into 2 pieces and place in bread pans. Let rise in a warm place until doubled in size. Bake at 350 degrees F for 30 to 35 minutes.

Slather with butter while it is hot, and enjoy some soul comfort.

HERBED HOMEMADE BISCUITS

A versatile recipe. Try substituting your favorite herb or those herbs whose tastes complement the dish you will serve the biscuits with.

2 c. whole grain flour (wheat or spelt)	3 tsp. baking powder
1 tsp. salt	⅔ to ¾ c. milk, soy milk, or buttermilk
½ c. butter, cut to pea size	

Other

1 large clove garlic and ¼ cup finely minced fresh oregano (1 tablespoon dried); or	¼ cup tomato paste and ½ cup finely minced fresh basil (2 tablespoons dried); or
¾ cup shredded cheddar cheese and ¼ cup minced fresh sage (1 tablespoon dried)	

Sift all the dry ingredients in a large bowl. Add the butter. Add milk and mix well. Herbal ingredients go in last and are mixed throughout dough. Roll out to ½ inch thickness and cut into interesting shapes. Bake at 450 degrees F for 12 to 15 minutes.

Enjoy these biscuits with soup or stew, or on a really bad day. Slather them with butter.

ROSEMARY BREAD STICKS

⅔ c. skim or soy milk	½ c. finely chopped chives
2 tsp. baking powder	1 tsp. finely chopped fresh rosemary (or dried)
1 tsp. salt	
½ tsp. black pepper	1½ c. whole grain flour (wheat or spelt)

Combine milk, baking powder, spices, and herbs. Stir in flour, ½ cup at a time, mixing thoroughly. Knead until smooth and elastic. Add more flour if it is too sticky. Cover and let stand for 30 minutes in a warm spot. Divide into 12 little balls, then roll these long and thin.

Bake on a nonstick cooking sheet at 375 degrees F for 12 minutes, then flip them over and bake 10 minutes on the other side, or until golden brown.

HEALTHY HERB BUTTER

½ c. unsalted butter   1 clove garlic, minced
1 tbsp. chives, finely diced   Pinch of salt
Shake of pepper

Bring butter to room temperature. Fold in herbs and blend carefully. Scrape mixture into a small bowl and refrigerate. Serve with hot bread or biscuits.

Garlic helps to stimulate the immune system, fights infection, and warms the system. Chives and black pepper also have antibacterial and warming properties.

For a little variety, keep the garlic in the recipe above, but substitute the following herbs for the chives, salt, and pepper:

1 teaspoon minced basil   ½ teaspoon minced oregano
1 teaspoon minced   ½ teaspoon minced sage
  marjoram

Nurturing and Nutritious

While you are longing for comfort foods, remember that savory may be as satisfying to the soul as sweet. The following recipes allow you to indulge in something comforting and nurturing—but also good for you. Don't be fooled, vegetables can be comfort food.

Dill and Potato Cakes

2 c. whole grain flour   3 tbsp. butter, softened
Pinch of salt   1 c. mashed potatoes
1 tbsp. finely chopped dill   2 tbsp. milk or soy milk

Sift all the dry ingredients into a large bowl. Add dill, butter, mashed potato, and milk and mix. It should make a soft malleable dough. Roll out to a ½ inch thickness and cut with cookie cutters. Place on a nonstick bake sheet and bake at 450 degrees F for about 20 to 22 minutes or until golden brown.

Herbed Grilled Mediterranean Vegetables

1 fennel bulb	1 yellow pepper
1 small eggplant	½ tsp. sea salt
1 red pepper	½ c. fresh herbs*
1 green pepper	2 tbsp. olive oil
3 zucchinis	

Any combination of parsley, thyme, rosemary, oregano, and basil

Cut all vegetables into bite-size chunks. In a large bowl, mix vegetables with olive oil until all have a thin coating of oil. Sprinkle herbs and salt into the bowl and mix thoroughly. Grill for 10 to 15 minutes, or until lightly browned on both sides.

Herbed Roasted Root Veggies

3 large potatoes	Salt and pepper to taste
6 carrots	¼ c. minced rosemary
3 sweet potatoes	¼ c. minced thyme
2 onions, peeled and cut into wedges	1 clove garlic, separated into cloves and peeled
3 tbsp. olive oil	

Cut all the vegetables into bite-size chunks. In a large bowl, toss the veggies first with oil, then add herbs and toss until the veggies are evenly covered with herbs. Place these on a large nonstick baking sheet and bake at 400 degrees F for about 1 hour, stirring occasionally. When everything is golden brown, remove from the oven.

Autumn Harvest Herb Soup

3 large leeks, sliced thinly	3 large sweet potatoes, shredded
4 tbsp. olive oil	2 large potatoes, diced
8 c. water	1 clove garlic, minced
3 tbsp. fresh sage, finely chopped	¼ c. fresh thyme
1 butternut squash, peeled and shredded	Salt and pepper to taste

In a large pot, fry leeks in oil until they soften. Add water; bring to a boil. Add all veggies and herbs and simmer for about 45 minutes. Use a hand blender or masher to blend out lumps. Add salt and pepper to taste. Serve with chunks of homemade bread or hot biscuits for dipping and wiping out the bowl.

Comfort

Though stress is a part of everyone's life, it doesn't have to destroy us or our good health. Take the time to create small satisfying rituals that can nurture and sustain you through times of stress. Make little lists of your favorite foods, and give yourself permission to enjoy as much as you want of the fruits, vegetables, and herbs on that list.

Whether it is the antioxidants found in herbs that hold an uplifting vibration, the superior nutritional content, or the deep emotional context of their remembered scents and tastes, remember that herbal ingredients have a deep connection to comfort. I hope you will find some tasty recipes for comforting treats that will get you through the long winter ahead, or a tough day.

Eat well, find comfort in everyday, simple pleasures, and let that comfort infuse your life.

SOY AND TOFU TUCKER

by Zaeda Yin

Tofu is made from soybeans and is the Japanese word for bean curd. The meat substitute originated in China in over 2,000 years ago and is one of the protein mainstays of Asian diets. Consumption of bean curd and associated soy products spread from China to Japan, Taiwan, Korea, and Southeast Asia, where it also became localized. When the written word came into being in China, much honor was accorded the humble tofu in poems, proverbs, recipe books, and in the odd medical tome that described it as "meat of the fields" and "meat without a bone." In Asian communities, tofu is indispensable because of its nutritional properties and suitability for all seasons and climates.

Bean curd is important to Asian cookery, but Japan's "traditional tofu masters" have turned tofu into an art form. Until a long sojourn in Japan introduced me to the versatile and nutritious aspects of tofu and soybean foods, like most people in the West I saw it as bland, limp, and boring. Japanese "tofu masters" in different locations have their respective methods for manufacturing tofu and soy products, which are closely guarded secrets. Families are not short of diverse recipes for tweaking tofu into savory, tasty, sweet, and nutritious culinary delights. In recent times, more types of tofu have been created by commercial manufacturers, gourmet chefs, and cooks motivated by new trends of haute cuisine, now popularly known as "fusion cuisine."

Supermarkets and health stores stock numerous varieties of tofu, tempeh, miso paste, soy milk, tofu-based yogurt, tofu ice cream, and other soy products. The gamut runs from silky to smooth, and soft to hard. Putty in the hands of whoever is preparing the dish, tofu renders itself easily to culinary transformations. Tofu cubes placed in a bubbling earthenware pot with vegetables, peas, corn, beans, or mushrooms make hearty fare that can be added to rice, noodles, and pasta (excellent for cold winters). Deep-frying turns tofu golden brown and crispy.

Nutrients

The soybean, and products made from it, is high in protein, low in saturated fats, a good source of calcium, free of cholesterol, and a useful source of vitamin E as well as manganese. Soy is also rich in amino acids, which in some cases cause the body to release the hormone glucagon (an anti-insulin hormone). Glucagon helps mobilize stored carbohydrates from the liver to keep the body supplied with energy, potentially eliminating hunger.

Soy foods also contain isoflavones, disease-fighting substances known as phytochemicals found only in plants. The two primary isoflavones are genistein and daidzein, with the respective glucosides genistin and daidzin. The ratio of genistein and daidzein varies among different soy products. Although the concentration of isoflavones may differ in various products, most traditional soyfoods, such as tofu, soy milk, tempeh, and miso, are rich sources of isoflavones. The only two soy products that do not contain isoflavones are soy sauce and soy oil.

Soy Health Benefits

Scientific studies show that protein contained in soybeans helps lower cholesterol. Soy is also believed to prevent some cancers and hot flashes in menopausal women. Researchers are still examining the possibility of soybeans being able to protect against breast cancer, prostate cancer, cardiovascular disease, menopausal symptoms, and osteoporosis. More than three decades of research has shown that people who consume a lot of soy foods and tofu experience some of the following health benefits:

Decreased Risk of Heart Disease

Populations in countries where soy products are eaten daily have less risk of heart disease. Soy decreases both total cholesterol and LDL (or "bad cholesterol") levels. Eating an average of 50 grams of soy each day can lower cholesterol by 9 percent, which, if applied to a nation's population, could reduce the number of heart attacks by 20 percent.

Cancer Prevention

In Asian countries where diets are rich in soy, breast cancer is less common. For example, Japanese women have one-quarter the rate of breast cancer of American and other Western women.

Reduced Rate of Prostate Cancer

Japanese, Chinese, and other Asian males who consume vast amounts of soy products have a far lower risk of prostate cancer. Soy products, mainly tofu, have been part of the diet in those cultures for many centuries.

Ease Menopausal Symptoms

Soy foods are known to ease menopausal symptoms such as night sweats and hot flashes. This is due to the isoflavone compounds, which are able to act as estrogen to counteract decreased natural estrogen production during menopause.

Prevent Osteoporosis

Diets rich in soy protein help diminish the rate of bone loss and in some cases may even increase bone density. Apart from isoflavones, some soy products contain more bone-building calcium than others.

Soy Sauces

Many Asian sauces used for cooking are extremely high in sodium. Soy sauce contains about 10 times as much sodium as barbeque sauce. However, low-salt soy sauce versions are readily available. Those on low-salt diets for health reasons should avoid any sauces that are high in sodium. A lot of soy sauces also contain wheat, and therefore are not suitable for those with gluten intolerance. Black and yellow sauces made from either salted or fermented soybeans are high in salt and thickened with wheat flour. Be sure to read labels carefully before purchasing.

Curdling Agents

Manufacturers use different types of agents for curdling soy milk, which determines the quality of the tofu you get. The best is the traditional Japanese coagulant *nigari*, a mineral-rich gray liquid that drips from hessian bags containing raw sea salt. Calcium sulphate, which occurs naturally as gypsum, is also widely used because it increases the percentage of calcium in tofu. If you intend to make tofu at home, shop around for the right source—poor quality calcium sulphate is an industrial byproduct.

Tofu or Bean curd

Tofu is a soft, white curd that when pressed, resembles fresh cheese. When soaked soybeans are ground with water, cooked, and strained, soy milk is made. By curdling soy milk and separating the resultant whey from the curds, tofu is formed. Hard tofu has a compact texture that will not disintegrate when fried or cooked in soups. Ideally, hard tofu should be used the day of purchase, but can be refrigerated for three to five days.

Soft tofu is called *kinugoshi* in Japan, meaning "silken" tofu. Throughout Southeast Asia, soft tofu is generalized as "tahu-fah." During production, it is not pressed and the curds mingle and set in the whey. Then the whey is carefully scooped off. Soft tofu has a delicate, silken texture, and can be served with ginger tea, tapioca, jelly, puffed barley, and lotus seeds.

Miso

Miso is a paste made from the fermented soybeans, cereal grain, and sea salt. Used extensively in Japanese cooking, miso is a hallmark flavor in many guises. Miso paste can be used to make sauces, gravies, dips, custards, milkshakes, stock, and soups. It also gives a distinct but delicious flavor to stews, casseroles, and stir-fried dishes. Miso paste can also be used as a marinade, pickling medium, salad dressing, and even as a nutritious bread spread.

Chinese miso, though a progenitor of the Japanese product, has not entered the Western market to the same extent as Japanese miso. There are more than 250 types of Japanese miso, as each Japanese locality produces different varieties and not all are exported to the West. Miso paste available outside Japan is usually light yellow miso made with polished rice as a major ingredient and is sweeter than darker miso paste. Rice miso is also called "kome" or "shiro."

Darker miso pastes are produced from a combination of soybeans and barley, soy, and brown rice, or simply soy without any cereal. Those made with barley are called "mugi miso," and are deep brown in color with a hearty, semisweet flavor. Brown rice miso, known as "genmai miso," is savory sweet. It can darken by the month, as well as change from a light flavor to a strong flavor as it "ages" from light brown to almost black. "Hatcho miso" originates from a region renowned for its Samurai warrior ancestors. Containing only soy, this black-brown variety has a totally different flavor from any other Japanese miso.

Soy milk

Supermarkets and health stores carry numerous brands of soy milk, which vary in flavor and texture. Read labels carefully, as some products are loaded with sugar, chemicals, or "soy isolate," which is not the real thing. Genuine soy milk is also kosher. In recent times, some Western communities began making "Toffuti" *(soy-based ice cream),* which evolved from a New York Jewish café. Be wary of commercial advertisements gushing about their brands being natural, having low cholesterol, and containing no dairy products. They make no mention that their products may contain heaps of sugar and chemicals. Be wary of natural-sounding ingredients such as "corn syrup," a chemical sucrose derived from cornstarch by industrial refining.

Tempeh

Tempeh originated in Indonesia and is made of hulled, cooked soybeans that are fermented with a white mold (mycelium) until they form into blocks, slabs, or cakes. It can be marinated, grilled, or added to soups, casseroles, and stews. As raw tempeh soaks up oil very quickly, it is best to brush each piece lightly with oil before browning in a nonstick skillet. Across Indonesia, tempeh is mostly fried or deep-fried after being marinated with local sauces. Fried tempeh is called tempeh goring. Depending on the additional ingredients combined with soybeans during manufacture, tempeh comes in many varieties. Pure soy tempeh has the strongest taste while other kinds made with grains and seeds have a lighter taste. Due to its texture, flavor, and high protein content, tempeh is the closest thing to meat the vegetable kingdom offers. Condiments that enhance tempeh are chili, coconut milk, cucumber, and raw or blanched vegetables.

Yuba

Yuba is Japanese for dried bean curd "skin," another favorite food consumed daily in many Asian households. It is made by allowing thick soy milk to simmer uncovered at a very low temperature until a "skin" forms on top that quite resembles scalded cream. To eat it at its freshest, insert a chopstick under the "skin" and lift it up. Yuba, widely available at Asian grocery stores in the form of cubes, sheets, and sticks, can be dried and stored for up to six months. Buddhist vegetarian cookery uses a lot of yuba, employing techniques that turn dried bean curd into mock smoked meats, mock chicken slices, mock ham, and other meaty-textured dishes with a wide variety of sauces, marinades, and condiments. In Chinese cooking, the cubes are soaked in water for use as wrappers for stuffing vegetables, fish, and other ingredients. Yuba sheets can be simmered in sauces and soups. The sticks are mainly shredded and used in vegetable stir-fries, soups, stews, and fried noodles. A warm dessert can be derived from an old Chinese folk recipe: Yuba sticks boiled in a sweet broth of barley, lotus seeds, and egg or quails' eggs.

Shoyu or Soy Sauce and Tamari

Soy sauce is called "shoyu" in Japanese. Its production involves soaking and cooking soybeans combined with cracked roasted wheat and inoculated with a culture known as "koji." When the wheat and soy are entirely covered by the culture, sea salt and water are added. The mixture is then poured into huge wooden barrels and left to ferment for two to three years. After this period, it is strained to remove wheat-meal, soy, and oil. The liquid substance is then pasteurized and bottled. Another type of soy sauce is known as tamari, which is similar to shoyu but contains no wheat. Naturally made shoyu and tamari from Japan are like fine, well-matured wines in epicurean value. Soy sauces from different countries have distinct flavors, colors, and textures. Traditional Chinese sauces differ from Japanese variations as much as Indonesian and Thai varieties do. All soy sauces contain unique local ingredients. They may be produced with wheat flour or soy flour and some even combine oyster sauce and shrimp.

Some Soy Recipes
Sweet Simmered Miso or Nerimiso Topping

This basic form of simmered sweet miso is generally prepared in small portions of 1 or 2 cups. It is preserved for use over several weeks as a topping or seasoning for cooked grains, vegetables, potatoes, salads, tempeh, and tofu. Unused portions will retain their flavor for 2 to 4 weeks if refrigerated in sealed containers. The following recipe renders half a cup.

5 tbsp. "red" or barley miso	2 to 4 tbsp. sugar (to taste)
1 to 2 tsp. sake (rice wine) or white wine	1 tbsp. water

Combine all ingredients in a small saucepan and simmer for 2 to 3 minutes on low heat. Stir constantly with a wooden spoon until the mixture becomes slightly firmer than regular miso paste. Remove from heat and let contents cool to room temperature before serving. Store extra portions in sealed containers for refrigeration.

Mushroom Miso Sauté

Miso sauté can be used with vegetables, nuts, and fruits, then served with fried tofu, rice dishes, porridge, noodles, fresh vegetable slices, or steamed vegetable chunks. This recipe makes a bit over half a cup, but a little goes a long way.

2 tbsp. oil	1 tbsp. miso paste of your choice
10 mushrooms, thinly sliced	1 to 2 tsp. sugar

Coat a wok or frying pan with oil and heat it up. Add mushrooms and sauté over medium heat until tender. Reduce heat to low, then add miso and sugar. As the mixture cooks, stir regularly until the mushrooms are evenly coated. Leave the sauté to cool to room temperature and serve.

Soybean Casserole with Tomatoes and Corn

1 c. cooked soybeans	¼ tsp. paprika
1 c. cubed tomatoes	½ tsp. sugar
¾ tsp. sea salt	2 oz. grated vegan cheese
1 tsp. minced onion	¼ c. chopped peanuts
1 c. cooked corn	

Preheat oven to 350 degrees F. Wash and thoroughly dry a casserole dish before brushing it with oil. Spread the first seven ingredients in the dish, sprinkle cheese and peanuts on top, and bake for 45 minutes to an hour.

Fried Crispy Tofu

12 oz. firm tofu

1 tsp. sea salt or vegetable salt

5 tbsp. flour

5 tbsp. oil

2 tbsp. shoyu (soy sauce)

Slice tofu lengthwise into halves and then crosswise into thirds, then use a clean cloth to pat each piece dry. Sprinkle with salt and roll tofu pieces in flour. Heat oil in a wok or skillet until quite hot. Add tofu and fry on both sides until golden brown and crispy. Drain oil onto paper towel. Serve with shoyu. Serves two.

Tofu and Miso Stew

1 large onion, thinly sliced

1 c. potatoes, cubed small

1 small carrot cut into thin rounds

3 c. water or stock

½ c. green peas, corn, or sliced
   green peppers

1 c. pumpkin, cubed in
   larger pieces

6 mushrooms, cut into halves

½ c. ketchup

2 tbsp. butter

½ c. miso paste of your choice

12 oz. firm tofu, cut into 16
   small rectangles

Combine the first seven ingredients in a large pot and bring to a boil over high heat. Reduce heat to low and cover. Let contents simmer for 15 to 25 minutes or until potatoes and pumpkin become soft. Stir in ketchup, butter, and miso. Cover and simmer for another 15 to 25 minutes while regularly monitoring the consistency. This recipe generally makes a brothy stew. For a thicker consistency, add a heaping tablespoon of corn flour to half a cup of water. Mix this well, pour it into the pot, and stir. Add tofu to the simmer and cover for another 5 to 10 minutes. Let sit for 5 minutes before eating. Serves four.

Making Soy Milk at Home

Making soy milk to a preferred taste and texture can be time-consuming and messy, but after experimenting a few times, the process should only take an hour. Utensils and implements required are a large pot, a huge heatproof glass bowl or stainless-steel container, a blender, a cloth sack or flour bag, and a saucepan. If possible, use high-quality organic soybeans and soak them overnight in lots of water. Strain off the liquid and wash the soybeans the next day. This recipe is for 1 cup soaked soybeans, so multiply when necessary as you go along. For a thicker and richer flavor, use 2 to 3 cups of soaked soybeans.

Boil 7 to 8 cups of water in a kettle. Pour 5 cups boiling water into the large pot over high heat. Purée the soybeans in a blender with the remaining 2 to 3 cups of boiling water until well ground and milky. Pour this into the large pot containing the other 5 cups of water and reduce heat to medium. Stir continuously until the mixture is well cooked or until foam rises. Pour contents into a moistened cloth sack set in a large bowl. Strain the liquid by pressing firmly with a large wooden spoon to extract soymilk. Rinse the large pot. Place the cloth sack in 1 cup of hot water in a saucepan and squeeze the bag again to ensure all remaining milk is extracted. Pour all the soy milk back into the pot and bring to a boil with high heat.

Those who like it sweet can add 3 to 5 tablespoons of raw sugar to the boiling soy milk. Stir the mixture very often to prevent the milk from burning. When the milk begins to boil, reduce heat to low and simmer for another 5 minutes before serving. This recipe makes about 4 to 5 cups of soy milk that is similar to that made in Southeast Asian countries like Singapore and Malaysia. (Japanese and Chinese recipes, which have different consistencies and tastes, are more difficult to make.)

Leftover soy milk can be poured into a container and refrigerated and served cold or warmed up later.

Tofu Ice Cream

18 oz. tofu, chilled	⅛ tsp. salt
3 tbsp. organic honey	1 egg yolk (pasteurized)
¼ tsp. vanilla extract	2 tbsp. almonds, chopped

Put 12 ounces tofu, honey, vanilla extract, and salt into a blender and purée for 1 minute. Pour into a container, cover it, and freeze the contents overnight. Next day, take tofu out of the freezer and cut into small chunks. Put these into the blender and purée with the remaining 6 ounces of tofu at high speed. While puréeing, add a few chunks of frozen tofu at a time and blend until contents are smooth. Before finishing the puréeing process, add an egg yolk and 2 tablespoons chopped almonds, some frozen fruits, or shredded coconut. Serves two.

Variation: For a green tea flavored ice cream, omit vanilla extract and add 1 teaspoon of powdered green tea (matcha) and 1 additional teaspoon of honey.

Note: Consuming untreated raw eggs carries a risk of salmonellosis as a result of the salmonella bacteria. Children, the elderly, pregnant women (the developing fetus), and people with chronic health problems that weaken the immune system or undergoing chemotherapy are most at-risk for food-borne illnesses. If possible, use eggs that have been pasteurized, which are safe to eat without further cooking.

Stew on This:
A History of Ingredients

by Nancy Bennett

Carrots, onions, potatoes, peas, and barley. The makings of a fine stew, some would say. Add in some lamb and you have a great Irish stew! Something to warm the soul and stick to the ribs, stew is one of the most nourishing meals you can make. But while you're cooking this delectable dish, did you know you are also cooking history?

Carrots

It is generally believed this orange root originated in Afghanistan, though the Greeks brought it into public view. The Greek called the carrot "Philtron" and used it as an aphrodisiac. It was said to make men more eager and women more surrendering.

It never really caught on as a food until the sixteenth century, when the Germans and French experimented with growing bigger ones of various colors. The Irish loved them, and the sweetness of the carrot was so admired that their writers referred to carrots as "underground honey."

In the Middle Ages, doctors said carrots would cure you of syphilis or the bite of a mad dog. Knowing it to be a favorite food of Queen Elizabeth I, one ardent fan once presented the queen with a wreath of carrots embellished with diamonds with a pot of butter in the middle. Elizabeth is said to have removed the diamonds and sent the rest to the kitchen to be cooked. The end result, of course, was buttered carrots.

Not only the Elizabethans but the Dutch made much of the carrot. In the sixteenth century, Dutch growers, overcome with patriotism, grew the orange vegetable to honor the "House of Orange." Carrots are a versatile food—great to eat raw, steamed and buttered, as a juice, as a flavoring in cakes and puddings, and of course, in stew.

Onions

Sacred enough to make one's eyes water with tears of joy, onions were fed to the workers on the great tombs in Egypt (and buried with the Pharaohs for the coming afterlife).

In Mesopotamia, in the oldest known body of law, the Code of Hammurabi, onions and bread are given to the needy in monthly ration. Romans started their day with a breakfast of raw onions and bread, sure to keep away any door-to-door salesmen. In America, cowboys in the West knew the onion as a "skunk egg," but still used it in their "son-of-a-bitch."

A folk cure for a cold is to eat a whole raw onion. Though I have never done this, there are many who swear by it.

Onions are not technically vegetables but part of the lily family. They have vitamins A and C and also a bacteria-destroying chemical called allyl aldehyde, so onions are great when you are feeling under the weather. What could make you feel better than a nice bowl of stew?

Potatoes

Gardeners in Ireland take spade to ground to plant their spuds on Saint Patrick's Day every year. Why? No one knows, but it is still a tradition. An old Irish saying goes, "If the beef's the king of meat, potato's the queen of the garden world." Both the Irish and potatoes were often looked down upon by Englishmen like William Cobbett, who referred to the potato as "Ireland's lazy root."

In South America, it was in the Andean region that potatoes were first reported. The Incas worshiped them, even though their version had purple skins. They called them "Papas," and in this prayer from the sixteenth century AD, they would speak in homage to the spud.

"O Creator! Thou who givest life to all things and hast made men that they may live and multiply. Multiply also the fruits of the earth, the potatoes and other food that thou hast made, that men may not suffer from hunger and misery." Though the South Americans exalted it, pregnant women were warned not to eat potatoes lest their babies be born with too large a head.

Around this time the first potato made it from the "new" world to the "old" world (in this case to Spain), and slowly spread from there. Some folks were none too crazy about it, saying it caused leprosy and scrofula.

Eventually, though, potatoes earned a place alongside other starches such as rice and pasta, as a staple "fill you up" food. In 1770, after a disastrous grain crop, potatoes became the food that kept many poor Europeans alive. Today you can find potatoes used in fish and chips. (This traditional dish was discovered by accident when fish was cooked in large oil vats to allow it to be shipped and the spud chips were used to cool the oil down when it got too hot.) Potatoes are also used in breads and breakfast dishes, and if you are a homemade wine maker you can turn them into potato champagne. Of course there is one meal that is synonymous with the potato—that would be stew.

Peas

If an army marches on its stomach, then peas must have their due. Both Greek and Roman soldiers had them as rations. Dried peas were easy to pack and provided good protein for fighting men. Though a great addition to a meal, peas were not favored by the upper classes who looked upon it as poor folks' food.

Peas were known to the early citizens of India, and have also been found in excavations of Bronze Age men living in Switzerland. Helen of Troy may have eaten them, as they were found in diggings in ancient ruins of that noble race. In Norse myth, Thor sent down those sweet edible peas not as a gift to the humans, but as a curse. Thor had sent his dragons to drop the peas down wells to foul up the water of his ungrateful followers below. But the dragons missed the target, and instead a new food crop was created. The people gave thanks and ate it on Thor's holy day of Thursday.

Peas were not really cultivated in Europe until the eighteenth century, though toward the end of the seventeenth they had become a much-favored delicacy for the upper class. "This subject of peas continues to absorb all others," Madame de Maintenon wrote in 1696. "Some ladies, even after supped at the Royal Table, and well supped too, returning to their own homes, at the risk of suffering from indigestion, will again eat peas before going to bed. It is both a fashion and a madness."

The French arriving on the shores of Quebec carried the dried pods for starter, and soon everyone was eating and growing peas. In the seventeenth century they made their way from England to the colonies of New England.

"Pease porridge hot, pease porridge cold, pease porridge in the pot nine days old" goes the rhyme. Pease porridge was a porridge made of peas, also known as pease pottage. Back then the poor would often cook one big meal and continue to heat it up every night, not wasting a bit. After nine days, I wouldn't recommend eating it, though peas do make a great addition to (you guessed it) stew!

Barley

In ancient times, barley was sacred to Demeter, and the secret orgies in honor of this goddess culminated in the unveiling of a spike of perfect grain, most likely barley. Isis also had a hand in bringing it into our wild roots. She discovered it while making sacrifices to the ancestors, and was later known as the Queen of Bread and the Queen of Ale.

As early as 5000 BCE, barley was being grown in Egypt, and in 3000 BCE, it had spread to the eastern Mediterranean area of Mesopotamia. From there it continued to flourish in Europe, China, Norway, India, France, Turkey, and finally North America. But barley can be traced back even further, into prehistoric times.

The grain can be made into flour (the Romans favored barley bread made with honey), soaked and combined with fruit to make a breakfast cereal, turned into fine ale, or added to stews.

Now that I have whetted your appetite, it's time to try a recipe. Cubed meat (lamb for Irish, beef for English) can be added to it. Make sure to dredge the meat in a flour mixture and brown it in advance before adding it to the stew for a nice taste and texture.

Athens Vegetable Stew

Olive oil	1 tsp. ground black pepper
1 onion, chopped	1 tsp. salt
1 clove garlic, chopped	½ tsp. dried oregano
3 potatoes, chopped	Splash of lemon juice
3 carrots, chopped	2½ c. water
½ c. frozen or fresh peas	Splash of Worcestershire sauce (optional)
½ c. pearl barley	

In a frying pan, heat olive oil and brown onions and garlic. Drain. In a large pot over medium-high heat, combine prepared onions and garlic, carrots, potatoes, peas, barley, pepper, salt, oregano, splash of lemon juice, and water. Bring to a boil and then turn down so that stew is simmering. (An old English saying that "a stew boiled is a stew spoiled" applies here.)

Continue simmering, stirring occasionally, until vegetables are tender and barley is cooked, about 50 to 60 minutes, adding more water if necessary. If you want a bit more flavor and a darker tinge, add a splash of Worcestershire sauce before serving.

....

BREAKFAST AND BRUNCH DELIGHTS
by Lynn Smythe

The ritual of taking a leisurely Sunday breakfast has occurred on a regular basis for many years at my house. It's the one day of the week when we usually aren't all rushing around like crazy people trying to get ready for school and work. There's nothing like waking up to the smell of my husband's freshly brewed coffee as he begins to prepare breakfast for the entire family. We often will serve breakfast for dinner one night of the week if we missed our normal Sunday morning meal due to one of our camping trips or mountain biking expeditions.

Brunch is a combination of traditional breakfast and lunch foods and is usually served between 10 a.m. and 2 p.m. A brunchtime feast features a variety of recipes to feature at your next home-cooked breakfast or brunch celebration.

The Appeal of Herbs

Fresh herbs are called for in most of these recipes. There is nothing to compare to the flavor of fresh herbs in your cooking. If you don't have these herbs growing in your own garden, most grocery and health food stores sell packages of fresh herbs in their produce sections. You may also want to check your local farmers' market to see if any of the vendors offer fresh herbs for sale.

If you don't have the time to cook all your meals from scratch, simply adding a few fresh herbs to prepackaged foods is a quick way to imbue the healing power of nature into your meals. Herbs such as parsley, chervil, and chives work especially well to add a fresh herb taste to your food without overpowering the other flavors of your meal.

Chervil Vegetable Scramble

Chervil is a very mild-tasting herb with a faint anise-like taste. Its delicate fernlike leaves give it an appearance similar to parsley. In the Middle Ages it was sometimes referred to as rich man's parsley. Chervil symbolizes new life and hope. The scientific name for this herb is *Antrhiscus cerefolium*, the second part of which derives from the Greek word *chairophyllon*, which means "happy or delightful leaf."

1 tbsp. vegetable oil	1 tbsp. heavy cream
½ c. green onions, sliced thin	½ tsp. salt
½ c. red bell pepper, seeded and diced	¼ tsp. black pepper
½ c. mushrooms, chopped	¼ c. fresh chervil leaves, chopped fine
6 eggs	⅓ c. shredded cheese (optional)

In a large frying pan, heat the oil over medium heat. Add the green onions, bell pepper, and mushrooms, and cook for 5 minutes, stirring occasionally. Remove the vegetables to a plate and reserve for later. In a mixing bowl, whisk together the eggs, cream, salt, and pepper. Then stir in the reserved sautéed vegetables and pour into the frying pan. Sprinkle the chervil on top of the egg mixture, then add the shredded cheese if you like. Stir the eggs around until they are firmly cooked. Makes 4 servings.

Cinnamon Pecan Muffins

Cinnamon was once an exotic and expensive commodity only available from a few spice dealers. In order to keep the price high, disreputable dealers concocted fantastic tales of how they obtained their supply of cinnamon. An incredible story was told that in faraway lands, large birds built huge nests using twigs of cinnamon. In order to collect the cinnamon, which was too high for humans to reach, the collectors would entice the birds with large pieces of meat placed at the base of the nests. The birds would take the meat to their nests, which would quickly become weighed down and cause the nest to come crashing down to the ground. This enables the collect or easily harvest the cinnamon twigs from the ground.

Sometimes I substitute regular or vanilla soy milk for regular milk in many of my recipes.

1¾ c. all-purpose flour	1 tsp. cinnamon
½ tsp. salt	6 tbsp. butter, chilled
3 tsp. baking powder	1 c. milk or non-dairy milk
½ c. granulated sugar	½ c. pecans, chopped

Preheat oven to 450 degrees F. Sift the flour, salt, baking powder, sugar, and cinnamon into a large mixing bowl. Add the chilled butter and cut into the dry ingredients using a pastry blender or two knives until it has the appearance of a coarse cornmeal. Stir in the milk and pecans. Grease a muffin tin and fill each section ⅔ full with dough. Place the pan in the oven and bake for 12 to 15 minutes or until golden brown. Use the icing to frost the rolls. Makes 12 cinnamon rolls.

ICING

1 c. powdered sugar, sifted	1⅓ tbsp. water
1 tsp. orange extract	

Add the powdered sugar to a small bowl. Add the orange extract and just enough water to make a thin frosting. When the cinnamon rolls have been removed from the oven, place them on a large serving platter. Drizzle the icing onto the rolls until all of the icing has been used up. The icing will harden as it cools to room temperature.

Herb and Cheese Biscuits

Parsley seeds were thought to have to go to the devil seven times and back before they would sprout and grow in your garden. Parsley seeds are notoriously difficult to germinate, but you can give them a head start by soaking them in a small container of warm water a few hours before you plant them in your garden.

I prefer to use flat-leaf parsley, also referred to as Italian parsley, in this recipe. But regular curly-leaf parsley would work as long as you chop it up extra fine.

1¾ c. all-purpose flour	1 c. milk or non-dairy milk
½ tsp. salt	⅓ c. fresh parsley, minced
3 tsp. baking powder	½ c. shredded mild cheese
6 tbsp. butter, chilled	(Swiss, Monterey Jack)
2 tbsp. melted butter	

Preheat your oven to 450 degrees F. Sift the flour, salt, and baking powder into a large mixing bowl. Add the chilled butter and cut into the dry ingredients using a pastry blender or two knives until it has the appearance of coarse cornmeal. Stir in the milk, parsley, and Swiss cheese. Grease a muffin tin and fill each section ¾ of the way with the dough. Pour the melted butter evenly over the top of each portion of biscuit dough. Place the pan in the oven and bake for 12 to 15 minutes or until golden brown. Makes 12 biscuits.

Lemon Basil French Toast

Basil is one of the many herbs that can be added and used in love spells, as it is thought to help promote peace and harmony between lovers. A container full of basil placed outside of your window was once a signal that a woman was ready to be courted.

I like to grow containers of the small-leaved, spicy-globe basil on my patio. They add a nice decorative element to my home and it's easy for me to go outside to harvest a bit whenever a recipe calls for basil. If you don't have lemon basil on hand, you can substitute an equal amount of sweet basil.

4 eggs	1 tbsp. fresh lemon basil, minced
1 c. milk or non-dairy milk	1 to 2 tbsp. butter
1 tsp. lemon extract	8 slices French bread (1-inch thick,
Zest from 1 lemon	day-old bread)

In a medium size bowl, whisk together the eggs, milk, lemon extract, lemon zest, and lemon basil. Melt the butter in a large frying pan placed over medium heat. You may use nonstick cooking spray instead of the butter to coat the frying pan if desired.

Dip each slice of bread into the batter, being sure to coat each side evenly. Place the bread into the frying pan and cook until well browned on both sides. Add additional butter to the pan if necessary to prevent the French toast from sticking. Serve with the lemon syrup recipe listed below or with maple syrup.

TOPPING

½ c. lemon juice   ½ c. granulated sugar

In a small bowl, mix together the lemon juice and sugar until all the sugar has been dissolved. Serve this syrup along with the French toast. The syrup also tastes great served on top of waffles or pancakes.

Lovage-Infused Tomato Juice

Sometimes known by the folk-name of love ache, lovage is thought to be a useful ingredient to add to love potions and a range of love spells. Lovage has a faint celery-like taste and aroma, making it a perfect complement for many tomato-based dishes.

The leaves from the heart of celery stems make an acceptable substitute if you don't have lovage growing in your garden. I have also used fresh cilantro leaves mixed into this juice. You can either substitute them in place of the lovage or add a 50/50 mixture of cilantro and lovage.

46 ounces tomato juice	¼ c. lemon juice
¼ c. lovage leaves, minced	1 tsp. hot pepper sauce, to taste
½ tsp. freshly ground black pepper	6 lovage stems (optional)

Add the tomato juice, lemon juice, black pepper, hot pepper sauce, and lovage leaves to a large pitcher and mix together. Let chill in the refrigerator for at least 2 hours. To serve, pour into individual glasses and use a lovage stem to garnish each glass of tomato juice if desired. Lovage stems are hollow and the larger ones can be used like a straw. Makes 6 to 8 servings.

Quiche Lorraine with Savory Crust

Winter savory is a perennial plant, while summer savory is an annual plant and must be replanted from seed every year. The small, thyme-like leaves of savory can be used to attract fairies to your garden. Most cooks agree that the tender leaves of summer savory have a better flavor than the tougher winter savory leaves. I have used the two varieties interchangeably in my recipes.

CRUST

1¾ c. all-purpose flour	3 tbsp. water
½ c. butter, chilled	1 tbsp. fresh winter or summer savory, minced
1 egg	

Preheat oven to 375 degrees F. Sift the flour into a mixing bowl. Add the butter and mix into the flour using a pastry knife or two knives until it has the texture of coarse cornmeal. In a small bowl, whisk together the egg, water, and savory, then stir into the flour mixture. Use your hands to thoroughly mix all the ingredients together. Use additional flour if necessary to prevent the dough from sticking to your hands. Press the dough onto the bottom and sides of a greased 10-inch tart pan. Prick the bottom and sides of the crust with a fork. Place in the oven and bake for 15 minutes. Remove the crust from the oven and set aside while you are preparing the filling for the quiche.

FILLING

3 eggs	¼ tsp. black pepper
¾ c. milk	1½ c. cheddar cheese, shredded
¾ c. heavy cream	¾ c. chopped onion
1 tbsp. fresh chives, minced finely	1 pkg. bacon (6 to 10 slices), well browned

In a large bowl, whisk together the eggs, milk, cream, chives, and pepper. Stir in the shredded cheese and onions. Crumble and spread half the bacon onto the bottom of the prepared crust, carefully pour in the egg and cheese filling, then crumble the remaining bacon on top. Bake the quiche for 40 to 50 minutes until the eggs are set and no longer runny. Let the quiche cool for about 5 minutes before serving. Makes 8 servings.

Spiced Coffee with Cinnamon and Cardamom

The spicy seeds of cardamom have reputed aphrodisiac properties and are called grains of paradise in some countries. Cardamom seedpods can be found in the spice aisle of most grocery and health food stores. Be sure to purchase light-green pods, as the light-beige ones have been chemically treated to remove the natural green coloring. To use cardamom, I place a few pods on a wooden cutting board and lightly crush the pods with a rolling pin or the smooth side of a meat mallet. Then I remove the small dark brown seeds from the interior of the pod to use in my recipes. This beverage makes a delightful change from regular coffee.

½ cinnamon stick, broken into pieces	8 c. water
Seeds from 6 cardamom pods	Half and half
6 tbsp. ground coffee beans	Sugar (if desired)

Grind the cinnamon and cardamom seeds together in a coffee grinder. Place a filter in the basket of your coffee maker. Place the ground coffee, cinnamon, and cardamom into the filter. Brew your coffee as usual. This makes a strong flavored coffee. I like to serve it along with plenty of half and half and sugar. Makes 6 servings.

Vegetable Latkes with Garlic Chives

Chives are thought to be capable of chasing away all diseases and evil entities. Garlic chives are also called Chinese chives or tender-leaved chives. They have a delicate flavor that is like a combination of mild garlic and a bit of onion. Common chives can be used as a substitute in this recipe if necessary. I have found small pots of both garlic and common chives in my local garden center, and in the nursery section of my local home improvement store, which I take home and transplant into my garden. Chives also make a wonderful plant to grow inside small containers.

1 c. carrots, peeled and shredded	1 tsp. garlic powder
1 c. leeks, chopped fine	1 tsp. onion powder
1 c. mushrooms, chopped fine	½ c. all-purpose flour
1 c. potatoes, peeled and shredded	¼ c. vegetable oil
2 tbsp. garlic chives, chopped fine	Sour cream (optional)
2 eggs	Salt and pepper (optional)

In a medium bowl, mix together the carrots, leeks, mushrooms, potatoes, and chives. In a small bowl, whisk together the eggs, garlic powder, and onion powder, then stir into the bowl of vegetables. Add the flour and stir until well blended. Heat the oil in a large frying pan over medium heat, adding additional oil if necessary. Make individual latkes by pouring ⅓ heaping cup of the batter into the pan and flattening each one with a spatula. Brown well on both sides, then remove to a paper towel–lined platter to drain off the excess oil. Serve with sour cream and salt and pepper on the side if desired. Makes approximately 9 latkes.

CONDIMENTS

·····················

HERBAL VINEGARS: AROMATIC DELIGHTS FROM YOUR GARDEN

by Susun Weed

Spring is in the air. Buds are swelling, sap is running, and night is alive with sounds after winter's long silence. It's too soon to plant anything in the garden, and there's still deep frost in the ground, but the snow is gone, the weeds are green, and my supply of herbal vinegars is low so I'll spend the morning harvesting herbs to make more vinegars.

A pantry full of herbal vinegars is a constant delight. Preserving fresh herbs and roots in vinegar is an easy way to capture their nourishing goodness. It's easy too. You don't even have to have an herb garden.

Basic Herbal Vinegar

Takes 5 minutes plus 6 weeks to prepare

1 glass or plastic jar of any size up to one quart/liter
Fresh herbs, roots, weeds

1 quart apple cider vinegar
1 plastic lid for jar, or waxed paper and a rubber band

Fill any size jar with fresh-cut aromatic herbs (see the accompanying list for suggestions of herbs that extract particularly well in vinegar). For best results and highest mineral content, be sure the jar is well filled with your chosen herb—not just a few sprigs—and be sure to cut the herbs or roots up into small pieces.

Pour room-temperature apple cider vinegar into the jar until it is full. Cover jar with a plastic screw-on lid, several layers of plastic or wax paper held on with a rubber band, or a cork. Vinegar disintegrates metal lids.

Label the jar with the name of the herb and the date. Put it someplace away from direct sunlight (though it doesn't have to be in the dark), and someplace that isn't too hot, but not too cold either. A kitchen cupboard is fine, but choose one that you open a lot so you remember to use your vinegar, which will be ready in six weeks.

Apple Cider Vinegar

Apple cider vinegar has been used as a health-giving agent for centuries. Hippocrates, the father of medicine, is said to have used only two remedies: honey and vinegar. A small book on Vermont folk remedies—primary among them being apple cider vinegar—has sold over five million copies since its publication in the 1950s. A current ad in a national magazine states that vinegar can give us longer, healthier, happier lives. Among the many powers of vinegar: it lowers cholesterol, improves skin tone, moderates high blood pressure, prevents/counters osteoporosis, and improves metabolic functioning. Herbal vinegars are an unstoppable combination: the healing and nutritional properties of vinegar married with the aromatic and health protective effects of green herbs (and a few roots).

How Does It Taste?

Herbal vinegars don't taste like medicine. In fact, they taste so good I use them frequently. I pour a spoonful or more on beans and grains at dinner; I use them in salad dressing; I season stir-fry and soups with them. This regular use boosts the nutrient level of my diet with little effort and expense.

Sometimes I drink my herbal vinegar in a glass of water in the morning, remembering the many older woman who've told me that apple cider vinegar prevents and eases their arthritic pains. I aim to ingest a tablespoon or more of mineral-rich herbal vinegar daily. Not just because herbal vinegars taste great (they do!), but because they offer an easy way to keep my calcium levels high (and that's a real concern for a menopausal woman). Herbal vinegars are so rich in nutrients that I never need to take vitamin or mineral pills.

Why Vinegar?

Why vinegar? Water does a poor job of extracting calcium from plants, but calcium and all minerals dissolve into vinegar very easily. You can see this for yourself. Submerge a bone in vinegar for six weeks. What happens? The bone becomes pliable and rubbery. Why? The vinegar extracted the minerals from the bone. And now the vinegar is loaded with calcium and other bone-building materials!

After observing this trick it's not unusual to fear that if you consume vinegar your bones will dissolve. But you'd have to take off your skin and sit in vinegar for weeks for that to happen. Adding vinegar to your food actually helps build bones because it frees up minerals to the vegetables you eat. Adding a splash of vinegar to cooked greens is a classic trick of old ladies who want to be spry and flexible when they're ancient old ladies. (Maybe your granny already taught you this?) In fact, a spoonful of vinegar on your broccoli, kale, or dandelion greens increases the calcium you get from the vegetables by one-third.

Vinegar helps build bones, and when it's combined with mineral-rich herbs, vinegar is better than calcium pills. Some people worry that eating vinegar will contribute to an overgrowth in candida yeast in the intestines. My experience has led to me to believe that herbal vinegars do just the opposite, perhaps because they're so mineral rich. Herbal vinegars are especially useful for anyone who can't (or doesn't want to) drink milk. A tablespoon of herbal vinegar has the same amount of calcium as a glass of milk.

A Walk in the Herb Garden

So out the door I go, taking a basket and a pair of scissors, my warm vest, and my gloves, to see what I can harvest for my bone-building vinegars.

The first greens to greet me are the slender spires of garlic grass, or wild chives, common in any soil that hasn't been disturbed too frequently, such as the lawn, the part of the garden where the tiller doesn't go, the rhubarb patch, the asparagus bed, and the comfrey plants. This morning they're all offering me patches of oniony greens. The vinegar I'll make from these tender tops will contain not only minerals, but also allysl, special cancer-preventative compounds found in raw onions, garlic, and the like.

Here, in a sunny corner, is a patch of catnip intermingled with motherwort, two plants especially loved by women. I use catnip to ease menstrual cramps, relieve colic, and bring on sleep. Motherwort is my favorite remedy for moderating hot flashes and emotional swings. They are both members of the mint family, and like all mints, are exceptionally good sources of calcium and make great-tasting vinegars. Individual mint flavors are magically captured by the vinegar. From now until snow cover next fall, I'll gather the mints of each season and activate their unique tastes and their tonic, nourishing properties by steeping them in vinegar. What a tasty way to build strong bones, a healthy heart, emotional stability, and energetic vitality.

Down here, under the wild rose hedge, is a plant familiar to anyone who has walked the woods and roadsides of the east: garlic mustard. I'll enjoy the leaves in my salad tonight, as I do all winter and spring, but I'll have to wait a bit longer before I can harvest the roots, which produce a vibrant, horseradishy vinegar that's just the thing to brighten a winter salad and keep the sinuses clear.

Chickweed is a good addition to my vinegars, boosting their calcium content, though adding scant flavor. In protected spots, she offers greens year-round.

Look down. The mugwort is sprouting, all fuzzy and grey. I call it cronewort to honor the wisdom of grey-haired women. The culinary value of this very wild herb is oft overlooked. I was thrilled to find it for sale in little jars in a German super-market, right next to the dried caraway and rosemary. Mug-wort vinegar is one of the tastiest and most beneficial of all the vinegars I make. It is renowned as a general nourishing tonic to circulatory, nervous, urinary, and mental functioning, as well as being a specific aid to those wanting sound sleep and strong bones. Mugwort vinegar is free for the making in most cities if you know where this invasive weed grows. To mellow mugwort's slightly bitter taste and accent her fragrant, flavor-ful aspects, I pick her small (under three inches) and add a few of her roots to the jar along with the leaves. I cut the tall, flowering stalks of this aromatic plant in the late summer or early autumn, when they're in full bloom, and dry them.

The sun is bright and strong and warm. I turn my face toward it and close my eyes, breathing in. I feel the vibrating life-force here. Everything is aquiver. I smile, knowing that that energy will be available to me when I consume the vinegars I'll make from these herbs and weeds. As I relax against the big oak, I breathe out and envision the garden growing and blooming, fruiting and dying, as the seasons slip through my mind's eye.

The air grows chillier at night. The leaves fall more quickly with each breeze. The first mild frosts take the basil, the tomatoes, and the squash, freeing me to pay attention once again to the perennial herbs and weeds, urging me to make haste before even the hardy herbs drop their leaves and retreat to winter dormancy.

The day dawns sunny. Now's the time to harvest the last of the garden's bounty, the rewards of my work, the gifts of the earth. I dress warmly (remembering to wear red; hunting season's open), stash my red-handled clippers in my back pocket, and take a basket in one hand and a plastic tub in the other.

My gardening friends say the harvest is over for the year, but I know my weeds will keep me at work harvesting until well into the winter. In no time at all my deep basket is full and I'm wishing I'd brought another. Violet leaves push against stalks of lamb's-quarter. Hollyhock, wild malva, and plantain leaves jostle for their own spaces against the last of the comfrey and dandelion leaves. I think dandelion leaves are much better eating in the fall than in the spring; they seem much less bitter to my taste after they've been frosted a few nights. The last of the red clover blossoms snuggle in the middle. Thought not aromatic or intensely flavored, a vinegar of these greens will be my super-rich calcium supplement for the dark months of winter.

My baskets are overflowing and I haven't even gotten to the nettles and the raspberry leaves yet. They're superb sources of calcium, too! Ah! The gracious abundance of weeds—or should I say volunteer herbs? I actually respect them more than cultivated herbs—respect their strident life force, their powerful nutritional punch, and their medicinal values that help me stay healthy and filled with energy.

The main work of this frosty fall morning is to harvest roots: dandelion, burdock, yellow dock, and chicory roots. I've been waiting for the frost to bite deep before harvesting the nourishing, medicinal roots of these weeds. With my spading fork (not a shovel, please), I carefully unearth their tender roots, leaving a few to mature and shed seeds so I have a constant supply of young roots. I love the feel of the root sliding free of the soil and into my hands, offering me such gifts of health.

I admire burdock especially for its strength of character and its healing qualities. I settle down to do some serious digging to unearth its long roots. For peak benefit, I harvest at the end of the first year of growth when the roots are most tenacious and least willing to leave the ground. Patience is rewarded when I dig burdock. Eaten cooked or turned into a vinegar (and the pickled pieces of the root consumed with the vinegar), burdock root attracts heavy metals and radioactive isotopes and removes them quickly from the body. For several hundred years at least, and in numerous cases that I have witnessed, burdock root has been known to reverse pre-cancerous changes in cells.

Dandelion and chicory are my allies for long life. They support and nourish my liver and improve the production of hydrochloric acid in my stomach, thus ensuring that I will be better nourished by any food I eat. I make separate vinegars of each plant, but like to put both their roots and their leaves together in my vinegar. A spoonful of either of these in a glass of water in the morning or before meals can be used to replace coffee. Note that roasted roots used in coffee substitutes do not have the medicinal value of fresh roots eaten cooked or preserved in vinegar.

Yellow dock is the herbalist's classic remedy for building iron in the blood. Like calcium, iron is absorbed better when eaten with an acid, such as vinegar, making yellow dock vinegar an especially good way to utilize the iron-enhancing properties of this weed. (It nourishes the iron in the soil, too, and is said to improve the yield of apple trees it grows under.)

At that thought, I awaken from my reverie and return to spring's sunshine with a smile. A white cat twines my legs and offers to help me carry the basket back inside to the warmth of the fire. The circle has come around again, like the moon in her courses. Autumn memories yield spring richness. The weeds of fall offer tender green magic in the spring. What I harvested last November has been eaten with joy and I return to be gifted yet again by the wild that lives here with me in my garden.

Notes on Making Herbal Vinegars

It is vital to really fill the jar. This may take far more herb or
root than you think.

A good selection of jars of different sizes will enable you
to fit your jar to the amount of plant you've collected. I
especially like baby food, mustard, olive, peanut butter,
and juice jars. Plastic is fine, though I prefer glass.

Always fill a jar to the top with plant material; never fill
a jar only partway.

Pack the jar full of herb. How much? How tight? Tight
enough to make a comfortable mattress for a fairy.
Not too tight and not too loose. With roots, fill jar
to within a thumb's width of the top.

For maximum visual delight, leave plants whole.

Regular pasteurized apple cider vinegar from the supermarket
is what I use when I make my herbal vinegars.

Rice vinegar, malt vinegar, wine vinegar, or any other natural vinegar can be used, but they are much more expensive than apple cider vinegar and have many tastes which overpower or clash with the tastes of the herbs.

I don't use white vinegar, nor do I use umeboshi vinegar (a Japanese condiment).

The reason that most recipes for herbal vinegar tell you to boil the vinegar is to pasteurize it. I don't find it necessary to heat the vinegar, as it is already pasteurized, and the final vinegar tastes better if the herbs are not doused with boiling vinegar.

Exceptionally Good Herbal Vinegars

Herb	Part of the plant to use
Apple Mint	Leaves, stalks
Bee Balm *(Monarda didyma)*	Flowers, leaves, stalks
Burdock *(Arctium lappa)*	Roots
Catnip *(Nepeta cataria)*	Leaves, stalks
Chicory *(Cichorium intybus)*	Leaves, roots
Chives	Blossoms
Dandelion *(Traxacum offinalis)*	Flower buds, leaves, roots
Dill *(Anethum graveolens)*	Herb, seeds
Fennel *(Afoeniculum vulgare)*	Herb, seeds
Garlic *(Allium sativum)*	Bulbs
Garlic Mustard *(Alliaaria officinalis)*	Leaves, stalks
Goldenrod *(Solidago)*	Flowers

Herb	Part of the plant to use
Ginger *(Zingiber officinalis)*	Roots
Wild Ginger *(Asarum canadensis)*	Roots
Lavender *(Lavendula)*	Flowers, leaves
Mugwort *(Artemisia vulgaris)*	New growth leaves, roots
Orange Mint	Leaves, stalks
Orange	Peel (organic only)
Peppermint *(Mentha piperata)*	Leaves, stalks
Perilla *(Shiso)*	Leaves, stalks
Rosemary *(Rosmarinus officinalis)*	Leaves, stalks
Spearmint *(Mentha spicata)*	Leaves, stalks
Thyme *(Thymus)*	Leaves, stalks
White Pine *(Pinus strobus)*	Needles
Yarrow *(Achillea millifolium)*	Flowers, leaves

Calcium Supplements

Herb	Part of the plant to use
Amaranth *(Amaranthus retroflexus)*	Leaves
Cabbage	Leaves
Chickweed *(Stellaria media)*	All
Comfrey *(Symphytum officinalis)*	Leaves
Dandelion	Leaves, roots
Kale	Leaves

Herb	Part of the plant to use
Lamb's-quarter *(Chemopodium album)*	Leaves
Mallow *(Malva neglecta)*	Leaves
All mints, including sage, motherwort, lemon balm, lavender, peppermint, etc.	Leaves
Mugwort (cronewort) *(Artemisia vulgaris)*	New growth leaves, roots
Nettle *(Urtica diocia)*	Leaves
Parsley *(Petroselinum sativum)*	Leaves
Plantain *(Plantago majus)*	Leaves
Raspberry *(Rubus species)*	Leaves
Red clover *(Trifolium pretense)*	Blossoms
Violet *(Viola ordorata)*	Leaves
Yellow dock *(Rumex crispus)*	Roots

Plain Vinegars

Herb	Part of the plant to use
Basil	Stalks (some color, taste)
Most flowers, aka rosehips	Flowers (no color, no taste)
Raspberries/blackberries	Leaves (nice color, but no taste)

....

MAKING HERBAL BUTTERS

by Carly Wall

Usually, on the first fine spring day, my mind is full of exciting herbal possibilities. There is the herb garden to check, new plants to grow, and the most exciting—new ways to put the herbs to use. If you don't make the effort, you'll never use the herbs. You have to set reasonable goals for yourself, choosing one or two new ways per year to incorporate herbs into your life. Otherwise, you could become overwhelmed; after all, there are thousands of herbs and thousands of uses.

As I look out my home office window, the herb garden looks a little barren at first. I decide it's time for a break and so I put on my jacket and boots and take a walk.

The grass is greening up a little. In the herb garden I push aside the winter debris and wet leaves to find my first hint that spring is indeed around the corner! Tiny green shoots of chives are growing and pushing their way out of the ground. The chives are always up first. Now my eyes are adjusting, and I notice other things around me. The winter has been kind to my rosemary plants this year—they've survived. My thyme is green in places. I look around and suddenly see that the clematis vines I planted last year have made it too.

Sometimes it takes time to adjust our eyes from the dreary winter days to the spring landscape. It is almost as if we have been put to sleep ourselves by winter's cold winds. Gardeners, just like their garden beds, seem to hunker in for the winter. All it takes to wake up again is one turn around outside on the first mild spring morning, and again the mind races with gardening ideas.

I plan to haunt certain plant nurseries again and to dream up new garden designs. In the meantime there's plenty of work to be done clearing out the old and preparing for the new.

As I clear away the debris, I realize that my eating habits change in the spring. I begin to long for fresh green things. It does not take long to snip a few of the pungent, oniony-flavored tips of chives. I can mince them, add them to omelets, sprinkle them over baked potatoes, or toss them into soup bowls with a few croutons. If you don't happen to have chives, many grocery stores now carry fresh and dried herbs if you want to try them before growing your own plants.

I'm still looking for that one special project to try this year and I finally hit on the idea. I'll experiment with herbal butters. They are delicious, unusual (yet easy), and they brighten up a spring table too. They are also quite elegant for formal occasions and parties. Did I mention versatile? You can use a wide variety of herbs for these butters. Fresh or dried herbs both work well.

If you too decide to experiment with herbal butters, you'll discover they are an easy way to add zest to your cooking—and it's the easiest way to try out herbal flavors. You can make them with one herb or a combination of your choosing and use them in various ways. That's the challenge and adventure. Perhaps you'll create an herbal butter that will become a tradition.

Choose Your Butter

The best choice for herbal butters is the unsalted sweet butter (the real stuff). It lets delicate flavors of the herbs come through. You can also use margarine or salted butter too, depending upon how you plan to use your finished product.

Various Uses for Herbal Butters

Basically, herbal butters are flavored butters you can use just like butter, only with that extra kick. They are wonderful drizzled on all vegetables: tomatoes, eggplant, zucchini, potatoes, carrots, peas, or corn. They also make a good baste for all types of meat: lamb, beef, pork, chicken, fish, and other seafood. Last, they flavor rice and egg dishes wonderfully and are great slathered on thick slices of homemade breads, crackers, toast, and biscuits. There's nothing better than flavored butters for the grill, or to use to make toast or to make toasted French bread slices.

Making the Flavored Butters

Here's the basic recipe:

¼ lb. sweet cream butter, softened   2 tsp. fresh lemon juice
3 tbsp. finely minced herbs

If using dried herbs, mix in with the lemon juice to moisten. Cream everything together with a wooden spoon until well blended. You can either use a melon ball scoop to make butter balls (in which case, drop the balls into a bowl of ice water, then drain) or roll the whole thing into a log from which to cut rounds. If you roll it into a log, you can roll it in additional minced herbs for a decorative touch. A neat idea is to use minced chives for the recipe then roll the log in minced chive blossoms to coat the outside. The pretty purple blossoms are eye-catching.

Wrap the log tightly in plastic wrap (or place the balls in plastic baggies) and refrigerate or freeze. If fresh herbs are used, keep in the refrigerator up to three days. If using dried herbs, keep refrigerated a week or so. You can freeze the butters for up to three months. Be sure to let the flavors blend before using (at least four hours, but overnight is best). Let the butter stand at room temperature 20 minutes before serving.

What Herbs Work Well Together?

I like to make a parsley-garlic butter to toast French bread slices. This goes nicely with pasta dishes. Another great combination is to use rosemary/chive butter to rub all over a whole chicken before roasting (be sure to keep basting). Dill butter is great with grilled salmon. Mint butter is great in cooked carrots or peas and for spreading on bread in making cucumber sandwiches. Try making a sweet violet butter. Here is a recipe to brighten up the table and to give you an idea of the varied uses of herbal butters.

Lemon Balm Muffins with Rose Petal Butter

2 c. flour	2 eggs
½ tsp. salt	½ c. applesauce
1 tsp. lemon zest	½ c. lemon juice
1¼ tsp. baking soda	3 tbsp. minced lemon balm
½ c. sugar	

Spray muffin tins with nonstick cooking spray. Blend together dry ingredients. In another bowl whisk the eggs until blended. Add applesauce, lemon juice, and minced lemon balm. Add wet mixture to dry ingredients. Mix well and drop into muffin tins. Bake at 375 degrees F for 20 to 25 minutes. Serve with rose butter.

HERBAL SALAD DRESSINGS

by Caroline Moss

I often feel I am blessed. I do not have a large or beautiful home, and I do not have a lot of money to spend on its maintenance. However, my little cottage is in the depths of the English countryside, and from my window I have a view of my small flock of small Hebridean sheep, of my chickens scratching and pecking at the ground, and of the children's pony gratefully tucking into the first of the winter hay.

Most important of all, just a few feet in front of this scene is the little plot that provides the inspiration for my writing, the materials for my workshops, and a ready supply of flavor for my cooking—that is, my herb garden. My herb garden is likely my greatest pleasure—to be able to step out of the back door on a warm, sunny afternoon and choose a bunch of parsley or chives, a sprig of lemon balm and a stem of mint; nothing brings me more joy! Most supermarkets sell only tiny prepackaged sprigs of herbs. And nothing compares to the use of fresh leaves, just picked from the plant, in salads or dressing.

In fact, salad herbs are easy to grow from seed. I list below some of the most useful salad herbs and have indicated the lifespan of each plant. Some are annuals, which need replacing each year, or even several times in a year. Others are perennials, which last for a number of years. A few, such as parsley, are biennials. These have a life cycle of two years. All the plants mentioned grow outdoors in an English climate. If you have very harsh winters or live in the heat of the southern United States, you will need to check an American reference book for zone suitability.

A Salad Herb Garden
Alexanders (Smyrnium olusatrum)

A perennial growing three to four feet. This is a rather large rampant plant to be planted close to rougher hedges and walls. It was, traditionally, a vital country food source. The young leaves are excellent in salads and the stems, lightly boiled, are known as "poor man's asparagus."

Basil (Ocimum basilicum)

A warmth-loving annual, this plant should be treated like lettuce, with periodic plantings during warm seasons. Indispensable in dressings for tomato salads, the leaves can also be used in mixed green salads. There are many varieties.

Chervil (Anthriscus cerefolium)

A delicate annual growing to nine inches or so. Chervil is common in French dressings and has a delicate, aniseed flavor.

Chives (Allium schoenoprasum)

An easy growing perennial about a foot in height. A lovely salad herb, chopped coarsely with other greens or finely into a dressing to give a mild onion flavor. The flowers are also edible and add a decorative mauve touch to a salad bowl.

Dandelion (Taraxacum officinale)

No need to plant this common weed on purpose; it is everywhere. The young leaves add a lovely, peppery bite to a green salad or with warm, very crisp bacon.

Dill (Anethum graveolens)

A feathery perennial reaching three feet or so. It is usually eaten with fish such as salmon.

Fennel (Foeniculum vulgare)

A decorative, feathery plant growing to five feet or more whose aniseed-flavored leaves give great interest to a green salad. The root, used raw or cooked as a vegetable is a slightly different cultivar of the same family.

Garlic (Allium sativum)

Where would robust, Mediterranean salads be without garlic? Great fun to grow outdoors and use in salads. You may either simply rub a clove round your salad bowl to add a mild kick, or crush a clove and add for a fuller effect.

Lemon balm (Melissa officinalis)

A perennial reaching three feet or so, its lemon flavor is best used uncooked. Too much will taste rather like cologne, but a hint adds a lovely summer freshness.

Mint (Mentha var.)

This is one herb which probably needs no introduction. A rampant perennial to be planted in pots unless you have a large, unfettered area of this herb to grow in. Great in starchy salads such as potato, rice, or couscous.

Nasturtium (Tropaeolum majus)

An annual, growing to eighteen inches or so. Its decorative flower is edible, and its leaves add a hot bite when added to lettuce or other mild salad greens. Look out for decorative flower variations and climbing cultivars.

Parsley (Petroselinum sativum)

Along with mint, this is one of the best known herbs—a biennial that barely reaches a foot in height. Parsley adds depth of flavor, not to mention nutrients, when added chopped to a dressing. Also, add sprigs of flat leaf or Italian parsley to a mixed leaf salad.

Arugula (Eruca vesicaria sativia)

An easily grown annual for pots or outdoors. Plant periodically, like basil, to ensure constant supplies, and add to mixed salads for a peppery flavor. A favorite in the wonderful food markets of France and Italy.

Salad Burnet (Sanguisorba rosaceae)

A delicate-looking but robust, foot-high perennial, this little plant is noted in most herb books as having a cucumber flavor, though I personally think you would need a good imagination to detect it. It does, however, make a pleasant addition to a salad that has nothing too overpowering in it; its flavor will be lost if combined with mint or basil.

Sorrel (Rumex acetosa)

A tenacious perennial and wonderful culinary herb. Its young leaves can be used in a mixed green salad to add a lemony note. The leaves can be finely chopped and used moderately in a dressing; and you will also find recipes for sorrel sauce, traditionally served with fish. The botanical name refers to common sorrel, but watch for other varieties such as French sorrel *(R. scutatus)*.

Tarragon (Artemisia dracunculus)

A robust perennial reaching two or more feet, tarragon is integral to classic French cooking and gained great popularity in the cooking revolution of the 1980s. The aniseed flavor can over-power but adds complexity if used with caution in a dressing. Be sure to get the correct variety, as named above and sometimes referred to as French tarragon. There is a coarser cultivar known as Russian tarragon *(A. dracunculoides),* which is not as good.

Dressings

Using the above guidelines and your own tastes, herbs can be added to your own favorite dressing recipes or even to store-bought ready-made mixes. So long as you like the basic flavor of the herb it is really impossible to make a mistake. If you overdo things and feel the flavoring is too strong, simply add more olive oil, mayonnaise, yogurt, or whatever base you are using and keep the leftover dressing in the fridge.

Having said that, you should know that one of the best ways to make up herb salad dressings is simply to experiment. I will give you my own favorite recipes in the hope that you enjoy them in your own home cooking, but eventually you will learn that there is a straightforward oil and vinegar base to which variations may be made according to taste and usage.

Herb Vinaigrette Dressing for a Mixed Green Salad

Crushed garlic (to your own taste)

1 part acid (wine vinegar or lemon juice)

4 parts oil (for a wonderful but heavy dressing use the best extra virgin olive oil you can afford, or use a high-quality vegetable oil)

A pinch of sugar or dab of honey

Salt and pepper to taste

1 part finely chopped herbs (parsley, chives, chervil, and maybe the slightest hint of mint)

Put all the ingredients into a lidded jar and shake well to mix.

Tomato Salad Dressing

In place of the acid element in the above recipe, use balsamic vinegar. Also, add two parts plain, low-fat yogurt (this reduces the fat content per tablespoonful and gives the dressing a creamy texture). Don't include any mint but do put in a generous measure of basil if you have any on hand.

Cucumber Salad Dressing

Start with the base vinaigrette, but use only the mildest of acid (white or apple cider, rather than balsamic, vinegar). Add two parts sour cream and omit the mint while including dill.

Potato Salad Dressing

Start with the base vinaigrette, and for each cup of dressing add one small, finely grated onion, a teaspoon of grainy mustard (mild or spicy depending on your taste), and a higher proportion of mint. For a creamy dressing, you may prefer to add two parts yogurt or mayonnaise.

Couscous Salad Dressing

To freshly cooked couscous, add a dressing of base vinaigrette to which you have added an extra part (giving a total of two parts) measure of herbs using equal quantities of parsley, chives, and mint. Also add a finely diced tomato, cucumber, and onion.

Note: Mint is a widely used flavoring in Middle Eastern and North African cuisine. Their favorite drink, other than coffee, is a strong, sweet mint tea made by pouring boiling water onto a handful of mint leaves and leaving it to steep for ten minutes or so before straining and sweetening. Some herb nurseries will stock the strongly pungent Moroccan mint for you to use in these recipes. Otherwise a simple spearmint or peppermint will do as well.

I do hope you try using a wide variety of herbs in your salad dressing, and that you enjoy some lovely herbal meals in your home as I have in mine.

In the end, perhaps you will be inspired to start your own small herb garden if you don't have one already, and you will always be assured of a plentiful supply of fresh herbs at a fraction of the cost of those in the shops. Not to mention the priceless joy you will gain by simply picking herbs or enjoying their fragrance on the light breezes of spring.

....

HERBAL HONEYS AND HONEY-CANDIED HERBS
by Sara Greer

For thousands of years, healers have been endlessly praising the medicinal virtues of honey. Some have also added to these virtues by infusing honey with aromatic healing herbs, producing honeys that gave a one-two punch to ailments ranging from sore throats to upset stomachs, from influenza to the grippe.

Sweet Herbal Medicine

It's relatively easy to make herbal honeys for your home medicine chest, or for your kitchen pantry. These honeys will serve a wide range of purposes, from medicinal to culinary. Furthermore, herbal honeys have important advantages as a way to administer natural medications to toddlers and older children who would otherwise refuse your doctoring efforts.

Note: Honey should never be given to children under the age of one year.

Herbal honeys also have the advantage of creating two products with a single process. The herb themselves, candied by the honey, also can be used in cooking, healing, or beautifying.

You should begin this process by selecting the honey you want to use. Many different varieties are available, depending on the season of the year and your local area. But any type of honey will do—delicate and light orange blossom honey and dark and intensely flavored buckwheat honey both can make excellent herbal honeys. Farmers markets are a great place to hunt for honeys, and many health food stores and grocery co-ops sell honey in bulk. Plus, there are a number of good mail-order companies that specialize in honeys—from the exotic and unusual to the plain and ordinary.

If you are feeling particularly creative, you may try to match the flavor and texture of the honey to the flavor of the herb you plan to use. This way, you can achieve a more harmonious marriage in your herb and honey mixture. For example, a strong herb such as lavender matches the strength of buckwheat honey, while a lighter herb such as rose petal mates well with orange blossom honey. Or, a hearty herb such as ginger root or thyme goes best with an exotic variety like carrot honey.

When in doubt about which honey will match up with a particular herb, you should generally use a fairly neutral honey, such as clover or wildflower—all of which work well with most aromatic herbs. Whatever honey you select, it should be at or above room temperature and should flow freely while you are working with it. If you have chosen a thick honey or one that crystallizes easily, such as buckwheat or star thistle, you may need to warm it gently until it thins or liquefies enough to pour readily. You will need at least a cup of honey to experiment with, and a quart would not be too much to buy at one time if you are likely to try more than one herbal honey.

Preparing Your Herbs

Once you have your honey, you should begin to prepare your herbs. The best herbs to use are the strongly aromatic and woody herbs such as rosemary, thyme, hyssop, and sage; very fragrant flowers such as rose and lavender; or strongly flavored roots and seeds such as ginger root and fennel seed. Avoid moist and juicy herbs such as comfrey and borage, and tonic bitter herbs such as gentian.

You may use either fresh or dried herbs for this project, though fresh herbs yield a stronger product. Make sure before you begin that your herbs are clean; wash and rewash fresh herbs to remove impurities such as dirt. If, as with many roots, you need to wash them just prior to using, be sure to dry them thoroughly. Small-leaved fresh herbs may be used whole or even in sprig form. Larger leaves should be chopped coarsely. With roses, the petals alone are used; remove the white areas. Lavender buds are used whole. Seeds should always be thoroughly bruised, and roots should be sliced or chopped. Dried herbs can be used as small pieces.

In general, to go with a quart of honey, you will need about one to two cups of fresh herbs or one-half to three-quarters cup dried herbs. If you are using roots and seeds, use the smaller amount; if leaves and flowers, the larger amount. For smaller batches of honey, reduce the amount of herbs accordingly.

When you are ready to make your herbal honey, you will need a clean and dry quart-sized glass jar to steep the mixture in. If the inside of the jar lid is unlined metal, use a layer or two of plastic wrap between the jar lid and the jar. This will keep the honey and herbs from coming into contact with the metal. Chemicals can leach into your honey if this occurs.

Making Your Herbal Honey

Now that you've got everything assembled, choose one of the methods outlined below to make your herbal honey. Base your choice of method on the herb you're using—its type and variety, and its freshness and form (that is, leaf or seed, dried or fresh, and so on).

Cold Method for Fresh Herbs

If you are using fresh herbs, the honey should be at room temperature. Place the prepared herbs in the bottom of a clean and dry quart glass jar. Pour the honey over the herbs, taking care to leave one inch of headspace at the top of the jar to discourage overflow. Cover the jar, tuck it into a cool dark place, and leave it undisturbed for one to two months. If you are using a highly aromatic herb such as thyme, the honey is likely to thin out and may overflow from the jar in spite of the headspace. Place a saucer or small plate under the jar to protect your shelf from overspill, and check the honey every few days.

Warm Method for Seeds, Woody Roots, and Dried Herbs

Warm the honey until it reaches about 100 degrees. Proceed as with the cold method, except allow the jar of honey and herbs to cool completely before covering it and putting it away to steep. This product takes a little longer to finish. I generally leave the mixture to steep for two to three months to give the seeds the maximum amount of time to release their medicinal qualities into the honey.

Hot Method for Fresh Roots

Gently heat the honey until it is very liquid and begins to steam slightly. Follow the details of the recipe for ginger honey given below. This is usually ready in two or three weeks.

As the mixture steeps, the honey, with its unique property of being able to draw moisture out of plants, will force all of the juices and essential oils out of the herbs you've used.

Note: many herbs in turn will thin the honey, although some (lavender, for example) will not. The honey may change color as well as texture.

If you want to taste your herbal honey now and then during the waiting period, go right ahead. Just be sure to use a clean, dry spoon and not your fingers. Often a layer of herbs will float to the surface, and you may want to dig down below this. It won't hurt to stir the herbs back in when you're done.

Herbal honeys in general make a great base for syrups, and a soother for sore throat or mouth. Ginger honey is a good tonic for upset stomachs, and with added lemon juice it helps to reduce the discomfort of colds. Hyssop or sage-infused honeys are wonderful for treating cold and flu symptoms. Honey-based salves are useful for rashes and dry skin. Honey infused with a soothing herb such as lavender is a pleasant treatment for healing a burn scar, and it does not have the warming effect of an oil base. Oxymel, a mixture of honey and vinegar which often included herbs, is an ancient remedy, and herbal honeys make excellent oxymels. Herbal honey makes a useful substitute for plain honey in homemade cosmetics or soaps. And herbal honeys can be cooked with or eaten out of hand. They're also great for sweetening medicinal teas.

The shelf life of many herbal honeys is in the six-month to two-year range, depending on the moisture content of the herb used. Honey itself, having antibacterial properties, rarely spoils or molds, but added moisture naturally dilutes honey's keeping qualities. When in doubt, store the honey in the refrigerator and use it within six to twelve months. Any honey or herb that develops an off color or odor, or any other signs of mold or spoilage, should be discarded. Never taste a suspicious product!

A Byproduct of the Process: Candied Herbs

Once the honey is finished steeping, you have two options. You can simply leave it as it is, herbs and all, dipping into it as desired. On the other hand, you can warm it gently and pour it through a strainer to remove the herbs. Then set the herbs aside and bottle the honey. Any herbal honey made with fresh soft flowers or juicy roots should be stored in the refrigerator. Honey made with dried herbs, or with fresh woody aromatics like thyme, can be stored in your pantry or on a closet shelf. If the honey crystallizes, use it in crystalline form or warm it gently until it reliquefies. If you warm it, I'd recommend storing in the fridge from that point on.

Either after straining the honey, or after using it up, you'll have a batch of candied herbs to enjoy. You can use or store them just as you take them out of the honey, since they keep well refrigerated. Alternatively, you can spread them out to dry and crystallize on a sheet of waxed paper or on a plate. If you choose this second option, allow the herbs to air-dry until either they crystallize at least partially, or they reach a texture you like. Some honeys don't crystallize readily, or tend to absorb moisture from the air, and humid climates also tend to discourage crystallization, so your herbs may not actually end up covered with crystals of honey. Even so, the herbs will still dry out somewhat, and if you want this effect you should be able to achieve it. In either form, honey-candied herbs should be refrigerated.

What can you do with honey-candied herbs? You can always eat them out of hand—ginger root, angelica stem, fennel seeds, and a number of other candied herbs make delicious healthy snacks. You can also brew teas from them, especially the intensely aromatic herbs such as thyme, sage, or lavender. Candied hyssop makes a pleasant tea to soothe coughs and congestion, and candied lavender tea helps soothe a tension headache. You can also cook with the herbs. Add them to salads, salad dressings, soups, stews, and baked goods. One of the tastiest uses is to enhance a simple dough—shortbread or biscuit—with lively herbal flavors and a touch of sweetness by adding candied herbs. See the recipe for herb shortbread listed below for a quick and easy way to take advantage of these delicate flavors.

Recipes

Herbal honeys are a lot of fun to fix, particularly if you enjoy cooking or medicine-making. You can share the pastime with children, who love to have tasting privileges, or you can revel in some solitary creative time with your herbs and honeys. The recipes below are my personal favorites to start you on the road to inventing your own herbal honey delicacies and remedies. Enjoy!

GINGER HONEY

Stockpot or large saucepan	8 oz. fresh ginger root
3 lbs. honey (about 1 qt.) in a glass jar	1 clean quart (or slightly larger) jar with lid

Fill the saucepan or stockpot about 4 inches deep with warm water. Put the open jar of honey in the saucepan. Add more water if necessary to bring the depth of the water halfway up the side of the honey jar. Warm the saucepan on low heat.

While the honey heats, peel the ginger and slice it into more or less square chunks ¼ to ½ inch thick. Put it into the clean quart jar. By now the honey should be fairly hot and liquid. Carefully lift the honey jar out of the saucepan, dry it off, and let it stand for about 5 minutes to let it cool slightly. Even after cooling the jar will still be hot, so either wear oven mitts for the next step or use a ladle. Pour or ladle the hot honey over the ginger root in the quart jar. Leave about 1 inch of empty space at the top of the jar. The ginger will rise to the top of the jar and release its juice into the honey. The level of the honey may drop slightly as hidden air bubbles emerge and rise to the top of the jar. If this happens, add a little more honey to bring the level back up to the one-inch mark. You'll have about a cup of warm honey left over which you can use for something else, perhaps a small batch of lavender honey.

Now set the jar of ginger and honey aside to cool uncovered. Once it is completely cool, that is back to room temperature, you can put the lid on the jar. If you must cover it before you can safely put the lid on, lay a piece of muslin or a flour-sack towel over the top of the jar instead of using the lid. This will allow steam to escape. If the jar is lidded too soon, the steam will condense and drip back into the honey, significantly increasing the risk of spoilage.

Once the jar is cool and you have put the lid on tightly, turn the jar upside down. This helps blend the ginger juice into the honey, and although it seems like a bizarre method, it works better than stirring. Put the upside-down jar into your refrigerator. After about 24 hours, turn the jar right-side up; a day later, turn it upside down again. Repeat this process every day for the next two weeks. At the end of this time, the ginger juice and honey will have completely blended into a fragrant liquid with the consistency of maple syrup. You can remove the now-candied ginger pieces, or you can leave them in the jar until the honey is gone. Both the ginger and the honey are ready to be used in cooking, medicine, and so on. The ginger pieces are an excellent nausea remedy for travelers or flu sufferers. Watch out, though. The ginger pieces are much spicier than you would expect. Use tiny pieces until you get used to the strong flavor.

Herb Shortbread

1 c. butter or margarine, at room temperature	2 tbsp. honey-candied herbs
¼ c. honey (may be omitted)	2½ c. flour

Cream the butter or margarine. When it is soft, cream the honey and the candied herbs into it. Stir the flour into the honey/butter mixture, beginning with the lesser amount and adding more if necessary. Mix until the flour is thoroughly incorporated and a stiff dough forms. Shape the dough into a sausage shape about 7 to 8 inches long and 1½ to 2 inches across. Wrap this in waxed paper and chill it in the fridge until it is quite firm. Slice this "sausage" into ½ inch pieces and bake on a cookie sheet at 325 degrees F until just beginning to brown, about 20 to 25 minutes.

I usually use lavender or hyssop in these cookies, but you can also make a delicious savory version by using sage or thyme, omitting the ¼ cup of honey and cutting the flour down by ¼ to ½ cup. If you have crystallized honey, this recipe is a great place to use some of it. The crystals improve the texture of the cookies.

Honey Salve

1 tbsp. herbal honey	¼ oz. beeswax
3 tbsp. extra-virgin, cold- pressed olive oil	3 drops tincture of benzoin

Warm the honey and oil together until the honey is liquid and no longer clumps to itself in the pan. Grate the beeswax into the mixture and let it melt. Take the pan off the heat and stir in the tincture of benzoin. Pour into a 2-ounce salve jar. Stir the salve every 10 to 15 minutes as it cools, or more often if the honey appears to be separating out. I use a plastic chopstick for this task. When the salve becomes stiff, you can stop stirring. When it is entirely cool, cover and label the jar.

Jams, Jellies, and Condiments

by Tammy Sullivan

A meal just doesn't seem complete without a few choice condiments. Salads seem naked without at least a little bit of dressing—and who wants French fries with no ketchup or salt? If those condiments happen to be fresh or home-preserved, so much the better.

Salt has been man's primary condiment since before recorded history. Other condiments have been around since at least 5000 BCE when the early Greeks began cultivating the olive. They soon developed a method to cold press the olives with a stone wheel and bottle the oil. Homer called olive oil "liquid gold."

Condiments are chosen for their ability to complement or enhance the flavor of various foods. Some possess intentionally overwhelming flavor because their past function was to hide the fact the food may not be fresh. Liquamen was an extremely popular condiment in ancient Rome—so popular, in fact, that it was the first mass-produced condiment with more than one ingredient. Liquamen, a salty fish sauce, is the precursor to the popular Worcestershire steak sauce.

Similarly, ancient China has manufactured soy sauce since the twelfth century BCE and it has survived with a few minor changes. They also developed dipping sauces and the precursor to modern-day ketchup. Surprisingly, both ketchup and soy sauce originally were fish-based too.

Ancient Greece developed the forebear to modern gravy with a flour, water, and spice paste used to thicken stews. The ancient Greeks also used grape leaves in their food and would frequently wrap meats in them before cooking to add flavor and keep the meat juicy.

Mustard was another important herb for the ancient Greeks. With a diet consisting of plenty of fresh seafood, mustard leaves were frequently thrown into the stewpot or the seeds were ground and added to wine for a sauce. Mustard is known to have been used throughout ancient Egypt and Asia as well.

Yogurt and cheese came to be known around 5000 BCE through accidental creation. Without a cool storage spot, milk would often begin to curdle within a few hours. Depending on the temperature, the resulting yogurt could be creamy or coarse. If it was coarse, it was used to make a soft cheese, as the process of making it butter was not discovered for another 2,000 years. Butter is the only man-made condiment deemed fit for the gods.

Honey, a pure substance that required only human discovery, is the only other condiment the ancient Greeks deemed fit for the gods. Fittingly, the first recorded use of honey dates back to Egypt circa 5500 BCE when the ancient Babylonian and Sumerian cultures used it as an offering to the gods. Honey wine, also called mead, was thought to be the earthbound equivalent of "nectar," the drink of the gods.

Some Native American tribes rarely used salt, preferring sugar as their primary condiment. Each spring they would tap the maple trees and cook down the sap until they had a fine syrup they called "sweet water." This tradition carries on today with maple syrup being among the most popular of syrups.

Mankind's search for an earthbound ambrosia surely precipitated the continued creation of condiments. The desire to consume foods thought to impart magical qualities must have played a part as well. Early man must have thought he had stumbled upon true ambrosia when sugar was discovered. In 510 BCE, Persian Emperor Darius spoke of the honey from the "reed without bees." He was speaking, of course, about cane sugar. Cane sugar took the place of fruit juice, date syrup, and honey as the primary sweetener almost as soon as it became available—and remains one of the most heavily cultivated crops in the trade.

The condiment world really began to heat up with the discovery of horseradish root. Horseradish root made its debut around 1500 BCE and the discovery is credited to none other than Apollo himself. According to legend, the Oracle at Delphi told him the root was "worth its weight in gold." Vinegar was usually added to the ground root to create a sauce. Eventually, it made its way to Japan and became the fabulous wasabi paste and dipping sauces of today.

The ancient Egyptians are credited with the invention of the first pickled items. In 500 BCE, Herodotus wrote about the pickled fish and fowl that was frequently consumed by the ancient Egyptians. The popular pickled cucumbers that we enjoy today date back more than 3,000 years and originated in India.

As new types of herbs became more widely known due to seafaring tradesmen, new ways to prepare food followed. People no longer found it necessary to cover the taste with an overwhelming sauce when it could be improved by adding a few spices. Spices became highly sought-after items and frequently used as currency. In fact, pepper was once demanded as a ransom payment in ancient Rome. Pepper was seen as the ultimate status symbol, for only the truly rich could afford it. Likewise, cinnamon was highly prized by the Romans, who considered it sacred because of its delightful aroma.

Ancient civilizations also prized their grapes. Fruit pectin was not understood yet, so most grapes were preserved as wine. Pliny the Elder researched and developed methods to keep wine from turning into vinegar. Today, flavored and wine vinegars are considered veritable staples on the spice shelf. Later on, spiced wine became all the rage in France and Spain.

Through the years, exciting new foods would be added to the rapidly growing list of condiments. In the late 1700s, condiments were revolutionized with the advent of home canning. It was now possible to taste sauces, relishes, and syrups from far-away lands, thanks to the longer shelf life.

Jelled sauces had been served since before recorded culinary history, although fruit pectin was not fully understood until the late 1800s. In the early 1800s, pioneers would boil their cider until it had a syrup consistency. Once the cider cooled, it formed into a jelly.

With so many varied condiments throughout the world, choosing new ones to try can be quite intimidating. Many go way beyond famous and into the infamous category. For instance, do you know what the leading sandwich spread is in Australia? I'll bet you can name at least one brand of hot sauce. Both condiments have been mentioned in numerous hit songs. Sugar and honey have become so synonymous with all things sweet that they are used as pet names for those we love—and let's not even discuss the many songs that feature them.

When you make your own condiments, you can tailor the recipe to suit your palate. An equally important consideration in making your own condiments is home preservation.

Why Preserve?

While it is certainly possible to make a small amount of a condiment, it is just as convenient to make several pints and save some. It's also practical if you are using vegetables, herbs, or fruits from your own garden—I have yet to see anyone consume an entire tomato harvest in one sitting.

When you preserve the food from your home garden, you are in control from planting the seed to preparing the finished dish. You know exactly which ingredients were used and what pesticide system you implemented.

How Do I Preserve?

There are many methods for food preservation available today. Whether canning, freezing, dehydrating, vacuum packing, or storing in a root cellar, you can be assured of fresh-tasting food all year round. Let's begin with the easiest.

Freezing

Assuming that you already own a refrigerator equipped with a freezer, the only additional item you need for this preservation system is a box of plastic baggies. Jams, jellies, and pie fillings are easily stored in the freezer along with the vegetables. Frozen food retains its moisture content, color, vitamins, and most importantly, its full flavor.

Most vegetables only need to be cleaned and sliced before sliding into the baggie. Berries and other fragile items should be frozen in a baggie with water added to it. The water will form an ice block and keep the berries from being crushed. Certain vegetables keep best when blanched a few minutes before packaging for the freezer.

The downside to freezing is if you don't package the food correctly, it could get freezer burn. Also, the frozen food must be maintained at a subzero degree temperature, so a prolonged power outage could damage your stock.

Canning

Home canning has many benefits. Along with a long shelf life, canned food can be stored at room temperature. Canning is appropriate for many types of food including sauces, soups, vegetables, relishes, fruits, butters, and pickles.

The home-canning system requires a small investment. You will need glass jars, lids, rings, and a large pot. The rims of the jars should be fully submerged under water and processed in a water bath. A water bath is basically boiling the jars to ensure that no bacteria remain to spoil the food.

If making jelly, you will also need fruit pectin and a strainer bag. The jars and rings can be used over and over, but the lids must be replaced each time. The United States Department of Agriculture says the only truly safe canning procedures are those that include processing in the water bath with new lids for a tight seal.

Dehydrating

Dehydrating is the oldest form of food preservation known to man. Primitive cultures would place berries, grasses, and herbs upon large rocks and leave them lying in the sun until they had thoroughly dried. Although modern society has many choices when it comes to preserving food, dehydration is still the preferred method for herbs, flowers, apples, and potatoes.

Dehydrated food takes up little space and can be stored at room temperature. The initial cost of a food dehydrator is minimal, but is also optional. Tomatoes that are dehydrated in the sun are considered a delicacy.

There are no chemicals needed for food dehydration. No added sugars or salts. All you need is a sharp knife and trays (these can be made from window screens) for your dehydrating unit. Slice the herbs, fruit, or vegetables and slide them into the unit or arrange them on the screen trays. Now, either place the trays in the sun or turn the unit on. That's it! That is all there is to it! Let the sun or unit do its job while you relax. Once the food is completely dry, simply bag it in plastic baggies and store. This is a fantastic method for making nutritious snacks for children.

Vacuum Packing

Vacuum packing requires the most expensive initial investment. Along with the machine, you must also purchase bags. While the bags are reusable, they are not cheap. But the process itself is simple and straightforward. Place the food in the bag, turn on the machine, and—presto!—you're done. Coffee is best preserved in this method. While this preserves shelf life, some items should also be frozen.

Herbs are best kept in dehydrated form or frozen in water. If choosing to freeze, freeze whole leaves fully intact. Chop or grind after thawing.

There are many books and websites to guide you through the process step by step (no matter which preservation system you choose), or you can contact your local county home economist. Since this article is about the condiments themselves instead of the preservation systems, let's get to the recipes!

The jam, fruit butter, and jelly recipes are prepared for use with the home canning system. It takes time for the jelly to "set" or gel properly.

Mayonnaise

1 egg	1½ c. olive oil
3 tbsp. lemon juice	1 tsp. salt
1 tsp. sugar	

Combine all ingredients and whip until the right consistency. Add other spices as desired.

Ocalee's Dandelion Jelly

1 qt. tightly packed dandelion petals (no stems)	Pinch of orange zest
2 qt. water	Squirt of fresh orange juice
1 pkg. fruit pectin	5½ c. sugar
2 tbsp. fresh lemon juice	

Rinse the petals thoroughly. Boil them in water until the water turns yellow, which normally takes 3 to 4 minutes. Remove the petals and squeeze the remaining moisture into the liquid. Take 3 cups of the petal liquid and add the pectin, lemon juice, and orange juice in a large boiler. Bring to a full boil and then add the sugar all at once. Boil for 2½ minutes. Pour into hot sterilized jars and process in the water bath for 5 minutes.

Blackberry Jelly

3½ c. blackberry juice	½ tsp. butter
1 pkg. fruit pectin	5 c. sugar

Sanitize the jars by placing them in boiling water for at least 10 minutes. Allow them to remain warm while you cook the jelly. Combine the juice, pectin, and butter over high heat.

Stir constantly until it begins to boil. Add sugar all at once and continue stirring. Bring the mixture to a full rolling boil and allow it to boil for 1 minute. Remove from heat. Skim the foam off the surface. Ladle the liquid into the jars and place the lids and rings on them. Process in a hot water bath for at least 10 minutes. Yield: Seven 8-ounce jars.

Caramel Apple Butter

3 lbs. apples	¼ tsp. ginger
2 c. sugar	¼ tsp. cloves
1 bag caramels	½ tsp. cinnamon

Peel and purée the apples. Take 7 cups of the fruit pulp and cook it in a slow cooker along with the sugar. Allow the mixture to cook for 3 to 4 hours or until the consistency of applesauce. Stir in the caramels and spices. Resume cooking until the caramel has thoroughly melted. Place in hot jars and set in a water bath for 10 minutes.

Banana Butter

3 c. mashed bananas	Cherries or pineapple chunks (optional)
6½ c. sugar	1 pkg. fruit pectin
¼ c. lemon juice	

Combine all ingredients except the pectin in a large pot. Stir constantly until it comes to a full boil. Boil hard for 1 minute. Add pectin and stir. Skim off foam and pack into hot jars. Process 5 minutes.

Flora's Rose Petal and Champagne Jelly

1½ c. rose petals   ¾ c. water

Juice of 1 lemon   1½ c. sugar

¾ c. champagne   1 pkg. fruit pectin

Place the rose petals, lemon juice, and champagne in a blender and blend until smooth. Place the remaining water in a saucepan and add the sugar and pectin. Stir constantly and bring to a boil. Allow the mixture to hard boil for 1 minute. Pour the hot mixture into the blender and blend all of the ingredients together. Pour into hot jars. Process 5 minutes.

Southern Style Chow-Chow

1 head cabbage	2½ c. vinegar
3 c. sliced cucumbers	1 tsp. white pepper
1 c. sliced red peppers	1 tbsp. salt
2 c. chopped green tomatoes	1 tsp. black pepper
2 c. sliced green peppers	1 tsp. onion powder
1½ c. sugar	1 tsp. dill

Place all the vegetables in a large boiler, sprinkle with salt. Let them rest for a few hours. Drain, rinse, and drain again. Combine sugar, vinegar, and spices in a saucepan and bring to a boil. Simmer for 10 minutes. Add vegetables and simmer 10 more minutes. Pack into jars and process 10 minutes.

Greta's Pepper Relish

1 red onion	1 yellow bell pepper
1 red bell pepper	Olive oil
Tarragon	Pepper

Slices or dice the onion and peppers. Pour a little olive oil in a skillet and toss in the vegetables. Throw fresh tarragon over the mixture. Stir-fry over medium heat until the red onion takes on a translucent appearance. Scoop the mixture from the oil and serve immediately.

ROMAN VINEGAR

Fill a decorative bottle about ¼ full with garlic cloves, basil, thyme, and oregano. Heat red wine vinegar in a small saucepan. Pour the vinegar over the herbs.

HONEY-VIDALIA MARINADE

Place one whole Vidalia onion in a blender. Add three tablespoons honey and blend on high. Continue adding honey until the mixture is the same consistency as a runny applesauce. Pour over meat and baste as needed.

GREEK GARLIC DRESSING

1 qt. yogurt	2 cucumbers, peeled, seeded, and diced
2 cloves garlic, minced	3 tbsp. fresh dill, chopped fine
Salt and pepper to taste	

Combine all ingredients. Serve as a dip or a salad dressing.

PESTO

Place 2 large cloves of garlic in your blender or food processor. Add 3 cups packed basil leaves, ½ cup black olives, 2 tablespoons Parmesan cheese, and ½ cup olive oil to the garlic. Blend mixture until crumbly. Add nuts if desired. Blend a few minutes more.

ALL-PURPOSE SEASONING SALT

Peel and slice garlic cloves. Run them through the dehydrator and grind. Add salt and pepper to the ground garlic. You may add a bit of powdered onion as well. Delicious on everything!

ROASTED GARLIC

Pop a head of garlic in a small baking dish. Add a bit of water and a bit of olive oil. Bake at 400 degrees F for 30 minutes. Squeeze the garlic flesh out of the papery shell.

BOUILLON CUBES

To make your own bouillon cubes, keep the stock from any homemade soup. Boil it down until it is a bit thicker and freeze in an ice cube tray. Each cube is equal to one cube of store bought bouillon. Keep in mind that yours will not be so highly concentrated in salt, so season accordingly.

HERBAL BUTTERS

To make herbal butters, allow the butter to soften at room temperature. Add in the herbs of choice and blend until it has a spreadable consistency.

HEALTHY SNACKS TO GO: A FEW OPTIONS

Nuts and dehydrated strawberry slices.

Sliced apples and coconut, dehydrated and tossed with fresh grapes.

Sliced bananas, dipped in honey and dehydrated.

The fruit pulp left over from jelly making can be used in the dehydrator to make fruit leather.

FLOWERS
AND HERBS

RECIPES WITH VIOLETS

by Delores Duchen

One wildflower that everybody knows is the violet. Ranging in color from white to blue to purple, it grows happily in our lawns and gardens whether we encourage it or not. Because it is so hardy, sometimes it makes a pest of itself, crowding out other plants. Most people, however, are pleased to tolerate some violets in their yards. They add a touch of color to the early spring and remind us that summer is on its way.

It is surprising that more people don't also realize that violets are also edible. Both the flowers and the leaves can be eaten, raw or cooked, and are good sources of vitamin C. The flowers contain four times as much vitamin C, weight for weight, as oranges. The leaves also provide high levels of vitamin A and iron.

Raw, the flowers can be added to salads or used as a nibble or garnish. They may also be cooked into lovely sauces or jellies. Here are some recipes.

Violet Jam

Put one tightly packed cup of violets in your blender, add ¾ cup of water and the juice of one lemon, and blend into a smooth, violet-colored paste. Slowly add 2½ cups of sugar and blend until the sugar is dissolved. In a small saucepan, stir one package of powdered pectin in ¾ cup of water, bring to a boil, and boil hard for one minute. Pour this hot mixture into the blender with the other ingredients and blend at a low speed for about a minute, then quickly pour into sterilized jars and seal. Keep this jam refrigerated. It will stay fresh for about three weeks. You may also freeze it. Serve violet jam in little dabs on vanilla wafers or other cookies or muffins.

Cooked Violet Leaves

Cook the leaves like spinach and serve with salt, pepper, and butter or with vinegar and hard-boiled eggs. Be sure to drink the pot liquor too. Violet greens can be used to thicken stews and gumbos and are sometimes called "Wild Okra" as a result.

Creamed Violet Leaves

If you find that you dislike the slight astringency of the leaves, you can add a cream sauce or a can of cream of mushroom soup thinned with ½ can of cream or milk, or the white sauce of your choice. This is a good way to serve the leaves after they have matured and become too bitter to enjoy raw.

Violet Leaf Tempura

You can make a simple tempura batter by stirring cold water into 3 tablespoons of flour until you have a thin paste. Add ¼ teaspoon of baking soda, if you desire. Dip the leaves into this paste to cover, then drop into an inch of hot vegetable oil. Brown evenly.

Blue Vinegar

Steep a generous quantity of violets in a jar of white wine vinegar for three to four weeks. Leave in a sunny place so that the "essence" of the flowers will be released. Use it alone or add vegetable oil to make blue vinaigrette dressing.

Candied Violets

You may also use this recipe to candy rose petals and yucca petals. Beat two egg whites at room temperature until frothy. Dip the flowers into the egg white, one at a time, until they are completely covered. (If you are concerned about contracting salmonella from uncooked egg whites, try pasteurized egg whites from the baking section of the supermarket.) Then dip each flower into superfine granulated sugar. (If you can't find "superfine" just put regular granulated through the blender for a minute or so.) Be sure to cover all surfaces of the flower. Place each flower onto a cookie sheet covered with wax paper. Connoisseurs then use toothpicks to restore the violet to its original shape. You may prefer just to shape it into an oval shape. Sprinkle any syrupy-looking places with more sugar. After cooling, store in a tin with a layer of waxed paper between each layer of flowers.

....

THE LUCKY CARNATION
by Carly Wall

Ever wondered why the scarlet carnation *(Dianthus caryophyllus)* is considered a lucky flower? In 1904, the red carnation was adopted officially as Ohio's state flower in memory of William McFinley. He considered it a lucky flower because during an early campaign for a seat in the U.S. House of Representatives, his opponent gave him a red carnation for his buttonhole. Since he won that election, he continued wearing this flower throughout his career.

A Literary Flower

The carnation is actually a member of a large genus called *Dianthus*, containing more than three hundred flowering plants. There are three main groups: sweet Williams, pinks, and carnations. All of these require full sun and a well-drained, slightly alkaline soil. All are delightful in their own way. For now, we'll explore the carnations: the perpetual-flowering and the hardy border types. This ancient flower was known and loved centuries before the Christian era, and many have referred to it as the "Divine" or Dianthus. The Greeks and Romans often used it in garlands for their best athletes. In fact, it is part of literary history, being mentioned in Chaucer's *The Canterbury Tales*, where he called it "clove gilofre," derived from the Greek *caryophyllus*. Later, Shakespeare took the liberty of calling them "gillyflowers" in *A Winter's Tale*. Before that, the monks of the Middle Ages grew them in their monastery gardens as ingredients for their winemaking.

The perpetual-flowering carnations are an all-year-round plant that can be grown in greenhouses in changeable climates, while the border carnations are the more easygoing characters, requiring only good sun and moist conditions for them to fill your summer with bright color. It's not hard to grow these beautiful, varied flowers, and it's a shame that the carnation has for the most part been turned into a "florist" flower, for the joys of growing this beautiful plant in your own garden or greenhouse are unmatched.

Cooking With Flowers

Please remember that some flowers are not safe to eat; know what you are eating. Also, florist shop flowers are for the most part treated with chemicals, so don't eat these. Eat only flowers that are pesticide and chemical free.

Whenever I tell someone that I'm cooking with flowers, they look at me in that wondering way, as if they aren't sure whether I'm joking or not. Many haven't even heard of such a thing, and the ones who have think it's mainly a decorative endeavor (garnish for a salad or drink). Actually, flowers (the edible kind) have exciting and varied tastes and texture that add zest and even health benefits. For years I've candied violets, made lavender bud cookies, and added chopped chrysanthemum petals to soups. I've also made dandelion jelly and wine, which is quite a welcome treat on cold winter nights. There are actually about five flavor variations that flowers fall into: very flavorful, mildly flavorful, sweet, slightly bitter, and very mild. The carnation falls into the very flavorful category. It has a spicy bite. What do you do with it? Add the petals to salads, soups, or sandwiches. I like to add the red to herbal vinegars because it adds a pretty pink sparkle to the finished product. The clove-scented varieties add something special to sweets. Here I share a few of my favorite recipes using carnations.

Carnation Butter

½ lb. sweet butter, room temperature   2 to 3 tablespoons milk
1¼ c. carnation petals, chopped

Whip or blend petals into butter until well mixed. Press butter into a pretty container or server. Cover tightly and store in refrigerator about a week before serving to let the petals impart their flavor to the butter. Good served on banana bread or shortbread.

Carnation and Lavender Sugar

This floral sugar can be used in cakes, puddings, or sugar cookies. Take a one-quart sterilized mason jar and fill it half full with white granulated sugar. Fill the rest with two parts carnation petals and one part lavender buds. Pour this into a bowl and mix well, then return to the mason jar and close tightly. Leave the jar sealed for one to two weeks, shaking every three days. Spread out the contents of the jar on wax paper and remove flower material, then store the sugar in the jar in a cool, dry place. Sprinkle on cookies or desserts.

Carnation Jam

¾ cup boiling water

1 cup carnation petals, chopped

1½ c. water

1, ¾ ounce package of powdered pectin

5¾ c. granulated sugar

Have six to eight sterilized jelly jars on hand. Pour boiling water over carnation petals. Mix remaining water with powdered pectin (such as Sure-Jell). Bring water-pectin to boil over high heat. Add carnation petals and sugar. Stir constantly. Bring to a full rolling boil and boil for 1 minute. Fill jars to within 2 inches of the top. Wipe edges, cover with lids. Screw bands tightly. Invert jars for 5 minutes, then stand upright. Check seals after one hour. If jars haven't been sealed, place in a boiling water bath for 15 minutes.

And That's Not All

The Victorians had an obsessions with flowers and created many ways to add them to daily life. They even adopted the use of the nosegay to add hidden messages of sentiment and fragrance. The nosegay is simply a small scented bouquet (usually no taller than 6 inches) which can easily be hand-carried or pinned onto a blouse or lapel.

Create a tiny nosegay of carnations by gathering a bunch of the smaller blooms. Cut the stem ends short and even. Tie together, wrap ends with a piece of wet paper towel. Cover the paper towel tightly and completely with tin foil. Take a paper doily and wrap around the stem and tie with a pretty ribbon.

....

COOKING WITH LOVAGE
by Carly Wall

My introduction to lovage *(Levisticum officinale)* occurred when I picked up a tiny plant at a garden center while I was on the road traveling years ago. I have a habit of just dropping into garden centers or nurseries whenever I travel, just on the off chance that I will discover an unusual or unique herb that I have not seen before. Most of the time, of course, I don't find any herbs. But very occasionally, I sometimes hit the jackpot and find a tiny nursery brimming with all kinds of exotic plants with exotic scents and lovely leaves and flowers.

On this occasion, I found lovage. I was a relative beginner gardener then, just getting into herbs, and I didn't know much about anything. The only thing I did know, at least as far as lovage was concerned, was that its name was beautiful and its leaves were dark. So, it was with a trusting heart that I decided to take the little fellow home and plant him in a place of honor in my herb garden, near the entrance to the garden very close to a walking path. I hoped that I might in time perhaps learn a little more about him.

Little did I know—the lovage grew so fast I could not keep track. It seemed one minute it was six inches high, and a few minutes later it was climbing toward six feet in height. Very quickly, I came to know that this was a plant to be reckoned with, at least in terms of growth, and that it was very lovely to look at, though I still did not know much about its background—what was it useful for, how did it taste? There wasn't much information to be found on lovage in contemporary sources; it seemed to have fallen by the wayside in usage.

The History of Lovage

In actuality, lovage is one of the world's oldest known salad greens and has been in cultivation for several millennia. Native to the Mediterranean region, it grows wild in the mountainous areas of France, northern Greece, and in the Balkans. It is a perennial herb that comes from the carrot family, and was actually one of the most popular herbs during the Middle Ages. Its seeds were long used in cordials and confection, as well as in a number of medicines. The Emperor Charlemagne required it in his gardens, and most monasteries were known to plant it. Monks often placed lovage leaves in the shoes of travelers in the belief that it soothed weary feet. The colonists brought the herb to the United States. Thomas Jefferson's home and famous gardens, Monticello, has a patch of lovage growing there to this day. After learning about this surprising herb, I tried it, and eventually lovage became a staple of my kitchen, appearing in my soups and salads regularly.

Medical Considerations

Lovage has many uses as a medicinal herb. First and foremost, it has been used as a diuretic. The infused leaves or seeds help reduce water retention and act as deodorizers. An old remedy for an upset stomach contained lovage, brandy, and sugar. It is also said to be good for relieving skin problems, and a preparation made from the roots was added to bath water or made into a salve. This herb was helpful for rheumatism and migraine when the leaves and stalks were made into a tea, and it is said the tea is helpful in relieving stomach pains caused by gas. Lovage has also been used as an aphrodisiac or "love charm," and so has been called "love parsley," or by extension, lovage.

Long ago, lovage cordial was a popular drink with country people who took it as a remedy for sore throats. John Gerarde, the noted author and herbalist, wrote in 1597 that lovage was one of the wonder drugs of the time.

Growing and Harvesting Lovage

One or two plants of lovage are probably all you need, as a little goes a long way with this particular herb. Lovage is a perennial that grows to six feet in height, though it may die back in the winter and shoot up again in the spring.

Grow lovage in full sun or partial shade. The plant is easily propagated by seed or by root division. But when you plant it, be sure to give it plenty of room for it will want to spread out. Place the young plant in a sunny plot in rich, well-tended soil. Lovage is a heavy feeder and will reward good soil preparation with rampant dark-green growth. If your plants have sickly looking pale-green leaves, then you need to add fertilizer to the soil. If you want to keep your plant well groomed, you have to cut it back regularly. This will cause a beautiful compact plant to form; however, this will hinder flower growth. If you let your lovage grow free instead, you will get beautiful yellow blooms, and in second and each subsequent year thereafter, you will also get ample and sturdy bloom stalks.

To assure yourself of bringing in a good crop of lovage, it is best to plant the seed in the very earliest of spring, as lovage requires a long cool period to germinate—usually around 70 degrees for three weeks. In setting seedlings, give much room between them—often as much as 12 feet. Work aged compost into each planting hole, water it well, and then mulch. The roots can be divided and planted in autumn to expand the lovage bed.

Lovage is a stout plant, resembling in some aspects the herb angelica. Lovage has a thick, fleshy root that grows up to 6 inches long and has a strong aromatic smell and taste. The thick, hollow stems grow 3 to 6 feet in height, and the plant's leaves are dark green and not unlike the leaves of a celery plant. When bruised, the scent of the leaves of a lovage plant is very similar to celery with an anise undertone.

In the summer, when the seeds ripen, they should be collected. You should later sow the seeds in autumn or very early spring. The lovage plants should last several years if well cared for. And if left to self-seed, lovage should be carefree in coming up by itself.

Cooking with Lovage

The wonderful thing about cooking with lovage is that you can flavor any food with it just as you would flavor with celery. The flavor of lovage is very similar to celery, yet it is much more concentrated. And whereas celery is so hard to cultivate, lovage grows with abandon, which will ultimately make things much easier for you in your garden. Keep in mind that all parts of the lovage plant can be used in cooking, including the roots and seeds. This is somewhat unusual in a plant.

You can blanch and freeze the leaves and stalks of lovage if you have more than you need, or you can dry them to save for later. To save the seeds, cut off the flowering stalks when the seeds are ripe and dry them upside down with a brown paper bag tied over the seed heads. As the seeds dry and fall off, they will gather in the bag and you will not lose them. After the plant has flowered, lovage leaves become a little bitter so be sure to harvest lovage leaves early on in the summer months if you want to use them in your cooking. The roots can be harvested from two- to three-year-old plants in late autumn.

If you use lovage in cooking, always be sure to err on the light side when adding for flavor. The flavor of lovage is very concentrated, therefore a little goes a long way. Add just a pinch at first and carefully taste to see how much more may be needed.

Lovage Seeds

Use the seed like celery seed in soups, stews, sauces, or dressings. Queen Victoria commonly had a hankering for lovage seeds in candied form. They are also good added to breads or meatloaf—adding an unusual flavor to these old-fashioned traditional dishes.

Lovage Leaves

The leaves can be added fresh or dried to salads, soups, or sauces.

Lovage Stems

Young stems can be candied. The celery-like stalks are a welcome addition to soups and stews. They can survive long cooking times without losing flavor. The stems can also make naturally flavored drinking straws that are fun for the whole family to use.

Lovage Roots

The roots are good added to the stockpot, or powdered and used for a seasoning. The roots can also be chopped and dried to use in a tea.

Recipes

Lovage is very versatile. It can be used to flavor tomatoes, potatoes, and rice dishes. It can be tossed into soups, stews, or pasta recipes. Lovage is also good with chicken, in stuffing, or in omelets. And this is a herb that works well in recipes with many other herbs—partnering especially well with such varieties as chives, thyme, and bayleaf.

Here are a few recipes of my favorite ways to use lovage.

Lovage Bloody Mary

1 qt. tomato juice	1 tbsp. Worcestershire sauce
1½ c. vodka	1 tsp. black pepper
1 tbsp. Tobasco sauce	6, 8-inch lovage stalk "straws"
½ c. lime juice	

Combine all ingredients except the lovage in a pitcher and stir well. Pour the mixture over ice in six glasses and garnish with the lovage straws.

Fresh Tomato Lovage Chutney

2 lb. tomatoes, diced	1 c. honey
2 tbsp. peeled, chopped ginger root	2 tsp. dried basil leaves
2 tsp. dried lovage	1½ tsp. salt
½ tsp. ground cloves	

In a medium-sized saucepan, combine all the ingredients. Over medium-high heat, bring to a boil. Reduce heat to low; cook uncovered for about 45 minutes or until thickened, stirring frequently. Put the mixture into hot, sterilized half-pint canning jars, filling to within ¼ inch of the tops. Seal with lids and screw bands. Place the jars on the rack of a canner. Pour in enough boiling water to reach 2 inches above jar tops. Process jars in a boiling water bath for 10 minutes. Using tongs, remove from canner and place on thick cloth or wire rack; cool away from drafts.

After 12 hours, test the lids to make sure they have a proper seal; remove the rings from the sealed jars and store them in a cool, dark place.

Potato Salad with Lovage

2 lb. potatoes, cooked in skins	½ c. mayonnaise
½ c. sour cream	3 tbsp. chopped chives
½ c. chopped fresh parsley	1 tbsp. sugar
½ c. chopped lovage leaves	Salt and pepper to taste

Peel and dice the cooked potatoes. In a small bowl, combine everything except for the potatoes. Gently toss in the potatoes to cover, then season with salt and pepper.

Lovage Vinegar

Wash some fresh lovage and place it in a glass bottle. Cover with a good wine vinegar. Close tightly and let sit for at least a month. Decant into another container, straining it first through cheesecloth. Use in salads, soups, or sauces to add a little zip.

Lovage Tea

Make an infusion as follows. Place 2 or 3 teaspoons of dried lovage in a cup of boiled water. Let the infusion steep for 10 to 15 minutes, then strain the herb away. Drink 2 or 3 time a day for diuretic action and to strengthen the body. People who are either pregnant or infirm should not take this tea because of its strong diuretic action.

Chicken Lovage Soup

2 c. chicken stock	2 tsp. finely chopped lovage
2 c. chopped potatoes	½ c. finely chopped fresh marjoram
2 c. fresh corn kernels	Salt and pepper to taste
2 c. cooked chicken, chopped	

Bring the chicken stock to a boil, add potatoes, cover, and cook until potatoes are barely tender. Add corn and cook for 5 minutes. Stir in the chicken, lovage, and marjoram. Add salt and pepper to taste. Cook at a simmer for about another 10 minutes.

Candied Lovage

American colonists, who could not run to the store to buy candy when they had a sweet tooth, made their own sweet treats out of herbs. They candied young angelica stems and ginger, and also lovage stems and seeds, thus preserving the herbs and bringing out their flavor in a crystal sugar shell. These are wonderful to use as dessert garnishes or as edible decorations on cakes and pastries.

Cookbooks of the 1700s recommended the following process for candying lovage.

1 lb. lovage stalks   1 lb. granulated sugar

The most important thing about candied lovage is to choose stalks that are young and tender. You are only able to candy lovage in April or May when the shoots are new and softly colored. Trim the young shoots into 3- or 4-inch lengths, put them into a pan, cover with water, and bring to a boil. Drain and scrape away tough skin and fibrous threads with a potato peeler, like how you might prepare celery.

Return the lovage to the pan, pour on the fresh boiling water, and cook until green and tender. If the shoots are properly youthful, this process will take 5 minutes or less. Drain the stalks and dry them. Put them into a bowl and sprinkle granulated sugar between layers, allowing 1 pound of sugar for every pound of lovage. Cover and leave for 2 to 3 days. Slide the contents of the bowl into a heavy-duty pan. Slowly bring to a boil and then simmer until the lovage feels perfectly tender and looks clear.

Drain, then roll or toss the shoots on greaseproof paper thickly strewn with sugar, letting the lovage take up as much sugar as will stick to it. Then dry off the lovage—without letting it become hard—in the oven, using the lowest possible temperature. I place the stalks directly on the oven shelves (with trays underneath to catch any falling sugar) and find they need about 3 hours to completely dry. Wrap and store the candied herb after it has cooled completely.

....

LOVELY LAVENDER

by Chandra Moira Beal

Lavender is my favorite herb. It reminds me of my mother, of her lavender steam facials, and of old-fashioned perfumes and hard candies. Lavender can be found growing all over the world—in royal gardens and in the gardens of French chefs. A recent trip to a lavender festival, where a vast array of lavender products was on display, inspired me to think about this herb's wide range of uses.

There are at least 28 distinct varieties of lavender, all of which are used for perfume, cosmetics, potpourri, and flavoring. Lavender is so versatile it can be used in linen drawers, or on the body as an insect repellent. It can be added to a bath, burned as incense, mixed with beverages, and even eaten.

Lavender easily grows in pots or gardens, and you may find the dried petals in most health food stores. Lavender oil is also readily available and generally inexpensive, as are an endless array of lavender perfumes, soaps, and toiletries.

History of Lavender

Lavender comes from the Latin verb *lavare,* which means "to wash." The herb was popular among Romans for use as a bath scent, and it was also used in perfumes in ancient Phoenicia. Solomon used lavender wands to sprinkle holy water and purify the temple.

Lavender has long been treasured for its medicinal qualities as well as its cosmetic applications. It was mentioned in the thirteenth century *Book of the Physicians of Myddvai* as helpful "for the panting and passion of the hart and for them that use to swoune much." Salmon recommended using lavender in his 1710 *Herbal* against "the bitings of mad dogs and other venomous creatures." In fact, lavender is considered a protector of snakes or goddesses with snake totems, and can be used to invoke Hecate and Saturn. Culpeper noted that Mercury rules the herb, and that the herbs carry his effects very potently. He also recommended steeping lavender in wine (see recipe below) to "help them make water that are stopped or are troubled with the wind or colic."

Like Mercury, lavender attracts energy of a high vibrational nature, making it a good tool for meditation and increased awareness. Lavender's scent brings a sense of inner calm, peace of mind, and freedom from stress—all helpful qualities in times of quiet reflection. It can be used as a tonic during times of concentration, such as when studying for extended periods of time. Lavender serves as an aid in visualization and clairvoyance, and can help make magical work more permanent. And finally, lavender can aid in sleep and brings a sense of tranquility to the wearer.

Useful in traditional Midsummer incenses, lavender makes a popular choice in handfasting rituals, and is sometimes used in aphrodisiacs and love spells. It has also been used in childbirth rituals, for welcoming a newborn into the world and encouraging serenity and peaceful awareness in the child.

Cooking with Lavender

Cooking with lavender is somewhat of a lost art. The flowers can be used in appetizers, entrées, and desserts to impart a complex taste that is sweet, herbal, and spicy at the same time. Generally you can use fresh and dried lavender interchangeably in recipes, but fresh lavender is stronger than the dried form. If you are infusing a liquid with lavender, taste it often, and remove the petals when the flavor is strong enough. Too much lavender can be unpleasant.

Try these recipes to start your experiments with lavender:

Lavender Cream

1 tbsp. dried lavender blossoms   1 c. heavy cream

Crush the lavender blossoms to release their scent and mix them into the cream. Cover and chill for three hours. Strain out the blossoms and use in place of regular cream in baking, coffee, or tea.

Lavender Sugar

1 lb. granulated sugar   ½ c. fresh or dried lavender blossoms

Mix the sugar and the lavender and store in an airtight container. Before using, sift out the lavender. The sugar will become more infused with lavender scent the longer it sits. Use in place of plain sugar.

Lavender Honey

2 c. clover honey   ½ c. fresh or dried lavender blossoms

Combine the honey and lavender in a stainless-steel pot and bring to a boil. Remove from heat and let it steep for 30 minutes. Strain out the blossoms and store the leftover honey in a tightly sealed container. This honey can be used in cooking or tea, or even spread on toast or drizzled over fruit.

Lavender Wine

Pick 8 to 10 corollas (the purple blossom) from a fresh sprig of lavender and float them across a glass of chilled white wine. Alternatively, place a whole lavender sprig in the glass. Enjoy.

....

THE STORY OF THE EDIBLE HERBAL FLOWER
by Lynn Smythe

The history of edible flowers can be traced back thousands of years. For instance, capers *(Capparis spinosa)* are the flower buds of a Mediterranean evergreen shrub and have been used as a condiment for more than two thousand years in Europe. Dandelions were one of the bitter herbs referred to in the Old Testament of the Bible. Edible flowers such as daylilies and chrysanthemums have been used by the Chinese and Greeks for centuries.

A Brief Survey of the History of Flower-Eating

The practice of eating flowers has a long and varied history that spans across the globe. The Romans used edible flowers such as mallows, roses, and violets in numerous dishes. The English learned to use edible flowers such as borage and roses through their contact with the Romans. Anglo-Norman cuisine of the thirteenth and fourteenth centuries utilized a variety of edible flowers, including roses, hawthorn blossoms, and elder flowers. Hugh Platt's 1602 book *Delights for Ladies* includes recipes for candying flowers. Violets, cowslips, pinks, roses, and marigolds were used as natural food colorings during the Renaissance. The Portuguese first used the safflower *(Carthamus tinctorius)* in the 1700s as a substitute for the more expensive saffron. Saffron comes from the dried stigmas of the crocus flower *(Crocus sativus)* and is very expensive to produce. It takes approximately 4,000 flowers to make one ounce of saffron. Necessity is the mother of a lot of food innovation.

Europeans continued to use edible flowers after colonizing the New World. Colonists arriving in America from Europe brought with them the seeds of a variety of plants to grow in their gardens. Among the seeds were a number of edible flowers, including pot marigold and dandelions, that were used for making candied flowers, flower jelly, flower wine, salads, and syrups.

Native Americans have used a variety of flowers in their cooking throughout the years. American colonists were exposed to the uses of these plants and their flowers through contact with various tribes. Among the flowers used by Native peoples are cattails *(Typha latifolia),* century plant *(Agave americana),* bee balm

(Monarda didyma), red clover *(Trifolium pretense)*, yucca *(Yucca spp.)*, and squash blossoms *(Cucurbita spp.)*.

Edible flowers were very popular during the Victorian era (1837 to 1890), especially in salads. The Victorians added a variety of items to their salads, including violets, borage, primroses, gilly flowers (clove pinks), and nasturtiums. Many of these flowers could also be pickled for storage during the winter months when fresh flowers were not available. Victorians also candied violets and other flowers to garnish baked goods such as wedding cakes. After the Victorian era, the use of edible flowers fell out of favor for a time.

But in the past 10 or 12 years there has been a resurgence of interest in and use of edible flowers as part of the organic health food movement. Upscale restaurants and home cooks are now using edible flowers in their recipes, and magazines such as *Country Living* and *Gourmet* have featured edible flower recipes in recent issues.

Modern-Day Uses of Edible Flowers

You probably have already consumed a number of edible flowers without even realizing it. When you consume cauliflower and broccoli you are eating the unopened flower bud of the plant *Cynara scolymus*. The flower receptacles of Carolina thistle *(Calina acaulis)* can be used as a substitute for artichoke hearts. Cloves *(Syzgium aromaticum)* are the dried, unopened flower buds of an evergreen tree from the myrtle family.

Cloves are commonly used to flavor baked goods and holiday hams. Saffron *(Crocus sativus)*, which was also used in medieval European cooking, is currently used to impart a regal color and subtle flavor to rice and other dishes. Do not confuse the edible saffron crocus with the poisonous autumn crocus *(Colchicum autumnale)*.

This article will inform the budding chef and history buff about some of the more interesting flowers and flower petals that can be safely used for consumption.

Obtaining Edible Flowers

Flowers obtained from nursery and garden centers and florists are probably not safe to eat. The flowers you use must be free from any harmful chemicals such as are found in many commercially applied pesticides and fertilizers. You should always only eat organically grown flowers.

Check out your local health food store and farmers' market to see if they offer edible flowers for sale. Flowers intended for consumption should only be purchased from businesses that label their produce regarding whether they are organic and free of chemical pesticides and fertilizers.

Another option would be to grow your own organically raised flowers, or to obtain them from a friend who has an organic garden.

Safety Precautions for Today's Flowers

Always make sure you know what you are eating. Do not begin to use flowers in your cooking unless you are positive of their identification. Consult a good reference book for a comprehensive list of edible flowers. It can get tricky. For instance, day lilies *(Hemerocallis species)* are edible, while other lilies *(Asiatic, Oriental)* are not. The flowers from garden peas are edible; however, sweet pea flowers *(Lathyrus spp.)* are not edible. Tuberous begonia flowers are edible; however, wax begonia flowers *(Begonia semperflorens)* are not safe to consume.

Make sure you know the Latin name of the flower you want to consume. Many plants share the same common name, but the Latin name is unique for each plant.

Moderation and thoughtfulness are key. Something as mild as lettuce can cause you to have an upset stomach if eaten in abnormally large quantities. If you are interested in incorporating edible flowers into your cuisine, first start off with small amounts to see how your body handles them.

Perform a taste test. Even if a flower is edible and your digestion can handle them without any problems, you may not like the taste of certain flowers. Taste a few before adding them to any of your recipes to be certain you will enjoy the flavor.

Avoid harvesting edible flowers from the side of the road. They may be contaminated from harmful vehicle emissions.

Do not harvest flowers from the wild unless you have permission from the landowner and are absolutely certain of their identification.

Certain flowers in the composite family (chamomile, chrysanthemum, daisies, sunflowers) should be avoided by people with asthma, allergies, and hay fever problems. The presence of large amounts of pollen on these types of flowers may produce an allergic reaction in sensitive individuals.

The following edible flower varieties should be approached with caution. I probably wouldn't eat them because they are not 100 percent safe to consume. There are so many other safe choices when choosing edible flowers, why take chances?

Apple blossoms *(Pyrus malus):* May contain cyanide precursors.

Bachelor buttons *(Centurea cyanus):* Some references say these are edible, while others say they are not.

Linden *(Tilia spp.):* Frequent consumption of linden flower tea may cause heart damage.

Snapdragons *(Antirrhinum majus):* As with bachelor buttons, some references claim these are safe to eat but others do not.

Sweet woodruff *(Galium odoraturm):* These flowers may have a blood-thinning effect if eaten in large quantities.

Tulips *(Tulipa spp.):* These flowers may cause certain people to develop a rash or upset stomach.

Types of Edible Flowers

Most culinary herbs produce edible flowers. They usually taste like a milder version of the herb; that is, rosemary flowers have a lighter tasting herb flavor than do the leaves. Some of the more palatable herbs with edible flowers include the following: basil *(Ocimum spp.)*, borage *(Borago officinalis)*, chervil *(Anthriscus cerefolium)*, cilantro *(Coriandrum sativum)*, common chives *(Allium schoenoprasum)*, dandelion *(Taraxacum officinalis)*, dill *(Anethum graveolens)*, English lavender *(Lavandula angustifolia)*, fennel *(Foeniculum vulgare)*, garlic chives *(Allium tuberosum)*, hyssop *(Hyssopus officinalis)*, lovage *(Levisticum officinale)*, lemon verbena *(Aloysia triphylla)*, marjoram *(Origanum majorana)*, Mexican tarragon *(Tagetes lucida)*, mint *(Mentha spp.)*, oregano *(Origanum vulgare)*, rosemary *(Rosmarinus spp.)*, common sage *(Salvia officinalis)*, society garlic *(Tulbaghia violacea)*, summer savory *(Satureja hortensis)*, thyme *(Thymus spp.)*, and winter savory *(Satureja montana)*.

Many vegetables and fruits also produce edible flowers. When you harvest the flower of many of these fruits and vegetables, you sacrifice the blossom that would have turned into the fruit or vegetable. In some cases the plant would have produced more fruits or vegetables than you could normally use, so sacrificing a few flowers should not adversely affect your harvest. Here are some examples of fruits and vegetables which have edible flowers: arugula *(Eruca vesicaria satvia)*, chicory *(Cichorium intybus)*, garden peas *(Pisum spp.)*, lemon flowers *(Citrus limon)*, mustard *(Brassica spp.)*, okra *(Abelmoschus aesculentus)*, orange flowers *(Citrus sinensis)*, pineapple guava *(Feijoa sellowiana)*, radish *(Raphanus sativus)*, runner bean *(Phaseolus coccineus)*, squash blossoms *(Curchubita spp.)*, and strawberry *(Fragaria ananassa)*.

Many ornamental flowers are also edible. Here is a brief listing of some of the specimens that are safe to consume: bee balm *(Monarda didyma)*, garland chrysanthemum *(Chrysanthemum coronarium)*, cowslips *(Primula veris)*, day lilies *(Hemerocallis spp.)*, English daisy *(Bellis perennis)*, evening primrose *(Oenothera biennis)*, fuchsia *(Fuchsia arborescens)*, gardenia *(Gardenia jasminoides)*, hibiscus *(Hibiscus rosa-sinensis)*, hollyhock *(Alcea rosea)*, jasmine *(Jasminum sambac)*, Johnny jump-ups *(Viola tricolor)*, lilac *(Syringa vulgaris)*, mallows *(Malvia spp.)*, moss rose *(Portulaca grandiflora)*, nasturtium *(Trapaeolum majus)*, pansy *(Viola wittrockiana)*, pot marigold *(Calendula officinalis)*, redbud *(Cercis canadensis)*, rose *(Rosa spp.)*, signet marigold *(Tagetes signata)*, and sweet violets *(Violet odorata)*.

Some Particularly Tasty Flowers

The following flowers have particularly marked or distinctive flavors that you can work into your regular dishes if you choose. A little experimentation goes a long way.

Anise hyssop *(Agastache foeniculum)*: Mild licorice or root beer flavor

Clove pinks *(Dianthus caryophyllus)*: Sweet clove flavor

Dame's rocket *(Hesperis matrolnalis):* Mild lettuce flavor

Japanese honeysuckle *(Lonicera japonica):* Sweet
honey flavor

Lavender *(Lavandula spp.):* A lemony perfume flavor

Redbud *(Cercis Canadensis):* A tart apple flavor

Rose of Sharon *(Hibiscus syriacus):* Sweet and mild flavor

Sweet violet *(Viola odorata):* Sweet and perfumed in flavor

Tuberous begonia *(Begonia x tuberhybrida):* A tangy
citrus flavor

Yucca *(Yucca spp.):* A delicately sweet flavor

Preparing and Storing Flowers

As a general rule, you should use only the flower petals of edible flowers. Certain flowers such as violets, pansies, and Johnny
jump-ups, however, can be consumed whole. Here are a few rules
to live by in using your own flowers.

Pick flowers early in the morning after the dew has dried
on them or in the early evening. Flowers that are picked during the heat of midday will quickly wilt or dry out before you
have a chance to use them.

Remove pistils and stamens, and gently remove any residual
pollen with a soft brush. Also remove the sepals unless using
pansies, violas, and Johnny jump-ups—in which case you will
want to consume the sepals along with the rest of the flowers.

Remove the white heel present at the base of some flowers'
petals, such as chrysanthemums, daisies, marigolds, pinks, roses,
and tulips. This heel imparts a bitter flavor to the petals.

Gently wash the flowers if any dirt or bugs are present.

Pat the flowers dry with a paper towel or use a salad spinner to remove any excess water.

Use the flowers immediately or store them in one of two ways:

Place the flowers in a plastic bag or other airtight plastic container, along with one or two moist paper towels, and store them in the vegetable bin of your refrigerator.

Flowers with longer stems can be placed in a bowl or vase of water, which can then be placed in the refrigerator.

The General Culinary Uses of Flowers

Among the various uses for flowers, below I've listed a number of possible recipes so you can enjoy this unusual culinary treat in the following: salads, both fruit and green salad; hot or iced teas; baked goods, such as cakes, cookies, and muffins; jams and jellies; vinegars, oils, and butters; ice cubes and punches; and soups and sauces.

Edible Flowers in Salads

My husband (aka Mr. Meat and Potatoes) has eaten a variety of edible flowers in salads that I prepare from organic ingredients picked from our garden. This is true testimony to the natural appeal of flowers. To make a salad, hold off adding any dressing until you are ready to eat the salad. Otherwise the acids from vinegar and lemon juice may affect the color of certain flowers.

1 to 2 tomatoes, chopped

Various mixed greens (lettuce, spinach, kale, etc.)

1 to 2 orange or yellow sweet peppers

A handful of edible flower petals

Various herbs (both the leaves and flowers). Try basil, thyme, and Mexican tarragon to start.

Add the first three ingredients to a large bowl, and toss to mix well. Sprinkle the petals of the edible flowers and herbs on top of the salad prior to serving. My favorite flowers to use in green salads are borage, calendula, chives, garlic chives, and nasturtium. When using chive and garlic chive flowers be sure to pull apart the individual florets prior to adding them to your salad or other dishes.

Floral Tea Blends

One of my favorite store-bought tea blends includes cactus flowers, sunflower petals, and blue bottle flowers among its ingredients. Certain edible flowers can be dried to preserve for later use such as in your own tea blends.

To preserve flowers and flower petals for later use, pick bunches of flowers in the early morning. Gently rinse the flowers in water to remove any dirt or insects that may be present. Pat the flowers dry with paper towels. Place the flowers still attached to their stems in a bundle and secure them with a rubber band.

Hang these bundles upside down and store them in a dark, well-ventilated area. For best results, dry one type of flower per bundle. When the flowers are dry, the individual flower petals may be removed from their stems and stored in an airtight glass container away from direct sunlight. I like to make up a mixture of herbs and flower petals chosen from the lists below. I like to use 1 teaspoon dried tea blend or 3 teaspoons fresh herbs or flowers infused in 1 cup boiling water. Let the tea steep for 5 to 10 minutes, then strain and pour into a cup. Sweeten with honey or sugar if you desire. I sometimes add dried stevia leaves to the tea blend. *Stevia rebaudiana* is a natural, low-calorie sweetener I have growing in my garden.

Harvest these flowers for use in tea: cowslip *(Primula veris)*, elder *(Sambucus nigra)*, English lavender *(Lavandula angustifolia)*, florist's chrysanthemum *(Chrysanthemum morifolium)*, German chamomile *(Matricaria recutita)*, hibiscus *(Hibiscus rose-sinesis)*, hollyhock *(Alcea rosea)*, Arabian jasmine *(Jasminum sambac)*, pot marigold *(Calendula officnalis)*, rose *(Rosa spp.)*, and sunflower *(Helianthus annuus)*.

Harvest these flowers and their leaves for use in tea: basil *(Ocimum spp.)*, bee balm *(Monarda didyma)*, clary sage *(Salvia sclaera)*, hyssop *(Hyssopus officinalis)*, Korean mint *(Agastache rugosa)*, lemon balm *(Melissa officinalis)*, mint *(Mentha spp.)*, pineapple sage *(Salvia elegans)*, roselle *(Hibiscus sabdariffa)*, and scented geraniums *(Pelargonium spp.)*.

Floral Ice Cubes

For a very clever and wholly artistic way to use edible flowers, place a whole flower (such as borage, Johnny jump-ups, sweet violets, scented geraniums), or flower petals (such as daisy, nasturtium, roses) in the bottom of an ice cube tray. Fill the tray halfway with water and freeze overnight.

Remove the tray from the freezer and fill to the top with water. Return the tray to the freezer until the entire ice cube tray has been frozen. These floral delights can be used in iced teas and lemonades or floated on the top of punch bowls to impart a festive touch to any occasion.

Other Flower Recipes

Edible flowers can be incorporated into a variety of conventional culinary creations. Get creative and try adding edible flowers to your favorite recipes. I have included a few of my personal favorites to help get you started.

Garlic Cheese Biscuits

1¾ c. sifted all-purpose flour

½ tsp. salt

3 tsp. baking powder

6 tbsp. chilled butter

1 c. milk

2 tbsp. minced garlic chive leaves

1 tbsp. minced garlic chive flowers

⅓ c. shredded cheddar cheese

¼ c. melted butter

Preheat your oven to 450 degrees F. Sift the flour, salt, and baking powder into a large mixing bowl. Add the chilled butter and cut into the dry ingredients using a pastry blender or two knives until it has the appearance of coarse corn meal. Add the milk, garlic chive leaves, garlic chive flowers, and cheddar cheese. Mix until well blended. Form the dough into 12 balls. Roll each ball in melted butter and place in a muffin pan. Place the pan in the oven and cook for 12 to 15 minutes or until the biscuits are lightly browned.

Roasted Rosemary Potatoes

6 flowering rosemary sprigs
  (each around 4 inches)

⅓ c. olive oil

6 large baking potatoes

Finely chop the rosemary leaves and flowers after removing them from the tough, woody stems. Peel, wash, and cut the potatoes into ¼ inch slices. Brush the bottom of a large baking dish with some of the olive oil. Place a layer of potatoes on the bottom of the dish, brush the potatoes with olive oil, and sprinkle with salt, pepper, and part of the rosemary. Continue layering the potatoes, olive oil, and seasonings until all of the potatoes have been used up. A 9½ x 13 inch pan will hold three layers of potatoes. Bake in a 400 degree F oven for 60 to 75 minutes. For even browning of the potatoes, remove the pan from the oven after 30 minutes and flip the potatoes with a spatula. Return the pan to the oven and continue baking.

I like my potatoes on the crispy side so I leave them in for a bit longer. If you like more moist, less-crispy potatoes, take the dish out after an hour.

Floral Icing

4 oz. cream cheese, room temperature

2 tbsp. pineapple juice

2 c. powdered sugar

2 tbsp. pineapple sage flowers, finely chopped

Place the softened cream cheese into a mixing bowl. Mix in pineapple juice and stir until well blended. Sift the powdered sugar into another bowl. Gradually add the sifted powdered sugar into the cream cheese and juice mix. When the desired consistency has been reached, stir in the pineapple sage flowers. This icing can be served on top of your favorite cake (angel food, pound, and so on). The cake can then be garnished with candied flower petals for a truly festive look. (See below for more details).

Other Uses of Edible Flowers

Edible flowers can be used to add a creative touch to a variety of beverage and food dishes. They work great as garnishes on your dinner plate or floating in a bowl of your favorite soup.

Candied Flowers

Candied flowers look elegant garnishing a variety of items such as fruit salads, pudding, and wedding cakes. Prepare the flowers as mentioned in the preparation and storage section above. Candy the flowers using one of two methods.

Method one: Brush the petals of the flowers with beaten egg while using a very small artist's paint brush and sprinkle with fine granulated sugar.

Method two: Mix ¼ cup of corn syrup with 1 teaspoon of vanilla, almond, or peppermint extract. Brush the petals and flowers with this mixture using an artist's paint brush. Sprinkle them with powdered sugar.

With either method you may want to use a pair of tweezers to help you hold onto the flowers and petals. Place the candied flowers and flower petals on a wire rack that has been covered with waxed paper to try for a day or two. If you are not using the candied flowers right away, you can store them for up to two months in the refrigerator or in the freezer for up to six months. Place them in an airtight container in single layers with a piece of waxed paper between each layer. Don't place more than three layers of candied flowers per container. The following flowers work especially well for candying, as they have the best taste and appearance: borage, clove pink, cowslip, Johnny jump-up, lavender, lilac, pansy, rose, scented geranium, and sweet violet.

Chocolate Flowers

1 c. edible flowers and flower petals	1 c. chopped pecans
1, 12 oz. package semisweet chocolate chips	Powdered sugar
1, 14 oz. can sweetened condensed milk	

Lightly spray a muffin pan with nonstick cooking spray. Evenly distribute the edible flowers and flower petals among the 12 muffin cups of a muffin pan. Melt the chocolate chips and sweetened condensed milk in a double-boiler. Remove the chocolate mixture from the stove and stir in the chopped pecans.

Cover the flowers by dividing the chocolate mixture among the muffin cups. Let them chill until the chocolate has hardened. Remove the chocolate flowers from the muffin tin and cut each one into four pieces. Place the chocolates onto a platter and sprinkle them with sifted powdered sugar.

Floral Spreads

Add two to three tablespoons of fresh chopped flower petals into one cup of any of the following: butter, cheese spreads, cream cheese, mayonnaise, sour cream, or yogurt.

Mix well and use these spreads as you normally would on top of toast, bagels, crackers, fruits, vegetables, and so on.

Edible Flower Uses in Ethnic Cooking

Many Hispanic culinary creations utilize hibiscus flowers, linden flowers, coral-tree flowers, and squash blossoms as staple ingredients. These flowers are used in a variety of dishes such as squash blossom soup and hibiscus flower water. Canned squash blossoms are even available from one of the major Mexican food distributors. Squash blossoms are also chopped, sautéed, and served in tortillas.

The flowers of **mock lime** *(Aglaia odorata),* which is also known as Chinese perfume plant, are used to scent Chinese tea. Mock lime flowers have a pleasant vanilla scent when they are dried. The flowers of the neem tree *(Azadirachta indica),* meanwhile, are used along with its leaves ot make a tasty tea in India. These flowers' sweet jasmine-like scent are utilized in chutney and other recipes.

Dried **daylily** flowers (also known as golden needles) are used in Chinese hot and sour soup. Its fresh petals and flower buds are used in stir fries in Asian cuisine. They have a fresh taste similar to asparagus or green beans. The flowers of gardenia *(Gardenia augusta),* meanwhile, are used to flavor Chinese tea.

Garland chrysanthemum *(Chrysanthemum coronarium)* is a traditional oriental chop suey ingredient with dainty orange-yellow flowers. The flowers' bright yellow petals, which have a flavor similar to the leaves (spicy and aromatic), can be sprinkled on top of salads, rice dishes, and stir-fries.

In Scotland, the dried flower heads of **heather** *(Calluna vulgaris)* are mixed with other herbs such as blackberry leaves, wild thyme, and wild strawberry leaves and brewed to create what is called Moorland tea.

Rose water, made from rose petals, is a popular flavoring in Indian, Middle Eastern, and Chinese cooking. Turkish delight is a Persian confection that includes rose water.

Winged beans *(Psophocarpus tetragonolobus),* also known as gao beans, have been cultivated in Asia and India for centuries. The flowers are edible and used in numerous dishes.

Water lily *(Nymphea odorata)* flower buds are very fragrant, and they appear in oriental cooking both pickled or cooked as a vegetable.

The flower buds of the **wax gourd** *(Benincasa hispada)* are used in Chinese cooking, both steamed and stir-fried.

The flowers and leaves of **wasabi** *(Wasabia japonica)* are used to make wasabi-zuke, a type of Japanese pickle.

SAGE: THE WISE HERB

by Magenta Griffith

Sage, a shrubby perennial herb of the mint family, is native to the Mediterranean region. Sage can be grown in most climates or anywhere in a pot on a windowsill, and it is now found all over the world. The plants grow to a height of about two feet and generally do not bloom until the second season.

Sage grows well in many parts of the United States and is grown to a limited extent for commercial markets as well. Sage leaves are silver- or gray-green with a fuzzy texture, but there are newer varieties that come in different colors. They have a slightly bitter flavor and a distinctive aroma.

The botanical name for sage is *Salvia officinalis.*

Culinary sage is related to various ornamental salvia varieties, such as scarlet sage, *Salvia splendens.* There are hundreds of species of salvia, but only a handful are used in cooking. Most varieties are ornamental. Culinary varieties include golden garden sage *(Salvia officinalis icterina),* which has green and gold irregularly variegated leaves. Purple garden sage *(Salvia officinalis purpurea)* has dark-purple new leaves that turn a soft green with age. Tricolor sage *(Salvia officinalis tricolor)* is cream, green, and pink. Dwarf garden sage *(Salvia officinalis minum)* grows well in a container. All of these have basically the same flavor as garden sage. The golden and tricolor sages can be less winter-hardy than the common garden sage.

A sweeter variety, pineapple sage *(Salvia elegans,* also called honey melon sage), has a more delicate flavor and can't stand up to long cooking at high temperatures. Add to salads or to cut-up fruit to serve as an appetizer. Pineapple sage has oils that are released at very low temperatures, and it will lose its flavor if cooked for a long time or at sustained high temperatures.

By the way, prairie sage, used by Native Americans as a purifying smudge, is a different species of plant, *Artemisia ludovicana*. The smell is very similar to European sage, so early settlers assumed it was a related plant. It is actually more closely related to wormwood *(Artemisia absinthium)*, mugwort *(Artemisia vulgaris)*, and tarragon *(Artemisia dracunculus)*. Prairie sage is not suitable for cooking, as its flavor is bitter.

Growing Sage

Sage can be grown from seeds, stem cuttings, or by dividing an existing plant. Sow the seed indoors six to eight weeks before the last spring frost, and transplant the young plants when they are two to three inches high. Sage starts from seed fairly easily; however, plants grown from seed are generally of mixed types. For this reason, cuttings made from desirable plants are often preferred. Sage needs to receive at least six hours of sunlight each day to develop its full flavor.

Sage needs well-drained soil to discourage slugs and rot. If your soil drains poorly, add organic materials like compost. Mulching can also help the soil. The mulch should be about three inches deep and pulled slightly away from the stem of the plant. Sage can attract both spider mites and aphids. Usually, beneficial insects will counteract the problem, although it is unfortunate that the first pesky bug must establish itself for the helpful bug to arrive.

Spraying with water should be the first method of insect control. Hose off the plants several times each week. If you need stronger measures, use a horticultural soap and follow directions on the label precisely. Encourage good air circulation to prevent mildew and heat problems. If your soil is healthy, you probably won't need to worry about how acid or alkaline it is. If your soil is very acidic, a little lime will help sage grow well.

A few plants set in a corner of the garden or in a perennial flower of herb bed will furnish sufficient leaves for ordinary family use. Six to eight inches of the top growth can be cut from the plant about twice during the season. Never cut farther down the stem than where there are leaves. Harvest before late fall since late harvesting can cause the plant to die over the winter.

Using Sage

For drying large amounts of sage leaves, cut the flowers before they bloom and wait until the plants have grown back. Otherwise the leaves could be harvested before the plant blooms. If possible, wash the plants in the garden with a fine spray of water the night before. Cut in the morning, as soon as the dew has dried. You can pick the individual leaves and spread them on screens to dry in a well-ventilated room away from direct sunlight.

When completely dry, pack them in an airtight container. If you cut whole stems, cut them as long as possible without cutting into old wood. Hang these in bunches of three or four in a dark, dry area. As soon as they are dry and crisp, strip the leaves whole, if possible, and seal them in an airtight container. The flavor should remain potent for three or four months.

Freshly picked sage can be woven into wreaths. Once dried, these can be hung in a room to keep the air fresh and smelling sweet. The individual leaves can be plucked off and used, as long as you keep the wreath clean and away from contamination. If you hang a sage wreath too near a stove, cooking grease can condense on it.

Sage is sold as fresh sprigs or dried leaves. Store fresh sage in the refrigerator, wrapped in paper towels and enclosed in a plastic bag. Fresh sage leaves should be aromatic, with no soft spots or dry edges. Use them within five days. Fresh leaves may also be covered in olive oil and stored in the refrigerator for up to two months. Use the flavored oil for sautéing or in salad dressing. To freeze fresh sage leaves, wash and dry them, removing leaves from the stems. Pack them loosely in freezer bags. These will keep for up to one year. Freezing will intensify the flavor of the herb so adjust recipes accordingly.

Dried sage can be found with other seasonings in most supermarkets. As with all dried herbs, store closed containers in a cool, dry place away from light. It will keep for up to one year.

Dried sage can be found with other seasonings in most supermarkets. As with all dried herbs, store closed containers in a cool, dry place away from light. It will keep for up to one year.

Dried sage is preferred by most cooks and comes in whole leaf, rubbed, and ground form. Rubbed sage has a light, velvety texture; ground sage is a powder. Crush dried sage leaves in the palm of the hand to release their flavor. Use ground sage sparingly, as foods absorb its flavor more quickly than leaf sage. Chopped leaves can be used to flavor salads, pickles, and cheese. It is one of the most popular herbs in the United States.

The country that most often uses sage is Italy, where the most common use is to flavor meat and poultry dishes. Veal, which is sometimes thought bland, can profit a lot from this herb. Saltimbocca alla Romana is probably the most famous sage dish. Very thin veal steaks are fried together with raw, salt-cured ham *(prociutto crudo)* and fresh sage leaves and then deglazed with red or white wine.

Sage leaves fried in butter until the butter turns brown make an easy and interesting, but not exactly light, sauce to be eaten with Italian pasta or gnocchi, a form of tiny dumpling.

Sage is a very powerful flavor and tends to dominate. Its slightly bitter taste is complex and strong and not appreciated by everyone. Use sage cautiously, as it can easily overpower other flavors. Because of its strong taste, sage does not combine well with weakly aromatic or delicate herbs. Sage is the primary herb in poultry seasoning. It is sometimes combined with other strong flavors, such as garlic and green pepper, for seasoning barbecued or fried meat.

Besides the traditional use in stuffing, sage is good with pork, sausage, other meats, and cheese. It is often combined with thyme and used with beans and in soups. Use sage with fruit in vinegars. The bluish-purple flowers of garden sage make an attractive garnish in salads, butters, and soft cheeses. You can also freeze sage leaves in ice cubes for an attractive garnish to add to fruit drinks.

Hamburgers can be seasoned with a blend of freshly chopped or dried sage, mint, rosemary, oregano, and basil. Sage can be used to flavor paté, eggs, pasta, sauces, soups, beef stews, and vegetables. It holds up well for long cooking, such as a turkey or a soup. It adds depth to the flavor.

When you add fresh sage to dishes, such as soup or beans, you can put in a whole sage branch, then remove it when the dish has finished cooking. The leaves cook off; you can pull the branch out with tongs or a slotted spoon.

Sage is a wonderful flavor enhancer for seafood, vegetables, breadsticks, cornbreads, muffins, and other savory breads. Rub sage, cracked pepper, and garlic into pork tenderloin or chops before cooking. Use the leaves sparingly with onion for stuffing pork, ducks, or geese. Crush fresh leaves to blend with cottage or cream cheese. Potatoes can also be boiled with a bit of sage. Here are a few recipes that use sage.

Sage Stuffing for Turkey

3 tbsp. oil

2 onions, finely chopped

4 stalks celery, finely chopped

1 apple, peeled, cored, and finely chopped

1 tsp. dried thyme

1 tsp. black pepper

1 tbsp. dried sage

1 tsp. salt or celery salt

6 c. cubed dried bread

In a large frying pan, sauté the onions in the oil until transparent. Add the celery and sauté until no longer crisp. Add the apple and herbs and sauté for another minute. Turn off the heat and add the bread. Mix thoroughly. This should stuff a 15-pound turkey.

Wild Rice Poultry Stuffing

1 c. wild rice, uncooked

2 tbsp. butter

1 large onion, chopped

3 to 4 stalks celery, finely chopped

½ lb. mushrooms, chopped

1 tsp. dried thyme

1 to 2 tsp. dried sage

Salt and pepper to taste

Soak the wild rice in 2 cups of water for 1 hour. Drain, add 2 cups of water and simmer until done, about 30 to 45 minutes. In a large frying pan, melt the butter. Add the onions, sauté about 5 minutes, then add celery and mushrooms and sauté another 5 minutes. Drain rice and add to vegetable mixture with seasonings. This will stuff a 12-pound turkey.

Slow Cooker Pork Roast

3 to 4 lb. pork loin roast

1 onion, cut into eighths

1 apple, peeled, cored, and chopped

4 large potatoes, peeled and cut into quarters

2 carrots, each cut into 2 or 3 large pieces

1 c. cider

¼ tsp. pepper

1 tsp. dried sage

1 tsp. dried thyme

1 tsp. salt

Place pork roast into a slow cooker. Surround it with onion and apple pieces, then potatoes and carrots. Pour cider in and add sage, thyme, and pepper. Cook on high setting about 6 hours. Check for doneness; pork should not have any pink in the middle. Serve it on a platter surrounded by potatoes and carrots. You can serve the cooking broth as is or make gravy from it.

Homemade Breakfast Sausage

1 lb. ground pork

½ tsp. salt

½ tsp. pepper

2 tsp. rubbed fresh sage

½ tsp. poultry seasoning

1 pinch ground allspice

Thoroughly combine all ingredients and shape into 6 patties. Chill at least 1 hour. Fry for 3 to 4 minutes per side or until the sausage patties are browned and no longer pink in the center.

Easy Onion and Herb Focaccia

1 load frozen bread dough, thawed

1 tbsp. olive oil

2 tsp. chopped fresh rosemary
   or ½ tsp. dried rosemary

1 tbsp. chopped onion

2 tsp. chopped fresh sage
   or 1 tsp. dried sage leaves

Heat oven to 425 degrees F. Grease a cookie sheet or 12-inch pizza pan. Roll out dough and place it on the pan. Press down dough into a circle moving from center to edge. Brush with oil. Sprinkle with remaining ingredients. Bake 10 to 12 minutes or until golden brown. Cut into wedges and serve warm or cool.

Savory Corn Bread

1 c. cornmeal	1 c. flour
4 tsp. baking powder	1 egg
1 tsp. dried sage	1 c. milk
¼ tsp. salt	1 c. oil

Mix the dry ingredients, then add the egg, milk, and oil, and stir just enough to mix. Bake in a greased 8 × 8 pan for 20 to 25 minutes at 350 degrees F or until slightly browned on top.

Sage Beauty

Sage has also been used as a beauty aid. Early Greeks drank, applied, or bathed in sage tea. Turkish women said sage was a wonderful hair dye, and it is still recommended today for use in dark hair. Put a handful of the leaves in a cup of cold water, boil it for 15 minutes; cool, strain, and use the tea as a rinse to darken faded or graying hair.

Sage was a sacred ceremonial herb of the Romans and was associated with immortality or, at least, longevity. It was also said to increase mental capacity. The Greek Theophrasutus classified sage as a "coronary Herbe," because it flushed disease from the body, easing any undue strain on the heart. The genus name, *Salvia*, comes from the Latin for "salvation."

Charlemagne had it grown in his royal gardens. There is an old Arabic belief that if your sage grows well you will live a long time. The early Dutch ate a handful of the leaves every day as a snack, a salad, or one course of a meal, because of its nutritive value. During the fourteenth century, three leaves a day were to be eaten to avoid the "evil aire" all day long. As far as medicinal uses, herbalists used sage for just about every complaint there was. Mrs. Leyel, a British herbalist, thought that it was particularly good for the lungs and brain.

In the Middle Ages, people drank sage in tea and used sage to treat colds, fevers, liver trouble, epilepsy, memory loss, and eye problems. It has also been used for aches, seasickness, sterility, nerves, coughs, hemorrhoids, snakebites, worms, palsy, ulcers, fever, hypertension, hoarseness, lethargy, measles, diabetes, cramps, and insomnia. Sage is considered useful in alleviating hot flashes associated with menopause.

Throughout French history sage was considered a major medical herb, primarily because of its antibacterial properties. Sage was held to be a preventative medication because its disinfectant properties cleansed the inner body of germs and diseases. Early in the eighteenth century, the strong-smelling herb was used to disguise the rancid flavor of putrefying meat when there was no other way of keeping meat fresh. Lewis Spence reported that sage was a favorite of Hungarian gypsies; they believed that it attracted good and dispelled evil.

The Chinese value sage for its healing properties. Sage tea was and still is primarily used as a gargle for sore throat and as an aid to digestion. A sage tea can be made by steeping one teaspoon of dried sage in one cup of hot water for about 10 minutes.

The origin of the word "sage" is itself somewhat unclear. Sage most likely came to Middle English as *sauge,* from Old French, and before that from Latin, *salvia,* or "healthy." Other dictionaries state that salvia means "saved," in allusion to the herb's reputed healing virtues.

No one knows for certain if there is any relationship between the meaning of "sage" as a healthy or saving herb and the meaning of sage as "wise."

No matter what the origin of the word, sage is a very useful herb to be used wisely.

....

COOKING WITH SOUTHWESTERN HERBS

by Chandra Moira Beal

The idea of Southwestern cooking conjures up all sorts of exciting, exotic flavors—fiery chilies, fragrant spices, smoky peppers, sweet corn, and earthy beans. But it's the regional herbs that bring these dishes to life, adding simple but flavorful aromas and tastes to the meal and flecking the plate with vibrant color. Fresh herbs balance the otherwise hot and spicy cooking with cool, green vegetable flavors. From the refreshing and cooling cilantro to the bitter estafiate, Southwestern cooking is incomplete without the addition of herbs.

Defining the Southwest

The regions of the Southwest include California, Arizona, New Mexico, Colorado, and Texas—although growing seasons, cultures, and cooking customs overlap geographical borders. Many recipes evolved from Native American tribal cooking and from Mexico where the influences of the Mayan, Aztec, and Spanish cultures are prominent. The herbs that grow wild and abundantly in these areas make frequent appearances in the region's recipes, in recipes ranging from kitchen staples to medicinal teas.

The typical Southwest climate is arid and dry with plenty of sunshine and mild winters, but there is a lot of variation. Texas along has five gardening zones, and Colorado winters are anything but mild.

Southwestern herbs typically don't need overly rich soil, just dirt that is loose and porous and drains well. They tolerate arid conditions and thrive in rocky, sandy limestone terrain. These herbs require at least six hours of sunshine a day, which is why they're ideal for growing in the southwest. Many will appreciate a few hours of afternoon shade. They do tend to need plenty of water, and mulching can help retain moisture in the intensive summer heat.

Many of these herbs will grow in the northern states if they're given plenty of sun and protection from the cold during winter. If you live in an area that freezes regularly, container gardens are a great way to enjoy these herbs year round. Just plant them in pots that can be moved indoors as soon as the temperatures drop.

Most Southwestern herbs do well grown from seeds or transplanted from rooted cuttings. These herbs can be grown in window boxes, old wine barrels, clay or wooden containers, pots on patios, and along walkways—making them versatile, easy, and convenient for all.

Using Southwestern Herbs
Cilantro (Coriandum sativum)

Cilantro is one of the most popular herbs in Southwestern cuisine. Its cool, refreshing leaves balance the fiery chilies that are ubiquitous in many regional recipes. The refreshing, bittersweet pungency of cilantro is what gives it its unique flavor profile. There is no substitute for cilantro's flavor, and it should always be used in its fresh form. Some people have an aversion to the strong aroma and slightly soapy taste of this herb, but most people love it.

Cilantro seeds are known as coriander, and they have a mellow, citrus-like flavor that is not interchangeable with the fresh leaves. Cilantro is to Southwest cooking what parsley is to meals in other regions of America. You may see it garnishing an entrée, find it floating atop soup, stuffed inside tacos, sprinkled over guacamole, or tossed in a salad. Cilantro is readily available in most supermarkets, typically sold in generous, inexpensive bundles.

Cilantro is an annual that likes loose, rich, well-drained soil and full sunlight. Sow the seeds in the fall about a half an inch deep, then spread the seedlings one foot apart. It will tolerate freezing temperatures and frost and thrives in the garden in the cooler months. This herb will grow about two feet high and one and a half feet wide, but the leaves are best used when the plant is about six inches high. The leaves become spindly and lacy as the flowers appear, detracting nutrients and flavor form the robust leaves.

Cilantro's leaves are flat and green, resembling Italian parsley. When rubbed between the fingers, they produce a strong, pungent aroma. Cilantro doesn't dry well and loses its flavor quickly, so always use it fresh. You can store a fresh bunch in the refrigerator with the stems in a jar of water loosely covered with a plastic bag.

CILANTRO SEASONED POTATOES

Use a combination of red, white, Yukon gold, and purple potatoes in this dish for a colorful blend of flavors.

This can be served hot as a side dish or at room temperature as an appetizer sprinkled with shredded Parmesan cheese and red chili powder.

2 lb. potatoes, washed and quartered	1 bunch green onions with tops, chopped
2 tbsp. butter	1 c. fresh cilantro, loosely chopped
3 tbsp. olive oil	1 tbsp. chili powder
4 cloves garlic, crushed or finely diced	Salt and pepper to taste
4 tbsp. fresh lime juice	½ c. shredded Parmesan cheese
2 tsp. coriander seeds, freshly ground	

Cover the potatoes with cold, salted water and bring to a boil. Reduce heat and simmer about 12 minutes, but do not overcook. Meanwhile, melt the butter in a small saucepan with the olive oil, garlic, lime juice, and coriander. Drain the potatoes and toss them gently with the butter, adding the onions, cilantro, chili powder, salt, and pepper.

Serve warm or at room temperature, generously sprinkled with chili powder and Parmesan cheese. If chili powder isn't available, you may use paprika combined with cayenne pepper as a substitute.

Epazote (Chenopodium ambrosioides)

Epazote is tenacious herb that grows like a weed and is able to withstand less than optimum growing conditions. The name comes from the Nahuatl Indian words *epatl* and *tzotl* meaning "an animal with a rank odor." Some describe epazote's potent aroma as similar to turpentine, but don't let that discourage you from employing it in your cooking. This pungent and minty herb is hugely popular in recipes from southern and central Mexico. For centuries, Mexican mothers have steeped it in milk and sugar to rid children of intestinal parasites, but it also help prevent the socially embarrassing consequences of eating beans, especially black beans. Add a couple sprigs of the fresh herb to the bean pot during the last 15 minutes to reap its benefits.

Epazote thrives along sunny streambeds with some afternoon shade, but does well in poor soil and full sun, even growing out of cracks in the sidewalk. The serrated leaves resemble a goose's foot. Sow the seeds in the fall, then thin the seedlings to about one foot apart. Epazote will grow into a shrub about three feet high and two feet wide and will reseed itself once it is established. It can be downright invasive, so pinch the seed heads back in the early fall or it will take over the garden.

Frijoles Negros en Olla

1 lb. dried black beans	1 bay leaf
Water or broth to cover the beans	1 to 2 whole ancho chilies
3 tbsp. olive oil	Salt to taste
1 onion, quartered and studded with 2 whole cloves	1 tsp. dried oregano
	3 large sprigs fresh epazote
4 to 6 garlic cloves, crushed or diced	
½ tsp. cumin	

Wash the beans well, place in a cook pot, and cover with cold water or broth two inches over the beans. Add oil, onion, garlic, cumin, and a bay leaf. Bring to a boil. Immediately reduce the heat to a simmer and cover. Add chilies and cook 2½ hours. If necessary, add hot water to prevent the beans from bursting.

When the beans are almost tender and cooked through, add the salt, oregano, and epazote. Uncover and cook another 15 minutes.

Serve with green onions, cilantro, sour cream, lime wedges, or salsa.

Estafiate (Artemisia ludoviciana)

Estafiate is a willowy plant with downy silver foliage belonging to the wormwood family. It has a sharp, bitter taste that acts as a tonic and aperitif.

Estafiate doesn't show up as a central ingredient in recipes very often, but makes a nice medicinal tea traditionally used to treat stomach ailments. Simply steep the leaves in hot water and sip. Add half a teaspoon of the chopped leaves to rich sauces and gravies to deglaze the pan. Estafiate's sharp, bitter flavor contrasts well with sweeter sauces based on lingonberries or currants and served with wild game.

Estafiate is an annual that grows straight and tall. It tolerates dry, arid conditions and, like most herbs, enjoys well-drained soil and a sunny location. The stems have a reddish color that are tipped with blossoms of 10 to 12 small red and yellow flowers.

The festive color of estafiate makes it pretty in the garden as background to brighter colored plants and a good choice for dried wreaths. The leaves make an attractive garnish on the plate.

Hoja Santa (Piper auritum)

Hoja santa is a semi-woody shrub with a large, velvety heart-shaped leaves. It grows into a multibranching bush shaped like an umbrella. This plant is sometimes called a "root beer plant," because when you rub the leaves they release a musky scent similar to sarsaparilla.

The generously sized leaves make great edible wrappers for shredded pork or a sauté of onions, squash, corn, and tomatoes. You can also tear up the leaves to use in tamale fillings, dried shrimp and fish dishes, and mole sauce. Remove the stems and the center veins before chopping or tearing the leaves with your hands. Hoja santa can be added to black beans toward the end of the cooking for a flavorful kick. Use half of a small leaf in the bean pot.

Hoja santa enjoys full sun with some afternoon shade and rich, well-drained soil. It can be watered daily. When mature, Hoja santa produces long, white, cylindrical flowers in the summer that have a slightly rough texture. Oil glands form gelatinous balls on the underside of the leaves. Hoja santa spreads like bamboo with underground linear roots. It dies back in freezing weather but new shoots will appear each spring.

MOLE VERDE WITH HOJA SANTA

2 c. unhulled, raw pumpkin seeds

2 c. chicken or beef broth

6 oz. tomatillos, husks removed, rinsed, and coarsely chopped

6 large sorrel leaves, rinsed, stems removed, and coarsely chopped

¼ c. vegetable oil for frying

4 leaves hoja santa, stems and veins removed, coarsely chopped

8 large sprigs epazote, 5 coarsely chopped, 3 whole

4 jalapeno or 6 Serrano chilies, coarsely chopped

Toast the pumpkin seeds in an ungreased pan, turning them over and shaking the pan from time to time to prevent them from burning. Set the seeds aside to cool and then grind them in a coffee grinder or food processor to a fine powder.

Pour 1½ cups of the broth in the blender, gradually adding the tomatillos, sorrel, hoja santa, chopped epazote, and chilies blending as smooth as possible.

Heat the oil in a flameproof casserole (in which you are going to serve the mole) and fry the blended ingredients, stirring and scraping the bottom of the pan to prevent sticking; cook for about 25 minutes. Add the rest of the epazote.

Stir ½ cup of the broth into the pumpkin seed powder until you have a smooth consistency, and gradually stir into the cooked ingredients. Continue cooking over low heat, stirring constantly for 10 more minutes. Take care that the pumpkin seed mixture does not form into lumps; if this happens, put the sauce back into the blender and blend until smooth. Add any remaining broth and salt to taste. If the sauce is too thick, add a little water to dilute.

Serve mole sauce over enchiladas, eggs, or any bean and rice dishes.

Mexican Mint Marigold (Tagetes lucida)

Mexican mint marigold grows throughout Central and Southern Mexico and is sometimes known as *hierba da las nubes* or "cloud plant." The Tarahumara Indians of Chihuahua and the Huichol tribes of Jalisco favored this herb and used it in religious rituals. The Aztecs purportedly used ground Mexican mint marigold as numbing powder. They blew it into the faces of sacrificial victims before their hearts were plucked out.

Mexican mint marigold features strongly anise-scented leaves that enliven salads, fish, and game dishes. It is sometimes called "Texas tarragon" and can be used as a substitute in recipes that call for tarragon. Mexican mint marigold has a less assertive or fiery flavor, making it superb in vinaigrettes. Traditional uses also include cooking the herb with boiled green corn or chayote squash. It makes a delicious tea all by itself; steep a large handful in a teapot for six or seven minutes.

Cheerful, bright golden flowers appear on Mexican mint marigold in the fall. A perennial, it likes loose, well-draining soil and full sunlight. Plant cuttings by rooting them first in water, then putting them in the ground in early spring, spaced one foot or more apart.

The shrub will grow one to two feet tall and can be invasive, reseeding itself in the fall. Glossy, lance-shaped leaves with serrated edges give Mexican mint marigold a distinct, striking look in the garden.

Mexican Mint Marigold Vinaigrette

This tangy golden dressing is particularly tasty over leafy green and pasta salads or as a marinade for grilled meats or potato salad.

½ c. Mexican mint marigold vinegar

White wine or apple cider vinegar

1 egg yolk

1 large clove garlic, minced

2½ tsp. Dijon mustard

½ tsp. ground pepper

1 tsp. honey

1 tbsp. chopped Mexican mint marigold

½ c. olive oil

First, make a mint marigold vinegar by filling a glass jar half full with fresh Mexican mint marigold, stems removed. Then cover with white wine or apple cider vinegar and allow to steep overnight. Strain and use.

The next day, blend the egg yolk, garlic, mustard, pepper, and honey with a fork. Add the vinegar and chopped fresh herbs. Mix well. Slowly whisk in the oil. Makes about 1 cup.

Mexican Oregano (Poliomintha longiflora)

Mexican oregano has smaller, paler leaves than the common Italian oregano, but packs more aroma and taste with a spicy, peppery flavor, making it a good complement to the spicy foods of the Southwest. Oregano comes from the Greek words *oro* ("mountain") and *ganos* ("joy"). Mexican oregano makes a zesty condiment when steeped in red wine vinegar and used in a marinade. You can also add sprigs to hot coals before grilling steaks, or toss a handful into a pot of beans.

Mexican oregano is an attractive perennial with glossy, highly aromatic leaves protruding from woody branches. The leaves are oval and slightly fuzzy on the underside. Abundant tubular flowers blossom in the spring and summer in a riot of pink and violet. It tolerates arid, dry conditions and is freeze-hardy. This oregano likes loose, sandy, well-drained soil and some shade. When mature it reaches a height of up to 24 inches.

OREGANO PESTO

4 to 6 cloves garlic	½ tsp. lime zest
2 c. loosely packed oregano	1 tsp. fresh lime juice
1 cup fresh parsley	1 to 2 Serrano peppers, seeded, finely chopped
½ c. pine nuts	½ c. olive oil
½ c. Parmesan cheese, grated	

Chop the garlic, oregano, parsley, nuts, and cheese in a food processor or blender. Add the lime zest, juice, and chilies. Slowly add the oil until it forms a thick, green paste.

Serve tossed with pasta, melted over steamed squash, or spread on a baguette. This pesto freezes well, so you can enjoy the fresh taste all winter.

Yerba Buena (Mentha sp.)

Yerba Buena, literally the "good herb," has been used by people of the Southwest for centuries as a soothing tea for stomachache, headache, and the pains of childbirth. When brewed with cinnamon, clove, and nutmeg, it's a time-honored cure for *la cruda*, a hangover. Yerba Buena is also good in tomato-based soups. Its flavor is similar to spearmint, but the leaves are smaller and darker green.

Yerba Buena is a perennial creeper, frequently rooting along the stems and making an attractive ground cover or shady border. Yerba Buena grows well in rich, moist but well-drained soil in partial shade. It produces tubular white or lavender flowers from April to August. Plant it somewhere where you will often brush against it, such as on a garden path, to give off a lovely minty fragrance.

Yerba Buena Tea

Add fresh or dried leaves to boiling water and let steep for a deliciously soft, minty tea.

Sage (Salvia officinalis)

Sage comes in dozens of varieties and is the quintessential Southwestern herb. Its grayish-green leaves are highly aromatic. This perennial grows into a three-foot-tall shrub with woody stems. Sage likes full sunlight and loose, sandy, alkaline soil. It does well in a climate with lots of heat and humidity; just don't overwater it as it's prone to root rot.

It is essential to give sage good drainage. Growing a small plant in a clay pot is ideal as the clay will warm in the sun and help keep the roots dry. Sage also starts well as a transplant or can be grown from root cuttings. If grown in an area with mild winters, sage will bear leaves year round. If it dies back in a freeze, it will perk back up in the spring.

SKILLET CORN BREAD WITH SAGE AND PEPPER

1½ c. cornmeal	1 egg
½ c. white flour	1 tbsp. honey or molasses
½ tsp. salt	3 heaping tbsp. fresh sage, chopped
3 tsp. baking powder	2 tbsp. green onions, chopped
½ tsp. chili powder	2 tbsp. grated Parmesan cheese
½ tsp. white pepper	2 slices bacon, optional
1 tsp. paprika	½ c. oil
1½ c. buttermilk	

Preheat the oven to 425 degrees F. In a medium-sized bowl, mix the cornmeal, flour, salt, baking powder, chili powder, pepper, and paprika. Blend with a fork. In a separate small bowl, mix the buttermilk, egg, and honey or molasses until combined, then mix into the dry ingredients. Add the sage, onions, Parmesan cheese, and bacon. In a skillet, heat the oil to near smoking and pour it into the cornmeal mixture. Immediately pour the whole mixture back into the skillet and bake 20 to 25 minutes until golden brown.

More Recipes
Using Southwestern Herbs
Quesitos (Little Cheese Balls)

1 log of goat cheese	Mexican mint marigold flower petals
Chopped fresh Mexican oregano	Chopped fresh epazote
Chopped yerba buena	Crushed ancho chilies
Chopped fresh Mexican mint marigold	

Cut the goat cheese log into half-inch slices and roll the slices into bite-size balls. Roll the cheese balls in the mixture of herbs. These can be made early in the day and will keep well in the refrigerator. Serve on a tray with bunches of red and green grapes.

Pescado con Hoja Santa

6 redfish or red snapper fillets	6 tbsp. butter
1 tbsp. Spicy Seasoning (see below)	6 large hoja santa leaves
1 orange, thinly sliced	6 sprigs Mexican mint marigold
3 green onions with tops, chopped	

Spicy Seasoning

½ tsp. whole black peppercorns	½ tsp. cinnamon
½ tsp. whole allspice berries	½ tsp. cayenne
1 tsp. whole coriander seeds	1 tsp. paprika
½ tsp. whole cloves	1 tsp. thyme
1 tsp. oregano	

Grind the whole spices into a powder and mix in the dried herbs.

Creole Sauce

3 tbsp. oil	1 medium green bell pepper, chopped
1 medium onion, chopped	1 tbsp. Spicy Seasoning (see above)
4 to 6 cloves garlic, minced	1 tsp. brown sugar
2 celery stalks, chopped	1 c. broth
3 bay leaves	4 large tomatoes, peeled, seeded, and chopped
2 Serrano or jalapeno peppers, chopped	

Heat the oil in a large skillet and sauté the onion, garlic, and celery for about 5 minutes. Add the bay leaves and peppers. Continue to sauté until vegetables are slightly tender (about 3 minutes). Add the Spicy Seasoning, sugar, and broth. Bring to a boil, then reduce the heat and simmer 5 minutes. Add tomatoes and simmer another 10 minutes. Sauce should be thick. Remove bay leaves. Add salt and pepper to taste.

Preheat the oven to 400 degrees F. Brush both sides of the fish fillets with melted butter and sprinkle with Spicy Seasoning. Place each fillet on a hoja santa leaf, cover with ⅓ cup Creole Sauce, 2 thin orange slices, a sprig of marigold, some chopped green onions, and roll up tightly inside the leaf. Place seam-side down in an oiled baking dish. Bake 15 minutes. Pour remaining sauce over the top and serve with black beans and rice.

Leftover Creole Sauce is good on eggs and in omelets.

....

HERBAL TREATS
BEAT THE SUMMER HEAT
by Elizabeth Barrette

Among their many powers, herbs can help us maintain harmony with our environment. The most flexible are "adaptogens," which help the body adjust to different challenges. Especially relevant are "refrigerants," which lower body temperature, impart a cold sensation, or otherwise make hot weather seem less oppressive. Cold foods and beverages, particularly made with the right herbs, can improve comfort while providing a nutritious, culinary pleasure. Here are some herbs with cooling properties:

Anise has a sweet, fresh smell similar to licorice; a popular flavor in candies and cookies. Used sparingly, it soothes digestion.

Basil has a spicy-sweet smell and goes with almost everything. It reduces fever and headaches.

Borage stands out with its hairy leaves and blue, star-shaped flowers. It has a faint cucumber flavor. Borage also eases dry coughs and lowers fever.

Catmint has a mellower smell and taste than catnip. It soothes headaches and reduces fever. Add tender leaves to salads.

Catnip is intoxicating to felines, but relaxing to humans. It relieves nausea and promotes restful sleep. It makes an excellent tea.

Celery is juicy and refreshing. It helps keep the body hydrated. Chop stalks and add to salads, cheese spreads, etc., for a crunchy texture.

Chamomile smells like fresh-mown hay warmed by the sun. Use it to prevent nightmares and bring peaceful sleep. Chamomile makes delicious tea.

Cilantro has a pungent, spicy character. Chop its feathery leaves for use in sauces, sandwiches, and taco toppings.

Coconut has a mellow, sweet flavor and fragrance that creates a tropical mood. Coconut milk, coconut cream, and shredded coconut are soothing and cheering. Use liberally in desserts.

Coriander is the dried seed of cilantro plants and has a mild spicy flavor. It aids digestion and reduces flatulence among other things.

Cucumber refreshes and rehydrates. Its crisp flavor makes it a favorite in salads, but it is also delicious in beverages.

Cumin is among the cooling herbs in Ayurvedic tradition. Its strong flavor adds interest to mild herbal dishes.

Dandelion may be the most widely available herb. Use tender young leaves in salads. The flowers make dandelion wine.

Dill has a tangy flavor, stronger in the seeds and milder in the feathery leaves. It reduces stomach pains and hiccups. Use in pickles and dips.

Echinacea is best known for strengthening the immune system, but has broader normalizing effects on the body. It reduces fever and allergies.

Fennel has a mild licorice flavor with a greener note. Chew the seeds to aid digestion. Leaves may be added to salads or dips. Bronze fennel adds a red hue to herbal vinegar.

Ginseng increases the body's efficiency. American ginseng is more relaxing than oriental varieties. Use in tea and desserts when appropriate.

Hibiscus lends a rich tangy flavor to tea. It helps cool the body. The flowers make a lovely edible garnish.

Lavender has a sweet-sharp, musky fragrance. It soothes anxiety and relieves flatulence and halitosis. The flowers flavor tea, jelly, cream, vinegar, and desserts.

Lemon is famed for its intensely sour, bright flavor and fragrance. It adds zest to salad, tea, dessert, and dishes of all kinds. Lemon uplifts the spirit and stimulates thirst.

Lemon balm is both lemony and minty. Use in tea or candy the leaves.

Lemongrass has a subtle grassy-citrus flavor. Relieves diarrhea and stomachache.

Licorice appears most often in candied form, with its dark, spicy taste. It reduces allergies and asthma among other things.

Lime belongs to the citrus family, with a greener flavor. It relieves anxiety and depression. Use in tea or desserts.

Linden is sometimes called limeflower, though it is not citrus. Its flowers and honey have a light, sweet quality that make them ideal for tea and desserts.

Peppermint is more cooling than spearmint, with a mellower, bluish taste. It soothes and refreshes. Use in tea and desserts.

Raspberry leaves have cooling and antispasmodic properties. Tea made from them tastes similar to green tea. Sweet, juicy raspberry fruit stars in many summer jams, ice creams, and other desserts.

Rose needs an intense, sweet scent to function as an herb. It revives and rejuvenates. Candy the petals and use the hips in tea or jelly.

Saffron has a mellow, nutty-spicy flavor. It lowers fever and stimulates the libido among other things.

Sarsaparilla is rich and spicy with a faint medicinal taste. Its cooling properties make it popular in tea and soda.

Sorrel starts out bland in spring, but summer heat gives it a sharp tangy bite. It quenches thirst and reduces fever. Use in salads, soups, and sauces.

Spearmint has a sharper, greener taste than peppermint. It cools and invigorates. Use in tea and glazes, especially with meat.

Thyme comes in many flavors, such as musky and nutty; it also mimics herbs like caraway and lemon. It reduces indigestion and flatulence. Use in spreads and vinegars.

Watercress has a crisp, pungent flavor. Use in salads or soups. It also makes a great bed for serving other things, such as cheese spread.

Wintergreen has a strong minty-medicinal flavor. Its leaves and berries are good for toothpaste and tea.

Edible herbal flowers: angelica, bergamot, calendula, carnation, chicory, chrysanthemum, clover, daylily, dianthus, elderflower, jasmine, lemon, marjoram, nasturtium, pansy, primrose, sage, viola, violet.

Freezing Herbs

One good way to preserve herbs is to freeze them. Frozen herbs may be added directly to soups, stews, or sauces. For uncooked foods, first defrost and drain the herbs.

Herbs with tough stems and leaves should be separated before freezing. Pick off leaves and brush them clean. Don't wash them; too much water dilutes flavor. Spread leaves on a cookie sheet, and place in freezer overnight. Then transfer to freezer cartons or bags for storage.

Delicate herbs like fennel or thyme may be frozen as sprigs. Snip off pieces of uniform length and shake gently to clean. Pack them in layers in a freezer carton to prevent crushing.

You don't have to freeze whole herbs. They can be chopped, then frozen in ice cube trays or other small containers. You can also purée juicy herbs such as basil or cilantro. Mince in a food processor and slowly add olive oil to form a paste. Freeze the paste in ice cube or popsicle trays.

Take this opportunity to combine herbs that you use together. Some excellent cooling blends include basil, Italian parsley, and thyme; dill, mint, and lemon balm; peppermint, spearmint, and wintergreen; dill and fennel; catmint and lavender.

Ice Cream and Sorbets

The food that most symbolizes summer is ice cream and its luscious relatives. Ice cream uses heavy cream as a base often with eggs added. Though usually sweet, it can be savory, and is the richest of frozen desserts. Sherbet is moderate, using milk mixed with fruit or juice. Sorbet is lighter, made from water or fruit juice blended with puréed fruit. Granita is a delicate fluff of ice crystals flavored with fruit or fruit purée. Herbs lend their flavor to sweet and savory frozen treats.

Basil Ice Cream

Pour 1 cup milk into saucepan and simmer until bubbly. Remove from heat; add 1 cup fresh basil leaves and 1 teaspoon coriander. Allow to sit for a half hour. Run mixture through a food processor until smooth. Strain and discard solids, then set basil mixture aside. Combine 1 cup milk, 2 cups whipping cream, and ½ cup sugar; cook in saucepan over medium heat until bubbly, stirring constantly. Remove from heat. Beat together 7 egg yolks and ½ cup sugar, then add to hot mixture, stirring constantly. Stir in basil mixture. Cook over medium heat, stirring constantly, until mixture thickens enough to coat a spoon (about 5 to 7 minutes). Allow to cool, then freeze in ice cream maker per manufacturer's directions. Garnish with sprigs of fresh basil and serve.

MINTY MELON SHERBET

In a small saucepan, add 1 teaspoon lime gelatin to ¼ cup water; wait 1 minute. Then add 2 tablespoons coarsely chopped mint leaves, 2 tablespoons light corn syrup, and ⅓ cup sugar. Cook over low heat until gelatin dissolves, then remove pan from heat. Cover and let stand for at least 1 hour. Strain out the mint leaves and discard them. In a metal-bladed blender or food processor, purée together 1 cup honeydew melon cubes and 1 cup cucumber cubes. Stir purée into the mint mixture; then stir in 1 cup milk. Freeze in ice cream maker. Garnish with sprigs of fresh or candied mint and serve.

ROSE-COCONUT SORBET

In saucepan, combine 1 cup sugar and 1½ cups water. Stir over medium heat until sugar dissolves, then bring to a boil for 5 minutes. Remove pan from heat. Carefully stir in ½ cup coconut cream and 2½ cups fresh red or pink rose petals. Allow to cool for 2 hours. Strain syrup to remove petals, then add a dash of lemon juice. Freeze in an ice cream maker. Garnish with candied rose petals, shredded coconut, and/or rose syrup.

WONDERFUL LEMONBERRY GRANITA

In a saucepan, combine ½ cup sugar and 1½ cups water; bring to a boil. Reduce heat; simmer until sugar is fully dissolved. Stir in 1 cup fresh red raspberries and 1 cup fresh yellow raspberries.

Allow to cool. Run through a food processor until smooth. Strain and discard solids. Stir 2½ tablespoons lemon juice into raspberry mixture. Pour into a shallow metal pan and cover. Freeze for 1 hour, then scrape crystals away from pan edge. Freeze again, scraping and stirring the ice as it forms, until granita is completely crystallized. Serve immediately. Garnish with raspberries, lemon slices, or fresh or candied lemon balm leaves.

Toppings

In summer, you don't want to cook any more than necessary. Herbs perk up cold foods to make them more exciting. Herbal vinegars and salad dressings are the perfect complement for a bowl of tossed greens. Syrups and glazes accent ice cream or fruit. Butter and cheese spreads go well with crackers or bread.

Better Butter

To 8 ounces soft butter, add 2 tablespoons chopped cilantro, 1 tablespoon caraway-flavored thyme, ½ teaspoon cumin. Beat herbs into butter. Add 1 tablespoon lemon juice, and salt to taste; mix until smooth. Pack into butter mold or dish; chill before serving.

Changeable Cheese Spread

In a bowl, stir together 16 ounces cream cheese (softened) and 8 ounces small-curd cottage cheese. Add a blend of chopped fresh herbs, such as 1 tablespoon each of lemon thyme and dill; 2 tablespoons celery, 1 tablespoon cilantro; or 1 tablespoon English thyme, 1 teaspoon coriander, 1 clove garlic. Serve on a bed of watercress or stuff into edible flowers such as daylily or hibiscus.

Elegant Vinaigrette

Combine 3 tablespoons olive oil and 1 tablespoon cider vinegar in a clear glass jar; shake well. Add one clove garlic (crushed) and a dash of salt; shake. Add fresh chopped herbs: 1 tablespoon thyme, 1 tablespoon basil, 2 teaspoons fennel, 1 teaspoon coriander. Shake well, then let it sit for a half hour. Shake again before serving.

Ginseng-Mint Glaze

In a small saucepan, combine ⅔ cup water, 2 tablespoons clover honey, 2 teaspoons cornstarch, and mix well. Add ⅛ cup each of fresh spearmint and peppermint, and a 1-inch piece ginseng root. Boil over medium heat, stirring constantly, until mixture begins to thicken. Cool for 10 minutes. Use slotted spoon to remove leaves and root. Stir in 2 tablespoons lime juice. Chill 1 hour, then drizzle over fresh fruit and serve.

Herbal Vinegar

Gently warm (do not boil) 3 cups white cider vinegar. Into a glass bottle, put 6 sprigs of bruised herbs, such as borage, cilantro, dill; spearmint and catmint with coriander seed; rose petals, violet petals, and lavender; dill, lemon thyme, and nasturtium. Allow vinegar to cool, then cover and store in a cool, dark place.

Many Lemon Sauce

In a saucepan, heat ¾ cup sugar and 4 tablespoons water until syrupy. Add 1 tablespoon each of lemon balm and lemongrass. Cook for five minutes, then remove leaves. Add 2 tablespoons butter, juice of 1 lemon, and a pinch of salt. Stirring constantly, cook until syrup reaches desired consistency.

Beverages

Drinking soda—or worse yet, alcohol—will not keep you cool and hydrated in summer. For that, drink water. Herbal tea is also a good choice, especially when made with cooling herbs. Herb/fruit blends also work well. Sweeten minimally or enjoy plain.

Moon Tea

A magical version of "cold infusion" is Moon Tea. For this you need 1 cup of fresh herbs (not tightly packed) and 1 quart room-temperature water. You may also add a slice of fresh lemon or dried licorice root. Place the herbs in a clear glass container where moonlight can reach it for a mystical touch. Let the herbs steep overnight, and drink your Moon Tea the next day.

Berry Good Tea

Fill a muslin tea satchet with 5 tablespoons rose hips, 4 tablespoons hibiscus flowers, 3 tablespoons blackberry leaves, 1 tablespoon raspberries. Prepare as Moon Tea. Uplifting and refreshing, this is a good breakfast drink.

Citrus Sipper

In a saucepan, combine 1 tablespoon chopped lemon balm, juice of 1 lemon, ¼ cup lime juice, 2 tablespoons sugar, 2 cups water. Heat and stir until sugar dissolves. Cool at least 3 hours, then strain. Makes two 1-cup servings. This sprightly tea stimulates thirst and cheers the spirit.

Cool Head Tea

Combine in a mug ½ teaspoon each of dried chamomile flowers, dried linden flowers, fresh lavender flowers, and fresh catnip flowers. Add 1 cup boiling water, cover, and steep for 5 minutes. Strain and drink. This soothing tea calms mind and body.

Doublemint Fizz

Start with 4 tablespoons spearmint and 4 tablespoons peppermint. Add the juice of 2 lemons and set aside. Combine 2 tablespoons sugar and ½ cup water in a small saucepan; heat until sugar dissolves. Cool and put in a glass jar; then add the herbal mixture. Allow to steep overnight in refrigerator. Strain out the herbs. Add 2 quarts of ginger ale, pour over ice, and serve.

Desert Cooler

Blend 2 teaspoons dried hibiscus flowers and 1 teaspoon dried mint. Add 2 cups boiling water, cover, and steep for 5 minutes. Strain out and discard herbs. Add dash of roseflower water or rose syrup to taste. Divide into two 1-cup servings and drink. This exotic floral tea refreshes and hydrates.

Garnishes

Finally, use herbs to dress up special summer dishes. Parsley is fine, but sprigs of any cooling herb work as accents—consider frilly cilantro, dill, spearmint, the striking color of golden lemon thyme. Robust lavender stems make pretty stirrers in drinks. Some herbs, such as watercress, make an excellent bed for serving fish, fruit, or other foods.

For a decorative touch in beverages, freeze edible flowers or herb leaves into ice cubes. Choose single leaves or flowers that fit into the holes of an ice cube tray: lemon balm, spearmint, borage flowers, and violas are idea. Gently shake them clean. Place one item into each space, fill the tray with water, and freeze overnight. If items floating on the water is a problem, try filling the tray just halfway; freeze for half an hour to an hour, then fill the rest of the way and return to the freezer. For a spectacular effect in punch bowls, lay sprigs of herbs and edible flowers in a ring mold, fill with water, and freeze to make a colorful ice ring.

Candied herbs or edible flowers have a delicious "frosted" look. Some herbs are famous for this: borage flowers, peppermint, rose petals, spearmint, and violets. Use them to garnish cakes, ice cream sundaes, fruit salads, beverages, etc. Pick leaves or flowers on a sunny day and brush clean. Separate one egg white and beat until it starts to stiffen. Dip items in egg white, or paint the egg on with a pastry brush. Hold each item over a small bowl of sugar and sprinkle sugar over it until fully coated. Place sugared items on a sheet of waxed paper and place on a wire rack. Bake at 225 degrees F until dry and crisp. Store in airtight container.

....

AFRO-CARIBBEAN GREENS
by Stephanie Rose Bird

Greens are a highly sought after soul food beloved in Jamaica as Callaloo, and in the United States where collards, mustard, and turnip tops are simply called "greens." Numerous healthy recipes abound in the Motherland itself for various leafy greens as well. This article explores the phytonutrients contained in greens, and ways of growing, preparing, and using greens that are easy enough for everyone to try.

One reason people often reserve greens—collard, mustard, and turnip, or even spinach and kale—for special occasions is the challenge of cleaning them. I remember my grandmother and mom soaking them overnight in the bathtub or sink. While following in their footsteps, I also found that soaking your greens in the sink and adding vinegar to the water accelerates the cleaning process—no more overnight soaking. For those craving convenience, more and more shops carry precleaned and chopped greens and spinach.

A Historical Healing Connection

Understanding gods, goddesses, angels, and nature spirits can help us understand a great deal about cultures and their healing ways in connection to foods. Practitioners of Ifa, a faith with origins in Nigeria, believe a variety of orishas (deities) populate the world. Today, there is popular discussion and appreciation of about a dozen orishas; however, there are at least six hundred.

A curious orisha every herbalist should know is Osayin, the patron of the herbal arts. Unlike most orishas, whose birth is of orisha parents, Osayin sprang forth from the womb of Mother Earth herself like a seedling. He stayed hidden within the forests and learned all there is to know about plants. Still, Osayin was the servant of Ifa, and, as such, he taught herbalism to Ifa and those knowledgeable of that particular path.

These days we would call this orisha physically challenged. He is called lame, as he has one arm, a very large ear that does not hear at all, and a tiny ear that hears extraordinarily well. This orisha has a high-pitched voice that is so irritating it is difficult to listen. Osaying is one-eyed and misshapen, according to griots who teach us through oral tradition. This complex orisha shows us what can become of greed and admonishes against hoarding our gifts. In modern language, his story is a cautionary tale to herbalists who become intoxicated with power, retaining it rather than sharing.

We know Osayin as the African Green Man, Yoruban orisha of herbal medicines of the forest, and patron of herbalists—known as curandeiros by the African-Brazilian people. Green is the color of health and healing in nature. Thanks to the chlorophyll that makes plants green, they are able to use the sun's energy to generate food through photosynthesis, a process that converts carbon dioxide and water into carbohydrates while releasing oxygen. Our Green Man, Osayin, is orisha of wild crafted herbs, berries, flowers, bark, and wood. One of the chief orishas, his presence has always captivated my imagination.

According to the griots, Osayin collected all the medicinal herbs of the forest as well as the knowledge of how to use them. As spiritual herbalist, he tucked all of his botanicals and knowledge in a guiro, or calabash. There were numerous other orishas with helpful characteristics to the business of the world, but Osayin wanted to keep the knowledge of herbs out of their reach—high up in a tree, hidden in a calabash.

Oya, orisha of weather and changes, generated a huge wind, followed by a storm that knocked the calabash of herbal knowledge down to earth. She did this with the blessing of numerous orishas who desired that herbal wisdom. In the Americas and Caribbean, a path influenced by Ifa called *Regla de Ocha* (Rule of the Orisha), Osayin is represented by the *guiro* (gourd) that hangs in the *Santería ile* (house temple). Tribute needs to be paid to Osayin before his herbal medicine can be used in ceremony, spells, and cures. Osayin's symbols include the gourd where his spirit resides and a twisted tree branch, as well as his color—green. In Catholicism, St. Benito, St. Jerome, and St. Joseph represent his spirit.

As herbalists, we celebrate the magic held within the calabash, but we also realize that this earth wisdom should be available to all—this is the lesson of Osayin and the calabash. With no choice left, Osayin's calabash of herbal information, recipes, rituals, and ceremonies for health and spiritual well-being is now open to all. If you dare to look deep within the calabash, who knows what knowledge might be waiting inside?

Osayin's Green Bounty

While the family Cucurbitacea and calabash tree fruit brings Osayin's calabash immediately to mind, there are few other precious gifts that are of him as well. These soul foods include greens. Green is Osayin's color and also represents the verdant essence of Mother Earth. Osayin's array of greens represents fertility, vitality, and health. Greens also instill these traits in us, building our resistance to illness and strengthening our entire body system.

In West Africa the preferred green is called bitterleaf, which is washed to remove its bitter taste. Cassava leaves are enjoyed, as are ewedu, red sorrel, yakuwa, lansun, and pumpkin leaves. Jamaica has made callaloo a much-loved vegetable and seafood stew featuring their unique greens called, variously, dasheen, Chinese spinach, taro tops, or callaloo bush. In Africa and the diaspora, beet tops, kale, and spinach are some other vegetable greens enjoyed. Here is a recipe for callaloo:

Callaloo

1 lb. callaloo leaves
   (can substitute spinach)
4 slices thick-cut,
   naturally cured bacon
1 medium Vidalia onion
3 cloves garlic, minced
¼ c. fresh thyme
1 tsp. sea salt

1 tsp. ground peppercorns
32 oz. organic free-range
   chicken stock
8 oz. crab meat
4 oz. coconut milk
1 c. young okra
Hot sauce to taste

Wash callaloo or spinach well. Chop and set aside. Cut bacon into ½ inch squares. Chop onion finely. Add bacon to Dutch oven or heavy-bottomed saucepan over medium-high heat. Fry for about 4 minutes. Add the onion and sauté until translucent. Mince the garlic. Wash, pat dry, then chop the thyme. Add thyme to pan, along with salt and pepper; cook another 3 to 4 minutes. Add the chicken broth. Allow this to deglaze the pan, then cover and cook on medium low for 10 minutes. Add the crab, coconut milk, and okra. Cook another 10 minutes. Check seasonings; add hot sauce if desired.

New Image for a New Age

When once people thought greens, such as collard, mustard, and turnip (tops), were a lowly food, now people all around the world celebrate the nutrient-rich gift of Osayin's greens. Greens are especially high in lutein, chlorophyll, and antioxidants. Lutein is the main antioxidant that helps the eyes. Greens are showing promise as a deterrent for macular degeneration. This ailment consists of a deterioration of the sensitive central region of the retina, which weakens the field of vision. The green vegetables with the highest concentration of lutein, in order, are kale, collard greens, and spinach.

Collard, mustard, and turnip greens need not to be overcooked or fatty to be tasty. The soul food we enjoy is packed with antioxidant vitamins and minerals—especially wholesome when not overwhelmed by animal fat. In Asian cuisine, such as Thai, collards and other greens are stir-fried and they are delicious, showing there is no real need to cook the greens until they are dull and lifeless. Try your leafy vegetables (collard, mustard, and turnip greens) seasonsed with apple cider vinegar, or sautéed in olive or palm oil with onion and cayenne. If you want to cook them more in accord with tradition, which amounts to stewed greens, by all means drink the broth (pot liquor) for additional optimal health benefits. Greens can also be braised with light olive oil, a dash of salt, apple cider, or balsamic vinegar, seasoned with cayenne and garlic, and simmered in chicken broth for about 20 minutes to retain their goodness. Traditionally our people have enjoyed cooking these vegetables in a cast-iron skillet, which is why I recommend a Dutch oven for cooking the callaloo. Cooking greens in cast iron and adding a dash of vinegar or splash of lemon makes them even richer in iron than they normally are, since some of the iron is leached from the pan. Some folks cook them with tomato, and the citrus interacts with the cast iron in the same way as vinegar or lemon, again enhancing their iron rich quality. Greens are an excellent food for young people who are having growth spurts, as well as pregnant women and the elderly, because they are high in calcium.

Lowly vegetable no more, greens in their various array of shapes, sizes, and shades are warming, energizing, tasty, healing foods. A gift for all seasons from Osayin!

· · · · · · · · · · · · · · · · · · · ·

SWEET, SWEET STEVIA
by Dallas Jennifer Cobb

With increased awareness of the rise in obesity and diabetes in North America, many of us are looking for a natural, healthy alternative to sugar.

Stevia rebaudiana has so much sweetness packed into its leaves that it can be used in place of sugar. One leaf of stevia is 10 to 15 times sweeter than an equal amount of sugar. Plus, it contains no calories and has an effective glycemic index of zero.

Extracts of stevia, commonly used as sweeteners in Japan, China, and South America, are now finding their way into the mainstream markets of North America.

Stevia also has other health benefits. It is said to help fight tooth decay and gum disease by inhibiting oral bacteria, restoring pancreatic function and correcting blood sugar problems, lowering high blood pressure, helping relieve nausea, softening skin and healing acne, and lessening cravings for sweets and smoking. With a repertoire so extensive, you may wonder why stevia is not widely used in North America.

The History of Stevia

The Guarani Indians of Paraguay, South America, have used stevia as a sweetener for centuries. Traditionally called *Kaa-he-he* (sweet herb), the Guarani gathered the wild stevia shrub and used it to sweeten their Mate, a traditional tealike beverage. In the 1800s, stevia use was documented throughout the region, in Paraguay, Brazil, and Argentina. Through trade links, stevia came to the attention of Europeans in the 1800s, was documented for analysis in a Hamburg, Germany, research laboratory, and noted in U.S. government releases of 1918.

Stevia rebaudiana was named by Dr. Moises Santiago Bertoni, director of the College of Agriculture in Asuncion, Paraguay, in 1887. The name honors Rebaudi, a Paraguayan chemist, who first extracted the plant's sweet constituent, stevioside.

Historically, stevia, a native herb, was wildcrafted. The first commercial crop in 1908 yielded a ton of dried leaves. Following that, plantations producing stevia grew throughout Paraguay and similarly spread to Brazil and Argentina. During World War II, stevia was planted and used in England because of sugar rationing. In the 1960s, Japan strictly regulated the use of artificial sweeteners, but allowed the use of stevia as a replacement for sugar and other synthetic sweeteners.

Current Commercial Considerations

In 1991, the U.S. Food and Drug Administration banned the sale of stevia products. In 1994 they approved their sale as dietary supplements, meaning that they can carry claims of providing health benefits, but they cannot be marketed as conventional foods or food additives. Because of this, stevia could not be sold as a conventional food or sweetener but could be purchased in a health food store and used at home in place of sugar.

Although it took some time and a good amount of testing by the department of agriculture, today stevia is commonly sold as a sweetener and is available in most grocery stores in the United States.

Growing Stevia

Stevia rebaudiana is a perennial shrub from the daisy family, native to mountainous areas of South America. In its naturalized environment, stevia is semitropical. Because stevia enjoys heat, it can be grown as a perennial in Zone 7 or warmer climates. In other climates and zones it can be grown as an annual, planted in a summer garden and harvested in the fall.

Stevia prefers a sandy loam with a slightly acidic to neutral pH. During the summer months, or through periods of intense heat, stevia enjoys light watering frequently. A generous layer of compost around the base of the plant will provide added protection and nutrition for the shallow feeder roots near the surface, preventing them from drying out. Though sensitive to drying out, stevia also dislikes too much moisture, so soil with a high sand content will ensure good drainage.

Stevia grows about two to three feet tall. The bushes have many branches bearing slightly serrated, opposing leaves. It also forms small white flowers at the end of summer, which must be removed to concentrate sweetness in the leaves.

While stevia can be grown from seed, it is a difficult and time-consuming process. Stevia seedlings can be ordered from herb nurseries and planted directly in your garden when soil temperatures exceed 65 degrees F. With one healthy plant you can make your own cutting by removing a three-inch tip, dipping it in rooting hormone and inserting it in sandy loam. Plant stevia in rows of 20 to 24 inches apart, with about 15 inches between plants to accommodate their bushy growth. In addition to pinching off flowers, prune and pinch off leggy growth to encourage a bushy shape.

Feed stevia about once a month with a balanced fertilizer, either an organic compost or a compost with a lower nitrogen content than phosphoric acid or potash content. Organic fertilizers work best because they release nitrogen slowly.

Stevia seems to have an insect-repelling quality that deters grasshoppers. Though nontoxic, stevia is thought to repel insects by its very sweetness.

Harvesting Stevia

Glycosides, specifically stevioside, are the substances responsible for stevia's sweetness. The glycosides are concentrated in stevia leaves just before flowering, a process triggered by the shorter days of late summer and early fall.

Since the shorter days and cooler weather of autumn promote the formation of stevioside and intensify the sweetness of stevia, harvest as late as possible in the fall, but before the first killer frost. Continue to pinch back flowers and monitor the weather, timing your harvest for peak levels for stevioside.

If you live in a climate colder than Zone 7, you can either pull the plants from the ground or use pruning shears to cut the stalk of the shrub near ground level.

If you live in a Zone 7 or warmer climate, your plants should be able to survive the winter outside. For these perennial plants, prune branches only—not the main stem—leaving about four inches of the branch. The first year's harvest may be minimal, but you will enjoy an abundant harvest the second year. But after this, the older a plant gets, the less productive it will be. Try to start new shoots of stevia each year so you always have some two-year-old plants in peak production.

Drying Stevia Plants

After harvesting stevia, the leaves need to be dried. Plants can hang upside down in the sun for a few hours on their branches before removing the leaves. When you remove the leaves, spread them on a screen or net for good air circulation. Because stevia doesn't require high temperatures to dry, air circulation is more important than excessive heat. Place the net or screen in the sun for a full day in warm autumn weather. Longer drying times may lower the stevioside content of the leaf. After drying, the dried leaves can be stored in a jar or airtight plastic container.

Using Stevia

Dried stevia can be stored as leaf, or ground up in a food processor, coffee grinder, or with a mortar and pestle and stored as powder. You can also make a liquid version by adding a cup of boiling water to about ¼ cup of finely powdered leaves. Let it set for 24 hours, then strain and refrigerate the liquid.

With these homemade products, you will need to experiment to determine the appropriate amount of ground stevia, or stevia liquid, to use in your recipes. Variances depend upon the concentration of steviosides in the plant.

Commercially produced stevia products are more reliable because they are commonly produced from plants containing a high level of stevioside. With these powdered extracts, you need only a miniscule amount of stevia to flavor a cup of tea or coffee. If you notice a bitter aftertaste, try reducing the amount of stevia and experimenting with taste. Brands higher in steviosides will provide a sweeter taste with less bitterness.

Stevia Conversion Chart

Although different stevia products offer different levels of sweetness, the chart below is based on the most common white powder extract form of stevia. When substituting stevia for sugar, use the following chart to determine proper amounts.

Granulated Sugar	Stevia Powder Extract
½ cup	⅛ teaspoon
¾ cup	⅓ teaspoon
1 cup	¼ teaspoon
10 pounds	⅖ ounce

Cooking with Stevia

Stevia can be used fresh, in its dried form, in its liquid version, or in a commercially produced white powder. One leaf of fresh stevia can be added to a glass of lemonade, iced tea, hot tea, or coffee. It can also be dropped into the cooking pot to sweeten sauces, jams, jellies, and sweets.

Most recipes requiring sugar can be adapted to use stevia. But because much less stevia powder is needed for the same sweet taste, you must adjust recipes to balance the liquid and dry ingredients. While many stevia products vary, in general, ¼ to ½ teaspoon of stevia powdered extract equals 1 cup of sugar.

Reducing the sugar in your diet helps reduce calories consumed and lowers the glycemic index of the baked or cooked food item. Mixing stevia with sweeteners like honey or maple syrup can provide a reduction in sugar and calories while maintaining good taste.

The most important thing to remember is to not use too much stevia. Start with a small amount, taste the effect, and then add more stevia to suit your taste. When you use too much stevia, you run the risk of adding that bitter aftertaste to your baking or cooking.

As stevia is sweeter than sugar, the dry volume of stevia used will be much less than sugar. So when you substitute stevia for sugar, recipes will need to be adjusted to maintain the same relative moisture content and consistency.

Stevia Drinks

Stevia Lemonade

2 c. fresh squeezed lemon juice   ¼ to ½ tsp. stevia powder

8 c. water

Combine lemon and water in a large pitcher. Add ¼ teaspoon of stevia powder and stir. Add additional stevia to taste. Add ice, garnish with mint leaves or fresh lemon if desired, and serve in tall glasses.

Stevia Iced Tea

½ c. fresh squeezed lemon juice   ¼ to ½ tsp. stevia powder

8 c. brewed tea, cold

Combine lemon and tea in a large pitcher. Add ¼ teaspoon stevia powder and stir. Add additional stevia to taste. Add ice and garnish and serve in tall glasses.

Stevia Hot Chocolate for Four

3 tbsp. cocoa powder   ½ tsp. powdered stevia extract

¼ c. boiling water   4 to 5 c. milk or non-dairy milk

2 tbsp. honey or maple syrup   7 mini marshmallows (optional)

In a saucepan, mix cocoa and stevia. Add boiling water and stir. Add the milk or non-dairy milk. Keep at medium heat—do not boil. Add honey or maple syrup to taste. Garnish with mini marshmallows.

Stevia Snacks
Stevia Chocolate Chip Walnut Cookies

1 c. butter	1 c. chopped walnuts
1 tsp. stevia powder	1 tsp. baking soda
1 egg	Pinch of sea salt
1 tsp. vanilla	2 c. semisweet chocolate chips
2¼ c. whole grain flour (whole wheat or spelt)	

Preheat the oven to 375 degrees F. In a large bowl, blend the butter, egg, stevia, and vanilla, creating a creamy mixture.

In a medium bowl mix the dry ingredients. Add the dry mixture to the creamy mixture slowly, stirring well after each addition. Add chocolate chips and walnuts and stir well. Drop heaping teaspoons of dough onto a nonstick cookie sheet. Bake at 375 degrees F for 10 to 13 minutes until the cookies are golden brown. Yields about 4 dozen.

Stevia Apple Crisp

1½ c. rolled oats	1½ tsp. stevia powder
1 c. whole grain flour (whole wheat or spelt)	Dash of vanilla
	6 medium apples
½ c. butter, melted	¼ c. applesauce
¼ tsp. salt	¾ c. raisins (optional)
1 tsp. nutmeg	½ c. walnuts (optional)
2 tsp. cinnamon	

Preheat oven to 375 degrees F. Mix the first 8 ingredients together. Use about ¼ of the mix to line the bottom of an 8 × 12-inch baking dish. Spread apples (peeled, cored, and thinly sliced) and applesauce evenly, add raisins and walnuts if you choose. Cover with the remaining dry mixture. Bake at 375 degrees F for 30 minutes, then turn up to 450 degrees F for 5 to 7 minutes to brown the top.

Brian's Stevia Banana Bread

2 very ripe, brown spotted medium or large bananas

2 c. whole grain flour (whole wheat or spelt)

½ tsp. powdered stevia

¼ c. oil

½ c. walnuts (optional)

½ tsp. baking soda

2 tsp. baking powder

1 tsp. mace

1 tsp. cinnamon

1 egg

¼ to ⅓ c. milk or non-dairy milk

Mash the bananas in a large bowl. Preheat oven to 350 degrees F. Beat in the egg, oil, stevia powder, and milk. Combine all dry ingredients in a large bowl.

Fold dry ingredients into the wet ingredients, stirring as little as possible. Add walnuts; stir briefly. Pour into a nonstick loaf pan. Bake at 350 degrees F for 50 to 60 minutes until a toothpick comes out clean. Yields 1 loaf.

Stevia Pumpkin Pie

10 to 12 oz. soft or silken tofu

¼ c. oil

1, 15-oz. can pumpkin

2 tbsp. maple syrup

⅛ tsp. stevia powder

½ tsp. stevia extract

¼ tsp. salt

1 tsp. cinnamon

½ tsp. ginger

¼ tsp. nutmeg

Blend all ingredients until smooth and creamy. Pour into an unbaked pie shell. Bake at 350 degrees F for 1 hour. Cool and serve.

Whether you try these recipes or experiment and develop your own, you will find stevia to be a versatile, sweet herb. May you find sweetness, one recipe at a time, and not feel that you have to forego sweet treats in order to invest in your health. Happy cooking with sweet, sweet stevia.

....

FEASTING ON ROSEMARY
by Anne Sala

Few culinary herbs thrive so happily in the environment that shaped rosemary, a native of the hot lands surrounding the Mediterranean. For thousands of years, its spiked, waxy leaves have been used to commune with the gods and to flavor a variety of foods, both sweet and savory.

As travelers began to expand their knowledge of the world, they carried rosemary with them. Now it grows naturally wherever the winters are warm and the climate dry.

Traditionally, rosemary is paired with rich foods such as pork and lamb because it is said to help with the digestion of fat. It also has antiseptic qualities, making it an indispensable herb in pre-refrigeration days. Even today, its strong pine-like flavor can hide the fact that a cut of meat is past its prime.

For most cooks in the United States, rosemary recipes end with savory dishes. In other cultures, however, its unique flavor has been used to enhance everything from fruits to dessert—beyond the realm of savories. In fact, rosemary could really be put to the test and challenged to appear in every course of a dinner menu, including the after dinner pick-me-up. This is only advised if all guests at the table are fans of the flavor.

There is just one species of *Rosmarinus officinalis*, so all cultivars can be eaten. Medicinally, rosemary has been used to quell upset stomachs and to bring on menstruation. For that reason, pregnant women ought to keep their intake of the herb to a minimum. Some parts of this rosemary-themed menu should be started the day before. Try to start the sorbet two days ahead. All of the following recipes serves four people.

Appetizer:
Grilled Shrimp with Rosemary

A friend told me the hip culinary use for rosemary is to showcase its aroma only. The resinous taste can be overpowering when combined with delicate foodstuffs such as shrimp. If you have a vigorous plant growing on your property, ask your guests to snip off a branch to sniff between bites of shrimp throughout this course. Otherwise, fresh rosemary sprigs can be found in the produce section of most supermarkets.

If grilling the shrimp outdoors, toss a few branches of rosemary on the coals to scent the yard and set the party's mood. Inside, burn sprigs as incense.

12 shrimp, shelled, deveined, tails intact

¼ c. olive oil

3 green onions, sliced (the white and green parts), or a handful of snipped chives

Juice of 1 lemon or ½ c. white wine

1 tsp. pepper

4 branches of fresh rosemary

Place the shrimp and next four ingredients into a nonreactive bowl or resealable bag and refrigerate for 30 to 90 minutes. If you are using wooden skewers, soak them for about 30 minutes before grilling. You may also broil the shrimp in the oven with or without the skewers.

Start the grill so the coals will be white when you are ready to cook, or preheat the broiler. Remove shrimp from marinade. Thread 3 shrimp on each skewer. To prevent shrimp from wobbling while flipping on the grill, use 2 skewers per bunch.

Grill—or broil on a broiler pan—for 1 to 2 minutes per side, or until cooked through. Serve immediately with a rosemary sprig. Encourage your guests to inhale the aroma throughout the course.

For future reference, or for a more pronounced flavor, sturdy rosemary branches—stripped of leaves—can be used as skewers. Be sure to soak them before introducing them to fire.

First Course: Mushroom and White Bean Mélange

Mushrooms and white bean mélange can also be mashed up or puréed and made into a savory spread. This dish could also serve as a meatless main course if accompanied by a green salad (use rosemary in the vinaigrette, of course).

1 tbsp. butter

1 tbsp. olive oil (or 2 tbsp. if no butter)

1 small white onion, chopped

8 oz. button mushrooms, wiped clean with a damp paper towel and roughly chopped

½ c. white wine or white wine vinegar (any mild vinegar) or vegetable stock

1 tbsp. fresh rosemary, chopped, or 2 tsp. dry, crumbled

1 tsp. thyme, fresh or dry

1, 15-oz. can white beans, such as cannellini or navy, rinsed and drained

Salt and pepper

1 lemon cut into wedges

Place large skillet over medium heat and melt butter with the olive oil. Do not let the butter turn brown. Once the butter is melted, or the olive oil slides easily across the pan when tilted, add the onion and sauté until translucent. Add mushrooms and gently stir until they give up their juices and reduce in size.

After most of the mushroom liquid has disappeared, pour in the white wine, vinegar, or vegetable stock to deglaze the pan. Add rosemary and thyme. Stir in the beans and simmer for 5 to 8 minutes until they are cooked through. If there is still a lot of liquid, continue cooking until it is mostly gone. Add salt and pepper to taste. Serve warm and with lemon wedges. The juice brightens the flavors.

Main Course

Rosemary is such a versatile herb. The main course and side dish are mere examples of how rosemary can be used to enhance meat and potatoes. Instead of chicken, try lamb. Since lamb is such a sweet meat, substitute green apple for the pear to create a more perky pairing. The recipe is written so that you can cook both parts of the course simultaneously. The sorbet is simply a way to add a bit of coolness to the meal. It is particularly welcome if you serve this meal in summer.

Main Course: Chicken with Rosemary and Dijon

¼ c. fresh rosemary, minced	1 c. Dijon mustard
1 tbsp. salt	4 boneless, skinless chicken breasts
1 tbsp. pepper	½ c. olive oil
2 c. breadcrumbs	3 tbsp. butter

In a bowl, combine the rosemary, salt, and pepper. Place the breadcrumbs in another bowl, and put the mustard in another bowl. Use your fingers to sprinkle the one side of the chicken with the rosemary mixture. Then, using a spoon, slather the same side with mustard. After pounding them flat, set the breast, mustard-side down, into the breadcrumbs. Move it around so that side is completely covered. Keep the breast in the breadcrumbs and repeat steps one and two on the second side. Then flip the breast over and dredge it in the breadcrumbs. Repeat this procedure with the three other chicken breasts. Cover the breasts and refrigerate for at least 10 minutes, allowing the breadcrumbs to set.

Heat skillet over medium-high heat and add olive oil and butter. When the oil begins to sizzle, place one or two breasts into the skillet. Sauté for at least 8 minutes on the first side before flipping. Sauté until the interior is no longer pink. Depending how thick the mustard layer, the breading may come off in some spots. Do not let it burn. Let it brown, then remove to use as a crispy topping.

Side: Roasted Sweet Potatoes and Pear

2 large sweet potatoes, peeled	¼ c. fresh rosemary
3 to 4 pears, such as Bosc or d'Anjou	½ tbsp. salt
2 garlic cloves, crushed then sliced	¼ c. olive oil

Preheat oven to 425 degrees F. Chop the sweet potatoes into ½ inch chunks and slice the (peeled and cored) pears. Spread the potatoes and pears in a roasting pan, trying to get as thin a layer as possible. You might need to use two pans. Sprinkle the garlic pieces, rosemary, and salt over the contents, then drizzle with olive oil. Carefully toss until all potato and pear pieces are glistening. You can include the rosemary stems if you like.

Place the roasting pan(s) in the oven and cook for 40 minutes, stirring occasionally until sweet potatoes are somewhat brown and pears are very soft.

Palate Cleanser:
Rosemary Wine Sorbet

Sorbets are so simple to assemble. They are just flavoring, water, and sugar that you pop in the freezer until they're frozen. It is easy to go wild with the flavorings, but the end result will be milder than you expect, due to the freezing. I strongly suggest starting this component of the main course two days ahead.

As a palate cleanser when the other two courses are so sweet, the sorbet is made with less sugar than usually recommended. Use a crisp wine that you would enjoy drinking—perhaps even the same one you are serving with your dinner—because its flavor will be in the forefront. If you would rather make the sorbet without wine, use an unsweetened white grape juice or a sparkling white grape juice. Or, add more lemon and water.

2½ c. water	¼ c. fresh peppermint, or peppermint and lemon balm
½ c. sugar	1 c. dry white wine
¼ c. fresh rosemary	Juice of ½ a lemon

Pour the water and sugar into a saucepan set over high heat. Stir to begin dissolving the sugar. Add the herbs and continue stirring occasionally. Bring to a boil, then reduce heat to simmer for 5 minutes. Remove from heat and let cool. Pour into a nonreactive container, cover, and refrigerate overnight.

The next day, strain the herbs from the sugar syrup. Combine the syrup with the wine and lemon juice. Place the container (plastic might be best) in the freezer. After an hour, check on the sorbet. Use a fork or spoon to roughly chop up the ice that has formed. Continue checking on the sorbet about once every hour for the next 4 to 6 hours, breaking up the ice crystals with a fork. The more often you break up the ice, the smaller the crystals will be, making for a smoother sorbet. Serve small shavings on the main course plate, or set each person's portion in a separate bowl.

Dessert:
Rosemary Scented Sugar Cookies

After so many strong flavors bombarding your guests' senses, a simple sugar cookie is a nice way to wrap up the meal.

½ c. butter, softened	2 tsp. baking powder
⅔ c. granulated sugar	2½ c. flour
2 eggs	¼ c. sugar for decoration
1 tsp. vanilla extract	¼ c. fresh rosemary, chopped

Cream the butter in a mixing bowl. Add the sugar slowly and cream with the butter until the mixture gets light and fluffy. Add the eggs one at a time, beating the first one thoroughly into the mixture before adding the second. Mix in the vanilla. Sift in the baking powder and flour. Mix well. Cover the bowl and chill in the refrigerator for at least an hour.

Preheat oven to 350 degrees F. Grease two cookie sheets with butter or shortening. Roll out the dough into more manageable sizes, if necessary. Leave the unused portions in the refrigerator until you are ready to roll them out. Cut the dough into shapes using cookie cutters or cardboard patterns. Pour the sugar for decorating onto a plate and sprinkle with the rosemary. Take each cookie and press one side into the mixture. Just a few pieces of herb will scent the whole cookie. Place the cookies on baking sheets (sugar and rosemary side up) and bake for about 10 minutes. They are done when the edges begin to brown. Cool on wire racks. Makes about 30 cookies.

Rosemary Tisane

As your guests begin to push away their dessert dishes, offer them a last bit of rosemary before they leave. This tea is said to prevent hangover and nightmares, so tell them it is for their own good. Just this once, another herb is at the forefront, but rosemary is certainly in there.

4 c. water	½ c. fresh thyme or 3 tbsp. dried
2 tbsp. fresh spearmint (or 1 dried)	2 tbsp. fresh rosemary (or 1 dried)

Bring four cups water to a rolling boil. Place herbs in a teapot. Pour water over herbs and let steep for 3 to 5 minutes. Strain into four teacups. Serve with lemon and sugar or honey on the side. Then, send your guests on their merry way to dream rosemary-scented dreams.

GET MORE AT LLEWELLYN.COM

Visit us online to browse hundreds of our books and decks, plus
sign up to receive our e-newsletters and exclusive online offers.

- Free tarot readings • Spell-a-Day • Moon phases
- Recipes, spells, and tips • Blogs • Encyclopedia
- Author interviews, articles, and upcoming events

GET SOCIAL WITH LLEWELLYN

Find us on Facebook

www.Facebook.com/LlewellynBooks

Follow us on twitter™

www.Twitter.com/Llewellynbooks

GET BOOKS AT LLEWELLYN

LLEWELLYN ORDERING INFORMATION

Order online: Visit our website at www.llewellyn.com to select your books
and place an order on our secure server.

Order by phone:
- Call toll free within the U.S. at 1-877-NEW-WRLD (1-877-639-9753)
- Call toll free within Canada at 1-866-NEW-WRLD (1-866-639-9753)
- We accept VISA, MasterCard, and American Express

Order by mail:
Send the full price of your order (MN residents add 6.875% sales tax) in U.S. funds,
plus postage and handling to: Llewellyn Worldwide, 2143 Wooddale Drive,
Woodbury, MN 55125-2989

POSTAGE AND HANDLING:

STANDARD: (U.S. & Canada)
(Please allow 12 business days)
$25.00 and under, add $4.00.
$25.01 and over, FREE SHIPPING.

INTERNATIONAL ORDERS (airmail only):
$16.00 for one book, plus $3.00 for
each additional book.

Visit us online for more shipping options.
Prices subject to change.

FREE CATALOG!

To order, call
1-877-
NEW-WRLD
ext. 8236
or visit our
website

Incense
Crafting & Use of Magickal Scents
Carl F. Neal

Carl F. Neal's classic, bestselling book on making incense with natural ingredients has now been expanded and updated. This new edition includes twice as many ingredients, twice as many base materials, three times as many incense binders, twice as many recipes, expanded information about natural charcoal, a new section on making incense from ingredients from the local supermarket, an extensively expanded and updated chapter on making incense, and two new rituals.

Incense is your complete guide to making your own homemade blends. Whether you want to make loose, stick, coil, or cone incense, you'll find detailed instructions for everything from finding the right ingredients to proper drying methods. Explore your "scent-uality" and celebrate your connection to the spiritual side of life.

978-0-7387-4155-0, 288 pp., 7½ x 9⅛   **$19.99**

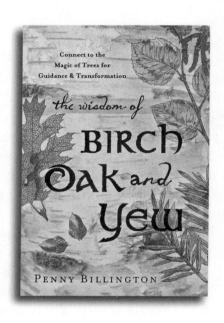

Connect to the
Magic of Trees for
Guidance & Transformation

the wisdom of

BIRCH
OAK and
YEW

PENNY BILLINGTON

The Wisdom of Birch, Oak, and Yew

Connect to the Magic of Trees
for Guidance & Transformation

PENNY BILLINGTON

Tune into the wisdom of three trees sacred to Druids—birch, oak, and yew—and use their powerful lessons and natural gifts to transform your life. Written by a Druid with more than twenty years of practical experience, *The Wisdom of Birch, Oak, and Yew* will guide you through a one-of-a-kind journey of magical self-discovery. Its unique invitation: change your perspective by "being as a tree" and consider yourself in light of the qualities of our arboreal friends.

Engage with the spirit of each tree and explore its relationship to the stages of your life and the rhythm of your days. Experience within yourself each tree's positive attributes, gain perspective by taking on each tree's role as "witness," and find respite from the frenetic pace of modern life.

978-0-7387-4090-4, 360 pp., 6 x 9 **$19.99**

CLIFF SERUNTINE

SEASONS
OF THE
SACRED EARTH

FOLLOWING THE OLD WAYS ON AN ENCHANTED HOMESTEAD

Seasons of the Sacred Earth
Following the Old Ways on an Enchanted Homestead
CLIFF SERUNTINE

Join the Seruntine family on a magical journey of green living at their homestead hollow in the Nova Scotia highlands. Share their magical experiences as the family lives in harmony with the land and respects nature's spirits. Growing and hunting most of their food, Cliff and his family share hands-on practical home skills you can use too.

With a warm, personal style, *Seasons of the Sacred Earth* chronicles the Seruntine family's adventures following the old ways. They celebrate the Wheel of the Year by leaving apples for the Apple Man, offering faerie plates during Samhain, and spilling goat's milk for the barn bruanighe. In return, the land blesses them with overflowing gardens, delicious ales, and the safety of their farm animals. Through their journey, you'll discover the magical and the mystical are never farther than Earth and Sky.

978-0-7387-3553-5, 336 pp., 6 x 9   **$16.99**

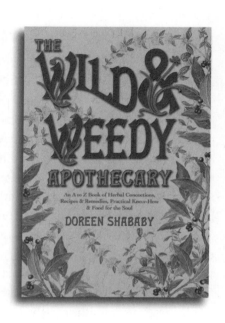

THE WILD & WEEDY APOTHECARY

APOTHECARY

An A to Z Book of Herbal Concoctions,
Recipes & Remedies, Practical Know-How
& Food for the Soul

DOREEN SHABABY

The Wild & Weedy Apothecary
An A to Z Book of Herbal Concoctions, Recipes &
Remedies, Practical Know-How & Food for the Soul
Doreen Shababy

Step off the beaten path and into nature's wild and weedy apothecary. In this warm and friendly guide, herbalist Doreen Shababy shares her deep, abiding love for the earth and its gifts. She invites readers to be playful and adventurous as they learn how to use herbs to make a soothing salve, fragrant tea, vibrant salads, and other dishes to delight the palate as well as the eye.

This extensive collection of herbal remedies, folk and food wisdom, and eclectic recipes from around the world represents a lifetime of the author's work in the forest, field, and kitchen. Organized in an easy and fun A to Z format, Shababy's extensive knowledge of the subject and unique collection of wit and wisdom will speak to beginners and herb enthusiasts alike.

978-0-7387-1907-8, 384 pp., 6 x 9   **$17.95**

---

the essential

guide *to*

natural

SKIN

CARE

Choosing

Botanicals,

Oils & Extracts

for Simple

& Healthy

Beauty

Hélène Berton

The Essential Guide to Natural Skin Care
Choosing Botanicals, Oils & Extracts for Simple & Healthy Beauty
Hélène Berton

Treat yourself—your face, hands, hair, and lips—to vitamin-rich, toxin-free nourishment from nature. *The Essential Guide to Natural Skin Care* maps the wondrous qualities and uses of botanicals used in homemade beauty products, making it easy to customize your own lotions, creams, milks, body butters, face masks, lip balms, ointments, toners, and more.

Choose from a wide variety of eco-friendly vegetable oils and butters, infused and essential oils, aromatic hydrosols, and emulsifiers. Discover the beneficial beauty and healing properties of each, as well as their practical traits, such as shelf life and absorption. You'll find ingredients that soften, tone, and hydrate skin and hair; tighten pores; fade scars; stave off wrinkles; prevent and heal acne; promote hair growth; treat dandruff; fight infection and fungus; and repel insects. This portable, compact DIY reference also includes practical advice and basic recipes that can be easily modified to your unique skin type, needs, and tastes.

978-0-7387-2927-5, 240 pp., 5³⁄₁₆ x 8   **$16.95**

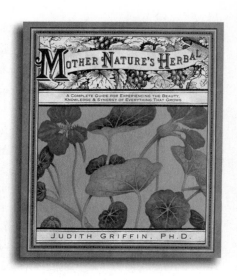

MOTHER NATURE'S HERBAL

A COMPLETE GUIDE FOR EXPERIENCING THE BEAUTY,
KNOWLEDGE & SYNERGY OF EVERYTHING THAT GROWS

JUDITH GRIFFIN, PH.D.

Mother Nature's Herbal
A Complete Guide for Experiencing the Beauty, Knowledge & Synergy of Everything That Grows
Judith Griffin

Step into a world of spiritual rejuvenation and radiant health with the restorative power of herbs. Brimming with herbal folklore, tips for growing and harvesting your own herbs, and over two hundred medicinal and culinary recipes from diverse cultures, *Mother Nature's Herbal* will become your trusted companion on the path to natural living.

Take a tour of the time-honored traditions and healing practices of cultures past and present, including Native and South American, Mediterranean, East Asian, and others. Create delicious and exotic entrees, brew soothing herbal teas, mix perfumes and salves using flower essences from your backyard garden, prepare elixirs and medicines to treat every ailment—and so much more.

With this wise book on your kitchen shelf, a rich heritage of herb craft and herbal tradition is at your fingertips.

978-0-7387-1256-7, 432 pp., 7½ x 9⅛   **$24.95**